The
Hyles Church Manual

by
Dr. Jack Hyles,
Pastor, First Baptist Church, Hammond, Indiana

Sword of the Lord Publishers
Murfreesboro, Tennessee 37130

ISBN 0-87398-372-6

Printed and Bound in the United States of America

*Colossians 4:11, "...my fellowworkers unto the
kingdom of God, which have been a comfort unto me."*

Dr. Jack Hyles

TABLE OF CONTENTS

*Actual public services or experiences recorded and transcribed for this publication.

INTRODUCTION

With pleasure and profit, I have read the manuscript, *Hyles' Church Manual*. I wish that this book had been published years ago so that many pastors and churches could have been blessed by its wise contents. This book, wisely divided into three sections: Church Business, Church Programs, and Pastor's Section, will be of invaluable help to all pastors who read it and to all churches that follow the detailed plans it sets forth.

I cannot praise enough this book which places warm and sympathetic hands on all matters that pertain to the welfare of the church.

Dr. Hyles has gone into details in such a wonderful way that pastors and churches will profit greatly by giving heed to the author's instruction.

The giving of the actual proceedings of a business meeting will guide pastors wisely in how to conduct a business meeting of the church. The same can be said for the chapter on the church budget and all matters concerning a building program, showing good plans and bad plans for building.

The chapters that deal with dedications and ordinations—the dedication of buildings and the ordination of deacons and preachers—is superb in directions given.

Superiorly superlative are all words in this book that set forth plans for building a great Sunday school, for conducting teachers' meeting, for securing and operation of buses.

The urgency of caring for the sick and shut-ins, for direction in youth programs, and well-organized and well-operated church nurseries, for having the right kind of music and singing, and the usefulness of the Women's Missionary Society is evident in all the author writes.

What the author writes about baptism and examples in soul winning add to the value of the book.

Every pastor on earth will find great profit and help in giving careful attention to the words of Section III—and being doers of the words.

If I could command pastors and they had to obey my command, all pastors would give careful attention to all the author says about weddings and actual wedding ceremonies, funerals and actual funeral services, spiritual counseling, pastor-and-people relationship and the pastor and the staff.

In what he writes about the invitation, Dr. Hyles, an expert himself in giving an invitation, expresses himself wisely as to how some wonderful gospel messages are ineffectual by a weak invitation.

I could use many strong adjectives in speaking of this book. But they would be inadequate to set forth its worth—written by a great gospel preacher, pastor of a great Baptist church, who has given much thought and prayer and time to the writing of a most excellently superb book—setting forth so many valuable things pastors and churches need to know and put into practice. I wish every pastor and evangelist and church in America would get a copy of this book, read it, and put into practice the wise instructions it gives.

Robert G. Lee

January 15, 1968

FOREWORD

"Dr. Hyles, could I come to Hammond and spend a week at your church just observing the work of the church, going soul winning with some of your folks, observing the bus ministry firsthand, and seeing how the work is done?"

These words were spoken by a pastor, and he did come to see the work. It wasn't long until another came, and another, and another — until our staff was spending much of its time training pastors, one at a time.

After talking with members of the staff, I decided to set a week when all of these pastors could come at the same time. One hundred sixty-nine preachers came for that week, and the First Baptist Church Pastors' School was born.

Some inquiries then came in concerning the possibility of another such school, and because of popular demand, another was conducted the next year. Approximately 250 pastors attended. The next year over 350 came, and in 1967 approximately 650 were registered for the Pastors' School. Then in 1968, there were 1,205 registered for this week of study.

Through the years requests have come that the material be put in print. Though such an endeavor would be nearly an impossibility, this manual represents at least an outline of much of the material covered at the Annual Pastors' School, which is conducted each year in the month of March at the First Baptist Church of Hammond, Indiana.

Jack Hyles
March 29, 1968

I. Church Business

1. The Church Business Meeting

In Romans 12:11 we are admonished to be "not slothful in business; fervent in spirit; serving the Lord." Since God's business is the biggest business in all the world, His business should be cared for in a businesslike manner. Nothing less than fervency and care should be taken in the business of the Lord Jesus Christ.

Because of this, many churches feel it is wise to have periodic business meetings. For some, the business meeting is once a year. For others, business meetings are conducted whenever there is special business. I have found it helpful through the years to have a monthly business meeting. Though brief, it is important. It keeps the people informed as to the affairs of the church and gives them an opportunity to speak out concerning such matters.

The Time of the Meeting

Perhaps the best time for such a meeting is after the Wednesday evening service. In the first place, the people are already there and this avoids having to call a special meeting on a special night just to take care of business. Then also, the people are in a spiritual frame of mind after a good service and fellowship around the Word of God. Many churches make a mistake, I think, in giving an entire Wednesday evening service to a business meeting. The people of the church have worked hard all day and, no doubt, have had their minds on carnal and material things. They are in no condition spiritually to do God's business. After a few great songs about Christ, some time of prayer, and a message from God's Word, people are in much better condition to transact the business of God.

The Order of Service for a Business Meeting

It is wise to start off with a prayer. This prayer should be a brief and simple one asking God to give wisdom to make the proper decisions and to give love in the transaction of the King's business. This prayer is followed by the pastor simply saying, "We will now have the reading of the minutes by the church clerk." The church clerk proceeds to read the minutes of the last business meeting. When the minutes have been read the pastor asks the congregation, "Are there any corrections or additions to the minutes?" If no one speaks, the pastor simply says, "The minutes stand approved as read." If someone makes a correction to the reading of the minutes, the pastor says, "The minutes stand approved as corrected."

Following the reading of the minutes come the recommendations from the board of deacons. The pastor may say, "We now recognize the chairman of our deacons, or the clerk of our deacons, for the recommendations from the board." The clerk (or chairman) reads the first recommendation and then closes it by saying, "Mr. Moderator, (the pastor) I move this recommendation be adopted." Then the pastor turns to the congregation and says, "Is there a second to the motion?" This should be done immediately as discussion on a motion should not take place until there has been a second. The clerk, or chairman, or pastor then should explain to the congregation, in detail, the action that is being recommended. The pastor, acting as moderator, should say, "Is there any other discussion?" Time should be allowed for discussion but irrelevant discussion should not be encouraged. Then the pastor says, "All in favor of the motion will signify it by saying, 'Aye.' All opposed may say, 'No,' and it is so ordered." In certain very important matters the vote may be taken by the raising of the hand or even by standing, or if the occasion warrants, a secret ballot may also be used. In our churches we have found that usually an "aye" vote is all that is necessary unless we are voting to borrow money, build a building, or to take some other major step.

The deacon clerk then reads the next recommendation and the above procedure is followed on each recommendation until they have all been read.

Following the deacons' recommendations we then come to the time of the treasurer's report. The treasurer's report may be read but we have found it more helpful to have a mimeographed report. Following is a copy of one page of a typical treasurer's report.

TREASURER'S REPORT FOR OCTOBER, 1967

BALANCE BROUGHT FORWARD	$10,874.17	
RECEIPTS FOR SEPTEMBER	40,037.81	
DISBURSEMENTS FOR SEPTEMBER	28,050.20	
BALANCE 9-30-67	22,861.78	

CHECKS FOR SEPTEMBER, 1967

7445	6	IBM Corporation	D.P.on Typewriter	29	82.50
7446	6	Munster Lumber	B & M Supplies	19	34.20
7447	6	Charles B. Miller	B & M Exp.	19	2.27
7448	6	Holiday Inn	Motel Expenses	38	39.17
7449	6	Bud Lyles	Motel Expenses	38	16.50
7450	6	VOID			
7451	6	IBM Corporation	Typewriter Rental	29	18.00
7452	6	Gateway Office Company	Adding Machine Ribbon	29	1.50
7453	6	Hammond Industrial Towel	Custodian Supplies	20	14.48
7454	6	Brewer's Small Engine Repair	Repairs - Pars.- Hyles	27	12.00
7455	6	Hammond Floral Company	Shut-In Expenses	79	2.00
7456	6	Maxine Jeffries	Shut-In Expenses	79	30.00
7457	6	Wulf's Cleaners	Laundry	35	4.53
7458	6	Hammond Times	Newspaper Ads	36	273.79
7459	6	Ad-Craft Sign Co.	Sign Lease	81	80.00
7460	6	Hitzeman's Flowers	Flowers	33	6.63
7461	6	Standard Equipment	B & M Exp.	19	5.44
7462	6	Huisenga Fur & Gift Shop	Ordinance Exp.	35	13.90
7463	6	Erminger's Food Mart	Grape Juice	35	12.00
7464	6	Texaco	Car Exp - Hyles	2	27.11
7465	6	Sinclair Refining Co.	"	"	14.87
7466	6	Del's Gulf Service	Car Exp - Hyles	2	18.98
7467	6	Dept of Water Works	Water Bill	25	3.67
7468	6	Dept of Water Works	"	"	35.15
7469	6	NIPSCO	Gas & Electric	23&24	845.34
7470	6	Sandra Plopper	Phone Expenses	26	2.37
7471	6	Illinois Bell Telephone	Phone Exp.	26&73	425.46
7472	6	Chapman Laundry	Laundry	82	23.15
7473	6	Addressograph-Multigraph	Machine Payment	29	76.02
7474	6	Farm Bureau Insurance Co.	Bus - Insurance	21	105.40
7475	6	Allied Electronics	Recording Tapes	28	44.50
7476	6	Calumet Farm Produce	Store Rent & Parking	81	80.00
7477	6	Pioneer Girls	Supplies	39	9.00
7478	6	BaptistBook Service	Girl's Supplies	39	7.95
7479	6	Kentucky Fried Chicken	Chicken - Wed Dinner	82	61.80
7480	6	South Shore Printers	Radio Envelopes	78	72.00
7481	6	Sherwin-Williams	B & M and Pars. Exp.	19&27	31.84
7482	6	Burger's Super Market	Wed Dinner - Groceries	82	15.53
7483	6	Parkmore Drive Inn	Wed Dinner - Fish	82	56.40
7484	6	Burger's Super Market	Groceries - Mission	73	52.81
7485	6	Hewitt Hardware	Mission Expenses	73	12.90
7486	6	John Clark	Deaf Visitation Exp.	79	10.00
7487	6	Earlyne Stephens	Salary		165.80
7488	6	VOID			
7489	8	Annabelle Kingery	Salary-Nursery-August	11	10.32
7490	8	Grace Hollinhead	"	"	6.45
7491	8	Opal Webber	"	"	20.67
7492	8	Mary Nagy	"	"	25.18
7493	8	Maxine Stromberg	"	"	11.61
7494	8	Ruth Zinn	"	"	3.87
7495	8	Virginia White	"	"	10.32
7496	8	Maudell Thompson	"	"	6.45
7497	8	Kay Stone	"	"	2.58
7498	8	Gail Slayton	"	"	12.90
7499	8	Nancy Reinert	"	"	3.01
7500	8	Neva Norrell	"	"	3.87
7501	8	Mary McCarley	"	"	1.72
7502	8	Kathy Hiles	"	"	3.87
7503	8	Druscilla Hayes	"	"	3.87
7504	8	Mrs. Sue Frizzell	"	"	2.58
7505	8	Dessole Frizzell	"	"	2.58
7506	8	Darlene Fisk	"	"	2.58
7507	8	Mary Douglas	"	"	3.87
7508	8	Jean Colbert	"	"	6.45
7509	8	Mrs. Kay Burden	"	"	1.29
7510	8	Jane Brock	"	"	2.58
7511	8	Lillie Baggett	"	"	2.58
7512	8	Judy Anderson	"	"	1.29
7513	8	Marie Darrah	"	"	1.29

You will notice that the number of the check, the date the check was written, the budget item from which the check is coming, the person to whom the check is written, the purpose for writing the check, and the amount of the check are all listed. This is very important. Every penny should be accounted for.

We find it helpful to pass out the treasurer's report at the door following the service. We announce to the people that if anyone has any questions about the expenditures, he may call the church office at any time and we will be happy to explain any or all of the treasurer's report.

We then ask if there is a motion to adjourn. Between the time of the asking for the motion and the making of the motion, of course, anyone who wishes to bring up something else may feel free to do so. This should not be encouraged but it should be allowed. The motion is made and seconded to adjourn. Then the pastor simply says, "All in favor of the motion to adjourn will signify by standing for the closing prayer." The standing to pray is the vote of adjournment.

The above order of service is a very simple one. The business meetings in our pastorates have usually lasted from five to thirty minutes, with an average of about fifteen minutes. The people know that nothing is being done under the table and that they have a right to speak on any issue. Because they do know it, normally they do not exercise this right. A right that is taken away is exercised more than a right that is granted.

Bear in mind that the deacons' recommendations are simply that— just recommendations. The deacons have no authority. All the authority rests with the church body. However, the church body has such confidence in the board of deacons that almost without exception, they readily accept the deacons' recommendations. This is as it should be. The church has confidence in the leadership of the deacon board and the pastor. Consequently, they are pleased and happy with the recommendations brought before them.

Helpful Rules to Follow

1. The pastor should be the moderator of the business meeting. There are a few things that I insist upon as the pastor. These are things that, if not granted, would prevent me from accepting a pastorate. Among these is the right to be the moderator in the church business meetings. This should be discussed before accepting a pastorate and thoroughly understood with the membership, pulpit committee, and the deacon board.

2. Insist on kindness. The membership of the church should feel that they may speak about any issue. They should not feel that they may speak rudely, or unkindly, about any issue. The moderator should insist that kindness prevail and that the right of anyone to speak freely on any subject be protected. People should have the idea that if they oppose something kindly, they will not be ostracized or ridiculed, but they should have a complete understanding that in caring for God's business a Christian spirit should prevail.

3. *The moderator should give all a chance to speak.* The smallest member of the church should feel that he has a right to speak concerning any issue. As mentioned before, when a church has this right, normally, fewer people will speak out. As long as one can see his privileges he need not fight for them, but when he sees his privileges being taken away he will often become obstinate and critical.

4. *Do not encourage opposition.* While each member feels that he has the right to speak and is offered the chance to speak, opposition should not be encouraged. For example, if it is obvious that the majority of the congregation is for a certain matter, when suddenly someone rises to speak in opposition, he should be allowed to say his peace, if he says it kindly. Then the moderator (the pastor) may say something like, "Thank you, brother, for that word," or "Is there any other word before we vote?" Statements such as these are dangerous: "Thank you, my brother, would anyone else like to speak on this matter?" or "What do the rest of you think of this opposition?" The opposition will rise to speak without any encouragement. It is wise to give the opposition a chance to speak but not to encourage their speaking. After the opposition has been expressed then simply take the vote. Remember through it all that the moderator should be kind and gracious even in the face of opposition.

5. *When big issues are involved the moderator should foresee the questions and prepare his answers.* When the moderator knows there is going to be a big issue he should predict the questions that will need to be answered and prepare the answers. On certain occasions I have taken as many as sixteen pages of notes to a business meeting when I knew questions would be asked me. I have prepared a page of answers for each possible question. This enabled me to answer carefully, thoughtfully, and with premeditation. This eliminated any possibility of my speaking hastily and in the heat of the battle making a mistake in fact or spirit. Then, when the question is asked, the moderator may simply pull from his little file his prepared answer and read it.

6. *Write letters of kindness and love to the opposition.* Following a business meeting where there have been differences of opinion and where someone obviously opposed the action taken, it certainly would be a Christian gesture for the moderator to write a letter of encouragement to the opposition. The following is an example:

Dear Mr. Doe,

I was thinking about you this morning as I reflected upon our business meeting last night, and I thought I would put my thoughts on paper. First let me tell you I thank God for your friendship and what you have meant to me through the years, and though last night we appeared to be on different sides of the fence, I do want you to know that I respect you and admire you as a Christian brother. I also want you to know that as long as you are in the church and I am moderator, and as long as you manifest the fine Christian spirit that you manifested last night, I will certainly fight for your right to speak your piece. You were gracious in your opposition and you have been a blessing to me personally. I thank God for the privilege of being your pastor and trust that He will give us many years of service together. I also thank God that on most issues you and I agree wholeheartedly, and I rejoice in what you mean to me and to your church. May God's richest blessings rest upon you.

Sincerely,

Signed by the pastor.

7. *The moderator should ask the church to table differences when the church is almost equally divided.* It has been my policy through the years that the church should be nearly unanimous on matters that do not include convictions. In such things as the building program, the borrowing of money, the buying of songbooks, the painting of the building, the remodeling of the building, the buying of new property, etc., there should certainly be a unanimity of spirit among the church members. Suppose, for example, that the vote was 55% for and 45% against, I would call for a motion rescinding the action taken and tabling the matter until the board of deacons could study it thoroughly and bring back another recommendation. Now, if it is a matter of conviction such as liquor or another moral issue, this should not be done. After a split vote is taken on something that does not involve a conviction the pastor could say something like this: "And the motion is carried. Now may I make a suggestion. The peace and harmony of our church is more important than any building or piece of property. Since the vote has been so close I would like to entertain a motion that we rescind the action just taken and place the matter in the hands of the board of deacons for further study in order that they might bring back, perhaps, a more suitable recommendation at our next business meeting." In every case this has been done and many church problems have been solved.

8. Have recommendations thoroughly thought out before being brought before the church. Now this is so important. The normal procedure of a recommendation in our church is from the pastor to the deacons to the people. The pastor should thoroughly think through his recommendations to the board of deacons. Then the deacons should thoroughly discuss and think through a course of action before recommending to the church that it be followed. Most church trouble is caused by a lack of thoroughness and proper planning on the part of the pastor and the deacons. The discussions, the opposition, the deliberations, etc., should be done in the deacons' meeting and not on the floor of the church where weak Christians may be present. Bear in mind that the deacon is supposed to be a mature Christian who is well seasoned in the work of the Lord. Consequently, he can disagree more agreeably than the weak Christian. The more discussion on the floor of the deacon board the less discussion there usually is on the floor of the church. When an issue is not thoroughly discussed and thought out by the deacons, it is oftentimes an issue of controversy on the floor of the church.

9. The moderator should never display his temper. There are several reasons for this, not the least of which is the fact that it is the person who hits the second blow that is usually penalized. In an athletic contest the man who hits first is seldom seen, but the man who retaliates is often seen and penalized. Many times people privately criticize, slander and rebuke the pastor but the other people do not see this. The pastor gets his fill of such actions and then goes to the platform and retaliates. The people only see the retaliation; hence, they penalize the pastor instead of the tormentor. The moderator should be very careful to be kind and gracious and the people should be aware of this spirit.

10. Always keep the people informed. An informed membership is a happy membership. An uninformed membership can be an unhappy and rebellious membership. As one has said, "Keep all the cards on top of the table" so the people know exactly what is going on.

11. Do not run ahead of the people. Many pastors prematurely borrow money, buy property, and build buildings. Now it is not so bad for the pastor to run a little bit ahead of the people on the program of the church or some other matter that can be rescinded, but suppose the pastor leads the people to borrow money when they are not ready to borrow money, then when he is called to another field they have to pay his debt. There is a note of a lack of wisdom in this. The pastor may be the kind of leader that will inspire his people to want to borrow, build, and give, but the people should be ready before a large project is started. Keep the people abreast with you. This is especially needful concerning the deacon board.

12. No business meeting should be held without the pastor. This is another one of those things that is a conviction with me. An understanding should be had with the pastor, deacons, and people that no church business meeting should be conducted in the absence of the pastor. When the people love the pastor and the pastor loves the people, this is usually no problem. They are more than delighted to grant his request.

13. It is wise to have a two weeks' notice before calling a business meeting of major importance. No secret business meeting should be conducted. In something of major importance such as the calling of a pastor, the building of a building, the borrowing of money, the buying of property, etc., an announcement should be made at least two Sunday mornings before the business meeting is conducted so as to give every member of the church adequate knowledge of what is to be transacted. Not only should the business meeting be announced but the matter to be discussed should be announced also.

14. It is very important that the pastor know parliamentary procedure. The pastor should know how to handle a motion and even an amendment to a motion. Suppose someone makes a motion; the pastor says, "Is there a second?" If there is no second, he then says, "The motion is lost for lack of a second." If there is a second, he says, "Is there any discussion?" Following the period of discussion the question may be called for, which means it is time to vote. The pastor then says, "All in favor say, 'Aye.' All opposed, 'No,' and it is so ordered."

However, suppose that during the time of discussion someone amends the motion. Someone could say, "I amend the motion as made and seconded as follows." Then the pastor, acting as moderator, should call for the vote on the amendment. He should say, "Is there a second to the amendment?" If there is a second, he then may say, "Is there any discussion about the amendment?" After the discussion about the amendment he then calls for the vote on the amendment of the motion. Following the vote on the amendment of the motion the pastor then returns to the previous motion as amended. He may then say, "All in favor of the motion as amended say, 'Aye.' All opposed, 'No,' and it is so ordered."

Following is an example of a typical business meeting as conducted in the First Baptist Church of Hammond, Indiana.

2. A Business Meeting

(Wednesday, May 18, 1967—9:00 p.m.)

A brief business meeting is conducted monthly at the conclusion of the Wednesday evening Bible study. This is usually the third Wednesday of each month.

PASTOR HYLES: Tonight we have a business meeting. We have plenty of time so you can get out on time.
We will now have the reading of the minutes.

Reading of the Minutes

CHURCH CLERK: "The April business meeting was called to order and opened with prayer by Pastor Hyles on Wednesday, April 19, 1967, at 9:00 p.m. The minutes of the regular meeting held on March 15, 1967, were read and approved. A list of 191 names was read by Pastor Hyles for church membership—169 by baptism, 17 by Christian experience, and 5 by transfer of letter. A motion was made by Dave Gifford and seconded by Dave Sharp that these applicants be received into our membership. The motion carried.

"On adoption of a motion by Bob Lail and seconded by Doug Hiles fifteen people were voted out of the membership—13 by transfer of letter and 2 were dropped by request.

"The board of deacons presented the following recommendations for the church approval:

1. That the church approve the same officers as last year for the new church year, May 1 through April 30, 1968, as follows: Church Treasurer, Glen Smith; Assistant Treasurer, Cliff Anglen; Church Clerk, L. J. Parr; and Assistant Clerk, Don Krueger. A motion was made by Ken Cunningham and seconded by Blanford Duff that this be approved. The motion carried.

2. That the church approve having steel guards installed on ten doors and six first-floor windows along the alley on all buildings except the Annex at the cost of $481.00, the money to come from the surplus fund. A motion was made by L. J. Parr and seconded by John Olsen, Sr., that this recommendation be approved. The motion carried.

3. That the church approve purchasing addressograph plates for the Beginner Department at the cost of $50.00, the money to come from the surplus fund. A motion was made by L. J. Parr and seconded by Jim Sprague that this be approved. The motion carried.

4. That the church grant a license to preach to Clarence Goren. A motion was made by L. J. Parr and seconded by Ed Rausch that this be approved. This motion also carried.

5. That the church approve leasing a new 'First Baptist Church' sign from the Ad Craft Sign Company at the cost of $600.00 down and $80.00 per month for five years to be installed on the corner nearest sidewalk approximately ten feet south of the red block wall and half way from the corner to the west wall of the auditorium. A motion was made by L. J. Parr and seconded by Walter Mitziga that this be approved. The motion carried.

6. That the church approve having the rear wall of the new Educational Building waterproofed with two coats of paint by the same contractor who did the new auditorium, at a cost of $750.00, the money to come from the surplus fund. A motion was made by L. J. Parr and seconded by Ray Boardway that this be approved. The motion carried.

7. That the church approve spending an estimated $200.00 from the surplus fund to have the present church sign repaired. A motion was made by L. J. Parr and seconded by Vic Nischik that this be approved. The motion carried.

8. That the church approve transferring $1,000 from budget item #59 to budget item #14 to increase the salary of custodian Mr. Sullivan, who will have increased responsibility with the completion of the new Educational Building, and this money to be replaced at the end of the year if the surplus fund so warrants. A motion was made by L. J. Parr and seconded by Earl Dukes that this recommendation be approved. The motion carried.

9. That the Church approve razing the apartment building to the east of the office building and the Knights of Christ building with the consent of Mr. Inkley, who holds the title to this building. A motion was made by L. J. Parr and seconded by Lewis Shoaf that this recommendation be approved. The motion carried.

10. That the church approve giving the bleachers in the Junior II Department of the Annex to the Bill Rice Ranch when this building is remodeled, following the completion of our new building. A motion was made by L. J. Parr and seconded by George Huisenga that this recommendation be approved. The motion carried.

"The meeting adjourned with prayer by Pastor Hyles at 9:20 p.m."

PASTOR: Thank you. You have heard the reading of the minutes. Are there any corrections or additions? If not, they will stand approved as read.

Voting in of New Members and Granting of Letters of Transfer

PASTOR: We have these requests for transfers. (Eleven names were read for transfer.)
Do I hear a motion that we grant these as requested? (Mr. Dunsworth raised his hand.)
Brother Dunsworth makes the motion. Is there a second? (Mr. Shoaf raised his hand.)
Brother Shoaf seconds it. Any discussion? If not, if you are in favor, say "Aye."

CONGREGATION: Aye.

PASTOR: If you oppose, "No." It is carried.

Recommendations From the Deacons

PASTOR: We have three recommendations from the deacons tonight. I think I should make this observation and explanation. I announced Sunday night that we had a life-changing decision to make tonight. That life-changing decision has been changed. We thought that we were going to buy the Wulf's Cleaners across the street but the matter has been postponed indefinitely, and we are not going to do it as of now.
All right, let us have the deacons' recommendations.

CHURCH CLERK: The board of deacons recommends that the church approves purchasing folding doors for the second floor of the present educational building assembly room for the additional classroom space. The cost will be $200.00 and the money will come from the surplus fund. Brother Pastor, I move that this recommendation be approved.

PASTOR: Is there a second to the motion? (Mr. Cunningham's hand was raised.)
Brother Cunningham seconds it.
This is what it amounts to: We have divided the rooms 200 and 300 of the present educational building (Miller Hall, as we call it) into classrooms, and we need one more folding door in room 200. The deacons are recommending that we buy this door and take the money from the surplus fund. Are there any questions or discussion? All in favor say, "Aye."

CONGREGATION: Aye.

PASTOR: Opposed, "No." It is carried.

CHURCH CLERK: The board of deacons recommends that the church grant a license to preach to Walter Ruskowski. Pastor, I move that this recommendation also be approved.
PASTOR: Is there a second to the motion? Okay, we have forty "seconds" to this motion. I saw Brother Duff here. He seconds the motion. Walter Ruskowski, of course, has been one of our own deacons for a number of years. Now he feels that God would have him to preach. We do not know what the future holds for him, but we wanted to go on record as being for him and recommending unanimously that the church license him to preach the Gospel. Is there any discussion about it? If not, if you are in favor, you will give a resounding "Aye."

CONGREGATION: Aye.

PASTOR: If you oppose (and of course, you do not), you may say "No" and it is so ordered.

CHURCH CLERK: The board of deacons recommends that the church spends $80.00 from the surplus fund to have the tile in the foyer of the new auditorium repaired. Brother Pastor, I move that this recommendation be approved.

PASTOR: Is there a second to the motion? (Mr. Streeter raised his hand.)
Brother Streeter seconds it. Back in the rear of this building there is ceramic tile. When the building was built, asphalt tile was installed. When we came in the first Sunday, it was raining, if you recall, and we slipped. We then decided to put down ceramic tile first. We didn't. We put the ceramic tile over the asphalt tile. When the fire came, the firemen came in here and, of course, the water got all over this floor. It seeped under the tile back there. The professional tile men say that the water has lifted up the edges of the asphalt tile. What they want to do is take one width of asphalt tile off all the way around, build up the concrete, and lay the ceramic tile directly on the concrete. They will fix it for $80.00. Does anybody want to discuss my intelligent explanation, or is it worth $80.00 to go home early? All in favor of spending the $80.00 by faith so that we can go home say "Aye."

CONGREGATION: Aye. (Laughter)

PASTOR: The opposed, "No," and it is carried.

As you go out tonight, you will find the monthly financial statements. You may get one as you leave. It has listed each check that is written and the purpose for its writing. If you have any questions, feel free to call the church office and we will do our best to answer. Every penny that this church spends is accounted for to the membership of the church. You may get your report as you go out tonight. Do we have a motion to adjourn? (Mr. Dunsworth and Mr. Lail raised their hands.)

All in favor may stand.

Let us pray.

Father, thank you for every activity of this evening and for the sweetness that prevails in our church. In Jesus' name. Amen.

Good night and God bless you.

3. The Church Budget

One of the more distasteful and yet more important phases of a church life is its financial life. In order to have the proper kind of financial arrangement it is wise to have a church budget. There are many ways to set up and adopt such a budget. By no means do we present the only way, but following is a system which has been proved successful in hundreds of churches.

1. *Deacons compose the budget committee.* In our chapter on the board of deacons we mention that the deacons form every committee of the church and that every church officer is chosen from the board of deacons. We also point out that the deacons have a meeting each Saturday evening, which means that every officer and committee of the church is present at the same meeting. This eliminates hundreds of hours of needless committee meetings. Now bear in mind that the committees are not chosen from the board of deacons but the board of deacons is every committee. The board of deacons is the nominating committee, the budget committee, the finance committee, etc. Hence, the budget is drawn up at their regular meetings.

2. *If the deacons plan to prepare the budget at the regular monthly meetings with no extra called meetings then it is best for the preparation of the budget to start in September.* Since the fiscal year should be the calendar year, that gives the board of deacons four months to prepare the budget for the following year. We have found it more practical and more timesaving, however, to have weekly budget meetings enabling us to start as late as the latter part of October or even the early part of November. In five or six rather lengthy meetings a budget can be prepared if proper preparation is made by the treasurer, the pastor, and the staff.

3. *A check should be made of the expenditures of the previous year.* Each item on the budget should be examined very carefully by the treasurer, pastor, or both, before the first meeting of the budget committee. Much care should be given to compare the budget item versus the expenditures for that item for the previous year. This will enable the budget committee in deciding whether to decrease or increase each particular budget item.

4. *A prediction should be made of the needs of the coming year.* Once again this should be done before the first budget committee meeting. Perhaps a building has been built which would necessitate the

increase of the utilities. Perhaps a new staff member has been hired
which would necessitate the increase of salaries. Perhaps there is a
building program being planned and the building will be completed before the end of the coming year. This should be taken into consideration. Using an old budget the pastor, or treasurer, or both, should
then write beside the old budget item what they feel the item would
need for the coming year. Following is a sample of such a page:

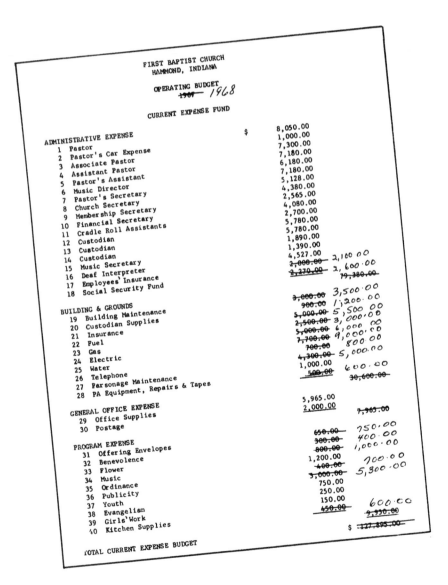

FIRST BAPTIST CHURCH
HAMMOND, INDIANA

OPERATING BUDGET
1967 *1968*

CURRENT EXPENSE FUND

ADMINISTRATIVE EXPENSE $ 8,050.00
    1 Pastor   1,000.00
    2 Pastor's Car Expense   7,300.00
    3 Associate Pastor   7,180.00
    4 Assistant Pastor   6,180.00
    5 Pastor's Assistant   7,180.00
    6 Music Director   5,128.00
    7 Pastor's Secretary   4,380.00
    8 Church Secretary   2,565.00
    9 Membership Secretary   4,080.00
   10 Financial Secretary   2,700.00
   11 Cradle Roll Assistants   5,780.00
   12 Custodian   5,780.00
   13 Custodian   1,890.00
   14 Custodian   1,390.00
   15 Music Secretary   4,527.00
   16 Deaf Interpreter   2,000.00   2,100 00
   17 Employees' Insurance   2,270.00   1,600·00
   18 Social Security Fund   79,380.00

BUILDING & GROUNDS   3,000.00   3,500·00
   19 Building Maintenance   900.00   1,200·00
   20 Custodian Supplies   5,000.00   5,500 00
   21 Insurance   2,500.00   3,000·00
   22 Fuel   5,000.00   6,000·00
   23 Gas   7,700.00   9,000·00
   24 Electric   700.00   800 00
   25 Water   4,300.00   5,000·00
   26 Telephone   1,000.00
   27 Parsonage Maintenance   500.00   600·00
   28 PA Equipment, Repairs & Tapes   30,600.00

GENERAL OFFICE EXPENSE   5,965.00
   29 Office Supplies   2,000.00   7,965.00
   30 Postage

PROGRAM EXPENSE   650.00   750·00
   31 Offering Envelopes   300.00   400·00
   32 Benevolence   800.00   1,000·00
   33 Flower   1,200.00
   34 Music   400.00   700·00
   35 Ordinance   3,000.00   5,300·00
   36 Publicity   750.00
   37 Youth   250.00
   38 Evangelism   150.00
   39 Girls' Work   450.00   600·00
   40 Kitchen Supplies   2,950.00

TOTAL CURRENT EXPENSE BUDGET $ 127,895.00

5. Outline the budget under main headings. For a church just starting a budget an examination of the expenditures for the past year would reveal that practically every expenditure could fall under one of a few headings. Our main budget divisions are as follows:

1. Administrative expense
2. Building and grounds
3. General office expense
4. Mission budget
5. Building
6. Program expense
7. Sunday school budget

6. The deacons, or budget committee, should discuss, at their meetings, each item and allocate its amount for the next year. One by one, carefully, prayerfully, and slowly the budget committee discusses the budget. When coming to each item, last year's expenditures are considered; the recommendation of the needs of next year as given by the pastor and/or treasurer should be considered; then an intelligent decision should be made concerning the needs of each item. When each item has been examined carefully the budget should be totaled and divided by the number of Sundays in the coming year to see what the total budget would be if recommended, as is, to the church. If the deacons feel that the average weekly budget is within reach of the people, then they should vote to approve the budget and recommend it to the church. Bear in mind at this point that the deacons have no authority to adopt a budget. This authority rests only in the church. The deacons are only an advisory committee as always and, as always, have no power to act apart from the church.

7. The proposed budget is then presented to the church. The first week in December is a good time for this. A mimeographed copy is given to each member and an announcement is made that a vote will be taken two weeks later to approve, reject, or modify the proposed budget. This gives the members two weeks to consider the budget and also gives ample time for absent members to secure copies and become acquainted with the proposals being presented by the board of deacons. Once again, an informed church is more likely to be a happy and satisfied church. Special care should be taken that nothing is being pushed through but that the church is kept aware of every step.

8. The church then votes to adopt the budget. Two weeks after the budget is presented the church meets in a regular business meeting and votes to adopt the budget as proposed by the board of deacons. This can be a brief meeting. Every member of the church has had ample time to carefully check every budget item. The pastor, acting as moderator, asks for questions or deliberations from the church floor. The budget may be changed by majority church vote. However, when the church has proper confidence in the pastor and deacons, and when the pastor and deacons have thoroughly thought out these proposals, we find that changes from the floor are very rare. In spite of this fact, however, the people should be aware that they may change the budget without bringing the wrath of the pastor and deacons upon them.

After ample discussion the pastor may then call for a motion for the adoption of the budget as proposed or as corrected. He may make such a statement as this: "Do I hear a motion that we adopt the budget as proposed by the board of deacons?" Someone makes a motion, the motion is seconded, the pastor then asks for discussion. Though discussion should not be encouraged it should definitely not be discouraged. We have found it wise to have the motion and second before any discussion whatsoever is given. After the discussion the pastor may then say, "All who are in favor of the budget as proposed will signify it by standing," and "All who are opposed may signify by like sign." (This is one of those few votes in the year when I prefer standing or the raising of the hand rather than simply the "aye.")

9. The operation of the budget. There are many successful systems for such an operation. In our ministry we have tried many but, following, you will find the system that has been best adapted to our needs:

(1.) A ledger book is prepared with a page for each budget item. Since each item on the budget is numbered, then the page for that item bears the same number. This way a running balance may be kept, not only for the extra budget, but for each item in the budget.

(2.) Each Monday the weekly allocation for each item is credited to its page as follows:

The annual allocation is simply divided by the number of Sundays in the year (usually 52) and 1/52nd of the annual budget is credited to the item each Monday.

10. *When an item is ordered the price is secured and subtracted from the balance of its budget item.* This is not done at payment. This leaves too much guesswork. It is done upon order. This means that the balance, when brought forward, will be the balance of money in the particular budget item after payment of everything that has been ordered. Hence, the balance on each page is an accurate one and will be even after outstanding bills are paid.

11. *The balance of each page must stay in the black.* This means that nothing can be ordered unless there is a sufficient balance to cover its purchase. Suppose, for example, that the secretaries need some stationery. They look to the ledger book under the item "Secretarial Supplies," "Office Expense," or whatever the appropriate title of that budget item is. They cannot order more stationery than this budget item will allow. Notice the following chart:

The above chart shows that we only have $94.62 in this particular budget item. Hence, we cannot order office supplies costing more than $94.62. Since EVERY ITEM MUST BE KEPT IN THE BLACK AND IF THIS ITEM IS KEPT IN THE BLACK, THEN THERE CAN BE NO DOUBT BUT THAT THE CHURCH IS STAYING WITHIN HER BUDGET.

12. Only one person should do the ordering. To make the above plan work, ordering should be in the hands of one person. If this is not possible, at least no one should be allowed to order without this person's permission. The financial secretary or church treasurer, as the case may be, finds it his job to see to it that nothing is ordered under any particular budget item that would throw that item in the red. Consequently, each person, before ordering, must contact the financial secretary or treasurer who in turn goes to the ledger book and checks the balance on the appropriate page in order to approve or reject the order. Again, let us reemphasize the fact that the entry is made in the book upon order and not upon payment and that the balance determines the amount that can be ordered.

Suppose, for example, that we pursue with the ordering of the stationery mentioned above. We have found that we have only $94.62. Suppose, then, that we order $75.00 worth of stationery; the following entry is made in the ledger book:

You will notice that we have a balance of $19.62. This will remain the balance until another order is made, or until next Monday when the weekly allocation is credited to this budget item.

13. The same deposit is made into the operating account each week. Let's suppose that a church's budget is $300.00 a week. The deposit each week is $300.00, no more and no less.

14. A surplus account should be set up. Because we are depositing the same amount of money each week in the operating account there must be another account where the surplus is deposited. Assuming that our budget is $300.00 per week as aforementioned, suppose the offering is $362.98. $62.98 of this is deposited in a surplus account and $300.00 is deposited in the operating account. Now, suppose that the offering is less than $300.00. Suppose, for example, that the offering is $283.10. This means that $16.90 is taken from the surplus account to make the deposit in the operating account exactly $300.00. This enables us to know, at all times, exactly how much money we have to spend for items over and above the budget. We know that the $300.00 deposit covers every item in the budget and since every item stays in the black we know that the $300.00 is more than meeting our needs. This gives us the assurance that we may spend anything in the surplus fund without affecting the budget.

This surplus fund cannot be touched unless the offering is below the budget or unless the church votes for an expenditure. This gives us direction and constant awareness as to our financial condition. Over the period of the year this surplus fund builds up and offers great security to the church. In case of emergency the church may decide to use some of it, and in case the offering is less than the budget, the surplus fund is used to make up the difference. This allows us to meet our budget every Sunday and to know exactly where we stand financially at all times.

15. Following is an actual copy of a church budget we have used in the past:

FIRST BAPTIST CHURCH
HAMMOND, INDIANA

OPERATING BUDGET
1967
CURRENT EXPENSE FUND

ADMINISTRATIVE EXPENSE

1	Pastor	$	8,050.00
2	Pastor's Car Expense		1,000.00
3	Associate Pastor		7,300.00
4	Assistant Pastor		7,180.00
5	Pastor's Assistant		6,180.00
6	Music Director		7,180.00
7	Pastor's Secretary		5,128.00
8	Church Secretary		4,380.00
9	Membership Secretary		2,565.00
10	Financial Secretary		4,080.00
11	Cradle Roll Assistants		2,700.00
12	Custodian		5,780.00
13	Custodian		5,780.00
14	Custodian		1,890.00
15	Music Secretary		1,390.00
16	Deaf Interpreter		4,527.00
17	Employees' Insurance		2,000.00
18	Social Security Fund		2,270.00
			79,380.00

BUILDING & GROUNDS

19	Building Maintenance		3,000.00
20	Custodian Supplies		900.00
21	Insurance		5,000.00
22	Fuel		2,500.00
23	Gas		5,000.00

24	Electric	7.700.00	
25	Water	700.00	
26	Telephone	4,300.00	
27	Parsonage Maintenance	1,000.00	
28	PA Equipment, Repairs & Tapes	500.00	
			30,600.00
GENERAL OFFICE EXPENSE			
29	Office Supplies	5,965.00	
30	Postage	2,000.00	
			7,965.00
PROGRAM EXPENSE			
31	Offering Envelopes	650.00	
32	Benevolence	300.00	
33	Flower	800.00	
34	Music	1,200.00	
35	Ordinance	400.00	
36	Publicity	5,000.00	
37	Youth	750.00	
38	Evangelism	250.00	
39	Girls' Work	150.00	
40	Kitchen Supplies	450.00	
			9,950.00
TOTAL CURRENT EXPENSE BUDGET			$127,895.00

MISSION BUDGET

TOTAL MISSION BUDGET		80,342.00
BUILDING		
Debt Retirement	45,000.00	
		45,000.00
SUNDAY SCHOOL BUDGET		
Sunday School Expense	11,763.00	
		11,763.00
MISCELLANEOUS		
Designated Offerings (Estimated)	30,000.00	
Nationwide Radio (Estimated)	16,000.00	
		46,000.00
		$ 311,000.00

16. *It is a good practice to have the checks signed by more than one person.* Perhaps the treasurer could sign and someone else could co-sign. This other person could be the church secretary, another deacon, and in some cases the pastor. (I personally do not think it wise for the pastor to sign the checks.)

The plan that we have used for years is having three men whose signatures are acceptable. Any two of these may sign. This enables one man to be out on vacation or sick, and still the Lord's work and business can go on.

17. *The counting of the money.* Under no conditions do we allow money to be counted during the services. We feel that everyone possible should be in the public services of the church, and so we discourage activities such as counting money to be carried on while the preacher is preaching. We have divided our board of deacons into four groups. One group counts each first Sunday, one group each second Sunday, etc. This means that each deacon counts money once each month. This is done on Sunday afternoon. The money is counted in a private, well-locked room with the best of money-counting equipment. The deposit slip is made up, the police department is called, and the deacons proceed to the bank under armed guard to make the deposit.

The money is placed in the night deposit vault where it is kept until the next day when the final and official deposit is made. Through all the years of my ministry I have left counting of the money in the hands of my deacons. We have found it wise not to let the same people count the money each week. Not only is there a security for the church; there is also a security for the counters in that the people realize that the counting of the money and the financial responsibilities are being spread out to many rather than controlled by a few.

18. *The keeping of financial records.* When a family is voted into the church they are given a packet of offering envelopes for the entire calendar year. There is an envelope for each Sunday of the year.

You will notice that there is no place for the name of the giver. You will also notice there is a number. This number becomes the financial number of the couple or of the child. A ledger card is made in the church office and on that card is placed this same number. The a-mount of the offering on the envelope is transferred to the ledger card for the permanent record of the family or of the child.

	Ledger Card	Acct.	464	
DATE	ENV. NO.	CONTRIBUTION		CONTRIBUTION THIS YEAR
JAN '67	464	50.00 +		50.00 •
FEB '67	464	40.00 +		90.00 •
MAR '67	464	40.00 +		130.00 •
APR '67	464	50.00 +		180.00 •
MAY '67	464	40.00 +		220.00 •
JUN '67	464	40.00 +		260.00 •

This enables us to keep an accurate record of the contributions of each person and family. Each six months we transfer the information on the ledger card to a statement and mail to each family its giving record for the six months' period. This gives the family official rec- ords for income tax purposes.

YEARLY REPORT

of your Contributions to the

FIRST BAPTIST CHURCH
523 Sibley Street
HAMMOND, INDIANA

Mr. & Mrs. John Doe
111 First Street   464
First Town, U.S.A.

DATE	ENVELOPE NO.	CONTRIBUTION	CONTRIBUTION THIS YEAR
JAN '67	464	50.00	50.00 •
FEB '67	464	40.00	90.00 •
MAR '67	464	40.00	130.00 •
APR '67	464	50.00	180.00 •
MAY '67	464	40.00	220.00 •
JUN '67	464	40.00	260.00 •

EC — Error Corrected
SP — Special Offering

"And all the tithe of the land, whether of the seed of the land, or of the
fruit of the tree, is the Lord's: it is holy unto the Lord." Lev. 27:30.

In summary, Mr. and Mrs. Doe take the envelope for the proper Sunday, place $10.00 in the envelope, write in the amount given on the outside of the envelope, and drop it in the collection plate. The deacons count the money on Sunday afternoon, taking the $10.00 from the Doe family's envelope and leaving the envelope for the financial secretary. The financial secretary takes the empty envelope, finds that the amount given was $10.00, turns to the ledger card of Mr. and Mrs. Doe, and credits them with a $10.00 gift. At the end of six months the financial secretary then sends to Mr. and Mrs. Doe their record of giving for this period.

19. *The treasurer's monthly report keeps the church family informed.* At each monthly business meeting a check-by-check report is presented to the church family. This keeps them informed as to every expenditure made. They are informed as to the total expenditures for the month, total receipts for the month, and present balance in the church account. Then an itemized check-by-check list is also given. A portion of such a report is below:

TREASURER'S REPORT FOR OCTOBER, 1967

BALANCE BROUGHT FORWARD	$10,874.17
RECEIPTS FOR SEPTEMBER	40,037.81
DISBURSEMENTS FOR SEPTEMBER	28,050.20
BALANCE 9-30-67	22,861.78

CHECKS FOR SEPTEMBER, 1967

7445	6	IBM Corporation	D.P.on Typewriter	29	82.50
7446	6	Munster Lumber	B & M Supplies	19	34.20
7447	6	Charles B. Miller	B & M Exp.	19	2.27
7448	6	Holiday Inn	Motel Expenses	38	39.17
7449	6	Bud Lyles	Motel Expenses	38	16.50
7450	6	VOID			
7451	6	IBM Corporation	Typewriter Rental	29	18.00
7452	6	Gateway Office Company	Adding Machine Ribbon	29	1.50
7453	6	Hammond Industrial Towel	Custodian Supplies	20	14.48
7454	6	Brewer's Small Engine Repair	Repairs - Pars.- Hyles	27	12.00
7455	6	Hammond Floral Company	Shut-In Expenses	79	2.00
7456	6	Maxine Jeffries	Shut-In Expenses	79	30.00
7457	6	Wulf's Cleaners	Laundry	35	4.53
7458	6	Hammond Times	Newspaper Ads	36	273.79
7459	6	Ad-Craft Sign Co.	Sign Lease	81	80.00
7460	6	Hitzeman's Flowers	Flowers	33	6.63
7461	6	Standard Equipment	B & M Exp.	19	5.44

Special Offerings

1. It is a good idea to take an offering each Wednesday evening. This enables those who do not attend the Sunday services to give their tithes and offerings. It also could be used to finance special projects. Many churches finance radio ministries through the Wednesday evening offerings. For a number of years we financed our bus ministry through the Wednesday evening offerings.

2. Easter and Thanksgiving offerings are taken. Twice a year we encourage our people to make a thank offering unto the Lord. This is over and above their regular weekly tithe. This can be used for radio, buses, rescue mission, or one of many other projects. Sometimes it is helpful to have such an offering for the purpose of meeting budget needs. Maybe the offerings have not met the budget for the year. The goal for these offerings could be to bring the offerings for the year up to the budget requirements.

3. There are several things to be considered in the taking of a special offering. Of course, the offering should be taken only when there is a need. The people should be given the true picture of the church's financial program. They should be trained that the pastor will take an offering when there is a need and that if he says there is a need, there is a need. The people must trust the pastor completely. If he says we need a dollar, then the people should know a dollar is needed. If he says we need $10,000, the people should know that the need is $10,000. They should never feel that they are being used by the pastor to meet an objective. Complete confidence concerning these matters should be developed.

In the taking of a special offering, the pastor should be serious. There is far too much joking going on at offering time. When a person gives, he should have the feeling that it is a spiritual activity. This is not to say that something humorous cannot ever be said, but the general atmosphere should be one of sobriety. The burden and the need should be laid kindly, lovingly, frankly, and sincerely upon the hearts of the people by the pastor. Following would be some words the pastor could use:

"Dear friends, we face a serious need today in our church's life. We find ourselves in need of $5,000 in order to meet our budget requirements for the year. Now you know that I would not come to you for this need unless it were a real one. You know how I have acted toward financial needs through the years and you also know that I am not an alarmist. If I act alarmed, then I am alarmed. Today I come to you presenting a serious need. Since I have been your pastor I have never presented a need that you have not met and I come to you sincerely and in faith believing that this one will also be met. Our receipts thus far this year have been $52,000. Our budget is over $57.000. That means that we need $5,000 in today's offering. This may cause some sacrifice on my part as well as yours. I plan to do my part. I trust you will do yours. Some will have to give $300.00. Some can only give a dollar or two, but let each of us give whatever he feels he can and each of us give whatever he would have to give to make it a sacrifice. I'm trusting God to lay on your heart the need. Let us meet it together."

Then the pastor should be honest concerning the raising of an offering. If an offering is taken for a certain matter, it should be spent for that matter. No money should ever be used for any purpose other than that which was told the people. It is certainly dishonest to take an offering and wrongly allocate the funds.

When the offering is taken and counted, the people should know the total given. Again, as we have said before, keep everything in the open. Never conceal anything from the people. Be honest with them and build their confidence in your financial responsibility.

It is often wise to have special envelopes for special offerings. Several of these are presented below:

You will note that there is always a place for an envelope number. This is the same number that is mentioned earlier in this chapter as is found on the ledger file and the regular envelope packet. This enables the financial secretary to credit every gift of every person.

By no means have we been exhaustive in this chapter. Simplicity has been our goal. We have not tried to confuse the reader with many plans but have tried to offer a simple, practical one that is being used and can be used. To be sure there are many others that God is using and the above is simply one of many plans. God has seen fit to bless it and use it in hundreds of churches around the world to carry out the greatest business in all the world—God's business.

4. A Building Program

The early church had no church buildings as we have today, yet it grew to tremendous proportions. It is true that church buildings are not necessary for growth, but certainly they are an aid to growth and progress in a New Testament church. We shall attempt to present in this chapter a simple and direct program for building. Since the problems of each church are unique, different adaptions of this plan will often be necessary, and in many cases, no doubt, a different plan entirely would be more suitable. Through the years I have found the following suggestions helpful in the building programs of my churches:

1. *Don't magnify buildings.* Buildings are only tools which enable us to reach people and teach people about the Lord Jesus Christ. They should not be magnified out of proportion. In the Grange Hall Baptist Church in Marshall, Texas, we grew a rather large rural Sunday school and church with only six or eight adequate classrooms. We used the shade of trees, the baptistry steps, the bedrooms of the parsonage, the attic, and church buses for Sunday school classrooms, and yet the church grew rapidly.

When I assumed the pastorate of the Miller Road Baptist Church of Garland, Texas, the total property valuation was $6,000. We had a building made of Arkansas tile with nothing but concrete on the floors, rafters for ceilings, and with no choir or pews. The first Sunday forty-four people attended to welcome the pastor. We had a little prefabricated building about sixteen feet by sixteen feet where we had two Sunday school classes and, other than this, we had only a nursery adjacent to the auditorium. We had five Sunday school classes meeting in the auditorium that seated comfortably only about 150 people. With these limited facilities we grew to an average of over 400 in Sunday school, with a high of 952. We used garages of the houses of neighbors. We borrowed an empty house across the street which we used for Sunday school classes. Since we had no pews, we came to an opening assembly in the auditorium and sat on folding chairs. We then went to our classes across the street in the borrowed house. Each person carried his chair with him across a busy street. Folks who came in early for the preaching service found an auditorium empty of chairs, and it remained so until Sunday school was over. Then they could see people carrying their chairs across the street to the auditorium.

We then built a one-story educational building but we could not afford chairs for this. I stood up and announced to our people that we were going to have the only Chinese Sunday school in America. Since the Chinese sit on rugs in school we would have a Chinese Sunday school with our children sitting on "throw" rugs. It was inconvenient, but the church grew. When we dedicated the aforementioned Sunday school building (which, by the way, I built myself), a strange thing happened. Bear in mind that I had never built a building. I knew nothing about buildings. We simply could not afford an architect, and we had only $13,000.00. With some wise counsel from a cement contractor, I led in the construction of the building. When the building was dedicated, we were very, very happy and proud even though it was a very simple building. On Dedication Day somebody asked me what kind of heat the building had. "What...err...kind of...heat?" I asked. Oh...Ah.... Yes, you guessed it right, I forgot to put heat in the building. We got some star drills, drilled holes in the walls and ran pipe along the ceiling to provide gas heat for the building. To this day the pipes are still visible. In spite of this the church grew.

To be sure a church can grow without adequate buildings but its growth will be faster and more solid if the building program can keep progress with the church's growth. Hence, do not magnify the buildings but plan for adequate facilities, if at all possible.

2. *Keep planning ahead of the needs.* The pastor and deacons should be planning ahead constantly for the needs of the church as far as buildings are concerned. Some churches even find it wise to have a master plan to provide continuity to their building program. This is certainly a wise step. As plans are made, they should be made within reason and common sense. Many churches build an auditorium that is entirely too big. Nothing hurts the spirit of a church anymore than such a mistake as this. An auditorium can be built with room for a balcony to be installed later or with plans for expansion later. I would rather have a smaller building that is packed than a larger building that is half empty. This is one reason that including a balcony in auditorium plans is usually a wise thing. When the balcony is not in use, the people will not be aware of this fact and the spirit of the church will not be hampered.

3. *Consider your needs, not your money.* Remember the promise, "But my God shall supply all your need according to his riches in glory by Christ Jesus." Sometimes the needs cannot be met immediately. Hence, the building program may have to be made in several steps, but it always seems to be a mistake when a church considers money before it considers its needs.

4. *Appoint a building committee.* Through the years I have asked the church to empower the board of deacons as the building committee. This is in keeping with our policy of church organization. (See chapter

on Deacons.) Be careful here not to choose people just because they are builders or well-to-do. Stay with the spiritual people of the church in this capacity. Now if the spiritual people happen to be builders or well-to-do people, it is much the better. It is better to choose the spiritual common man than the carnal well-to-do man.

5. *Look at many church buildings.* Acquaint yourself with the church architecture of the day. Especially should you acquaint yourself with the buildings of churches that are the same type church as yours. For example, our church is very evangelistic; hence, we want our buildings to look evangelistic. We have found it wise to visit numbers of evangelistic churches and look at their facilities. The deacons, or building committee, should take many trips together, carefully taking note of different advantages offered by different type structures. Do not limit your building to copy another but rather make it include the best features of many others.

6. *Employ an architect.* This is a vital part of a building program. I have found it best to use Christian architects who draw plans for many church buildings. It is amazing how much such an architect can help and how many ideas he has accumulated of which the pastor and deacons would never think. Much prayer should be given in the choosing of an architect. Remember, just because a man is a good architect does not make him qualified to draw church plans.

7. *Employ the architect to draw preliminary plans.* By preliminary plans, I mean a floor plan along with an artist's sketch of both interior and exterior of the building. This is normally done at a very nominal fee.

8. *Have the architect explain the floor plan, the elevation, and the architect's sketches to the deacons.* Such a meeting would probably last several hours, and the architect should go into much detail as he informs the deacons of his suggestions.

9. *The deacons should then adopt these preliminary plans.* A vote should be taken by the board concerning the plans, and if the plans are adopted, they can proceed with the building program.

10. *The pastor and deacons should then present the plans, as adopted, to the church for church approval.* Of course, this meeting is announced at least two weeks in advance and must be well attended by the membership. I have found it helpful to make slides of the architect's sketches, floor plans, and elevation showing them to the people and explaining them in detail. Caution must be taken not to run ahead of the people. Be sure deacons are in complete agreement as to the building program and be sure the people are ready to go into such a program.

11. *The church may then vote to employ the architect to draw the complete set of plans, to adopt the preliminary plans, and to empower the deacons as a building committee to see the building through to*

completion. If the church enthusiastically adopts the plans, then the architect may proceed with the drawing of the completed set of plans.

12. *Be looking for money.* All the time the pastor and/or deacons should be looking for finances. Local banks should be contacted as well as savings and loans associations, insurance companies, brokers, bonding companies, etc. Though final action on a loan by a lending agency is not usually taken until the plans are completed, it is important that steps be taken to secure finances even before the completing of the plans.

13. *It is wise for a church to limit its debt retirement to one offering a month, or one-fourth of its income.* This has been our policy through the years and we have found it to be a sound one. Allocate one entire Sunday a month for debt retirement or 25% of the income. Explain this to the lending agency and they will be impressed by your financial farsightedness and conservatism.

14. *Raise all of the money that you can.* Through the years I have steered clear of the money-raising campaigns that interfere with the evangelistic program of the church. I have also steered clear of an every-member canvas, etc. First, the pastor can decide what he himself can give. It should be sacrificial if he expects the people to sacrifice. Then he may call a meeting of his staff and explain to them that he is sacrificing. He can then show them the need and ask them to join him. A little card could be passed out asking the staff to indicate at the bottom of the card how much they could give during the days of the building program. For example, if the building program is going to last six months, ask them to write on the card how much they can give over the six-month period. We do not ask the people to sign the card. We simply want to know how much we can expect. We have no idea who it is that is going to give that much. It is between them and God.

Then a similar meeting is held with the board of deacons, explaining to them what the pastor and staff are going to do, laying the burden upon their hearts and leading them to join you in sacrificing. Then a meeting could be held with the teachers and officers and other leaders of the Sunday school and church. This meeting is similar to the one conducted with the staff and the deacons. Again, cards are passed out. The people indicate their promises but do not sign their names on the cards. After these meetings, a called meeting of the church should be conducted. It should be handled along the same lines of the aforementioned meetings. The Sunday school hour would be a good time for this since the Sunday school workers have already made their promises. In this meeting the remainder of the church can decide what would be a sacrifice for them, again using the blank card method.

After the pastor, the staff, the deacons, the teachers and officers, and the people have written their intentions, a total can be added and a victory report given to the church. It is very important that during this period the pastor be very honest and sincere with the people. He should keep them informed as to how much money is coming in and the needs that remain. I have found it unwise to use high-pressure methods, and I have also found that when the pastor is honest and sincere with the people, God's people will always meet the need.

Attractive envelopes should be printed for people to use during the building program. Below is a sample of one we have found most effective:

15. *When the plans are completed, the contract should be let.* We have found it wise to use local builders. We have also found it wise to let only reputable builders make bids.

It is also wise to have at least four bids. To get four bids a church would probably have to contact six to eight contractors. The date should be set for the opening of the bids. The bids should be sealed and given to the architect. At the date of opening the deacon board, or a designated portion of the deacon board, should meet with the pastor and the architect for the opening of the bids. The architect opens the bids and reveals their contents to the deacons and pastor. The deacons may then vote their preference and let the contract.

16. *There are varied types of agreements with contractors.* There are several different ways to employ a contractor. The best way is what is normally called "a turn key job." This means the contractor gives his bid and agrees to build a building for so much money. He does all of the labor and then presents the building to the church upon completion.

A very popular way of building is "cost plus 10%," which means the contractor agrees to build the building at what it costs him plus 10% for his profit.

An interesting way to build is called "contract plus percentage of savings." Suppose that a builder agrees to build a building for $100,000. An agreement can be made with him that a percentage of all he saves the church will go to him. For example, suppose he can build it for $90,000. Then he will get one-half of the $10,000 he saves. In other words, the original agreement is that the contractor makes 10% of the

$100,000 which is $10,000. If he can build the building for $90,000, he makes $15,000. If he can build the building for $80,000, he makes $20,000. So the more he saves, the more he makes.

Sometimes a church finds it impossible to employ a contractor and must build a building with volunteer labor. This is the worst of all the plans but it can be done and has been done very successfully.

In some cases the church will let the contract for a portion of the building and use volunteer labor for the rest. Perhaps the church members would want to paint the building, or lay the tile floor. Then these items simply could be left out of the contract and left to the church members to complete.

17. *As soon as the contract is let, the church could have a big ground-breaking day.* Goals should be set and a record attendance should be present. This should be a day of joy and victory. Often it is wise to have visiting dignitaries such as mayors, governors, congressmen, etc. The ground should be broken by the pastor, deacon chairman, or some other important member. Pictures should be taken to be used for future publicity purposes, for newspaper articles, etc.

18. *During the building program there should be a weekly meeting of the deacons.* This meeting is for the purpose of alerting the deacons to the progress of the building and allowing them to make necessary decisions as the building committee. Again the pastor should be very careful to keep the deacons informed and abreast with him in the building program.

19. *The pastor and deacons should work closely with the contractor.*

20. *Lighting should be considered very carefully.* Some architects and builders are a little aesthetic and tend to make the building a little dark. A light building is very important to a church, and care should be made to provide sufficient lighting.

21. *The building should depict the personality of the church.* It should reflect the church, and it certainly should not clash with the church's personality or profile.

22. *Give much attention to the public address system.* This is very vital. I like big speakers near the platform in preference to many little speakers scattered throughout the auditorium. The speaker should be able to hear himself. The pastor should certainly work closely with the architect and builder in this matter as the pastor is the expert involved as far as the public speaking is concerned. It matters not how beautiful the building; if the people cannot hear, the entire program is in vain.

23. *Following are some suggestions and sketches concerning the building of auditoriums and Sunday school classes with brief explanations of each:*

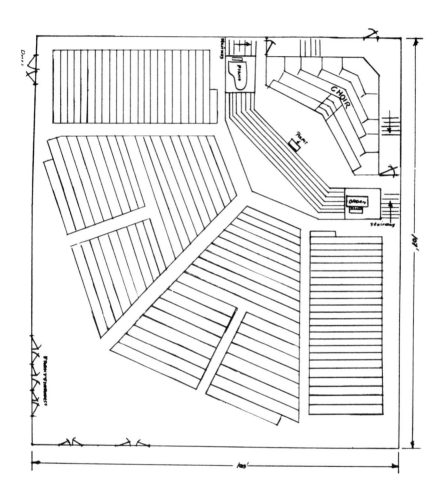

The fan-shaped auditorium shown above is for many the best audi-torium for speaking. This enables the speaker to be close to each person. It makes for good eye contact as well as acoustics.

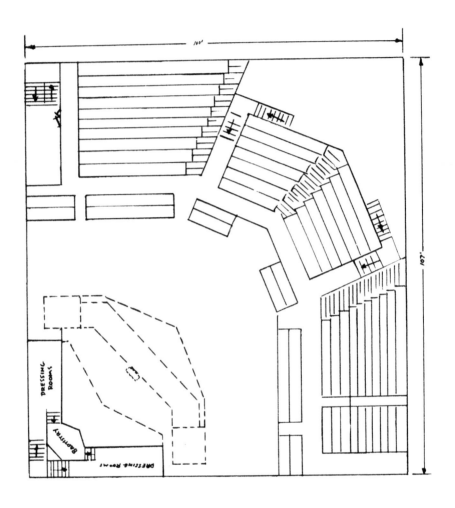

Using the type of balcony shown above, the seating capacity can be nearly doubled and with proper engineering, posts can be completely eliminated on the lower floor.

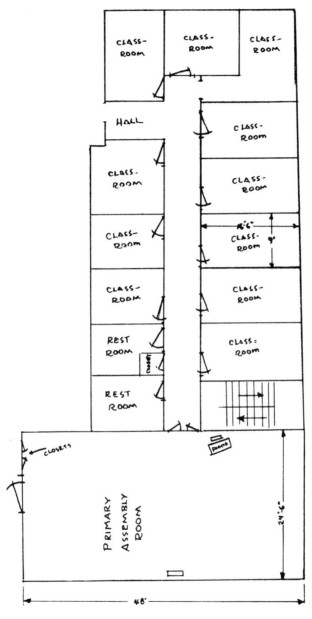

Many churches have used the above departmental plan. Notice the big assembly room and the small classrooms. The assembly room can also be used for classroom space by the use of modern folding doors. Though this is a good plan, one disadvantage is the amount of space used for hallway.

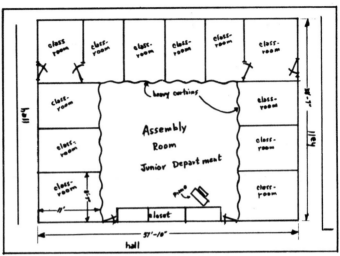

Above is a splendid departmental plan. Notice that the classrooms are located around the assembly room. The entrances to the class-rooms may be modern folding doors or heavy cloth. Many churches have used velour or velvet for this. These heavier materials keep out the sound very well. The advantage of this arrangement is that the assembly space is not limited to the big room but the classroom space can be used for assembly space when the folding doors or drapes are open. Suppose 200 children could be cared for in the classrooms. An assembly room seating 100 would be sufficient and the other 100 could sit in the classrooms during the opening assembly. This is a tremendous space saver.

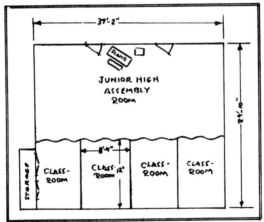

The above plan is similar to the previous one. The idea is the same. The classrooms can be used during the assembly time and much space is saved.

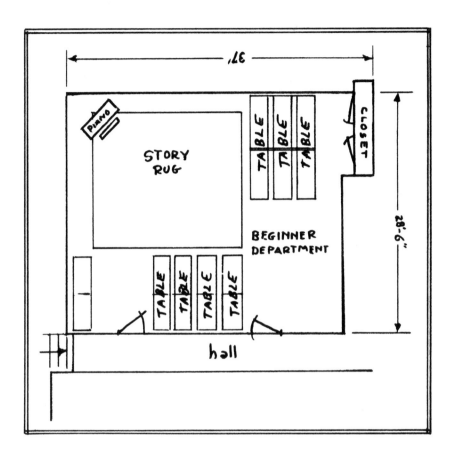

Here is a suggested arrangement for the Beginner Department. The previous sketches are only suggested for primary age and up. It seems to be a wise thing for the beginner and nursery children, ages 2 through 5, to be in open rooms. Notice the tables. Each class sits with its teacher at a table. At the tables the records may be taken, the handwork may be done, etc. Then the lesson is taught by a different teacher each week who teaches all of the children. The teacher stands at the edge of a rug shown above and known as the "story rug." The children gather around, sit on the story rug, and listen to the teaching of the lesson. Back to the tables they go for other handwork, etc. We have found it wise to use individual classes for the first grade and up and open rooms for preschoolers.

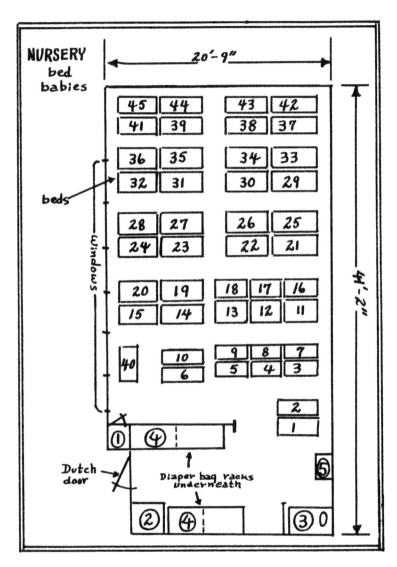

The above is a suggested nursery plan. You will notice several things:

1. Adequate closet and storage space
2. A half kitchen for the preparation of formula, warming of baby food, etc.
3. A diaper washer for the convenience of the workers
4. Diaper-changing tables
5. Diaper bag racks

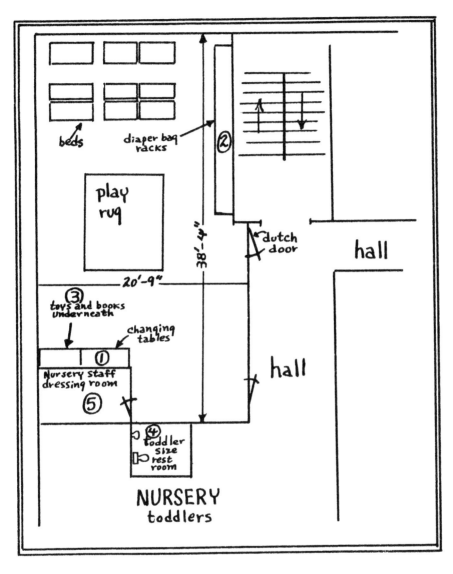

This is a suggested toddler nursery plan. You will notice several things:

1. Diaper-changing tables
2. Diaper bag racks
3. Toy boxes
4. Toddler-size restroom
5. Nursery staff dressing room

5. A Dedication Service for a New Building

(Sunday, June 18, 1967—7:30 p.m.)

Below is the dedication service for a new Sunday school building. At the closing of this service there were twenty conversions and additions, making a total of 122 for the day. Thirty-three were baptized.

CHOIR:

> To God be the glory, great things He hath done,
> So loved He the world that He gave us His Son,
> Who yielded His life an atonement for sin,
> And opened the life-gate that all may go in.
>
> Praise the Lord, praise the Lord,
> Let the earth hear His voice!
> Praise the Lord, praise the Lord,
> Let the people rejoice!
> O come to the Father, thro' Jesus the Son,
> And give Him the glory, great things He hath done.

MUSIC DIRECTOR: Thank you, choir. Shall we all stand, please. Turn to number 204 in your hymnals, please, 204, and all sing together this wonderful song, "To God Be the Glory," the second stanza. Everyone singing 204, the second stanza.

CONGREGATION:

> O perfect redemption, the purchase of blood,
> To every believer the promise of God!
> The vilest offender who truly believes,
> That moment from Jesus a pardon receives.
>
> Praise the Lord, praise the Lord,
> Let the earth hear His voice!
> Praise the Lord, praise the Lord,
> Let the people rejoice!
> O come to the Father, thro' Jesus the Son,
> And give Him the glory, great things He hath done.

Great things He hath taught us, great things He hath done,
And great our rejoicing thro' Jesus the Son;
But purer, and higher, and greater will be
Our wonder, our transport, when Jesus we see.

MUSIC DIRECTOR: Remain standing, please.

PASTOR: Thank you, Brother Terry. We normally do not sing the "Doxology" at First Baptist as a ritual but we sing it when we feel like singing it, and I feel like singing it right now. It has been a wonderful day, hasn't it? We have had tremendous blessings. We had 102 people saved or added to our church this morning. Isn't that something? This building was filled and thirteen to fifteen hundred people were having their own services outside this auditorium in other rooms. Tonight the building is packed and jammed. We are delighted that you are here. We appreciate your coming. It has been a wonderful day. Thank the Lord. So let us sing the "Doxology," not through ritual but from our hearts. Brother Terry, lead us in singing, "Praise God From Whom All Blessings Flow."

CONGREGATION:

Praise God, from whom all blessings flow;
Praise Him, all creatures here below;
Praise Him above, ye heav'nly host;
Praise Father, Son, and Holy Ghost!

PASTOR: Many people have made it possible for this day to be a reality. Among them few would have a higher place than Deacon Mel Graves. Mel Graves has been blessed of God with many gifts. He does a little bit of everything. His job is working for the Lyon-Healy Piano Company. Mel has worked in the business field and has done so many things. When our fire took place three years ago, he was the man who guided us in the securing of the insurance settlement. No one knows how many hours Mel worked at this. I thought it would be fitting for him to come lead us in the opening prayer for our Dedication Service. God bless him for all of the hours that he spent in helping the church in this matter.

MR. GRAVES: Our Heavenly Father, we are thankful for the privilege we have of being here this evening for this great occasion. We thank You for Jesus who made it possible. We thank Him for saving our souls. We thank Him for salvation and for the many people here in the great family of First Baptist.

Lord, as we think back over the years of the services here together with Brother Jack in this pastorate, we are thankful for every hardship that we have been through, for the lessons that we have learned, and for the fact that we have been shown how all things work together for good to them that love God and how great Thou hast been. You have opened doors for us to move ahead in Thy work. Lord, as the song said just a moment ago, may we always remember to give Thee all of the praise and glory for all of it.

We thank Thee, Lord, for these friends who have come to join us on this happy occasion. We pray that they will go away from here with a great blessing from having been here. We are thankful for everyone who had a part in the building and how smoothly the building program has gone. Lord, now would You open our hearts and guide us forward from this point on in greater service for Thee. In Jesus' name, Amen.

CHOIR:

My wonderful Lord, my wonderful Lord,
By angels and seraphs in Heaven adored!
I bow at Thy shrine, my Saviour divine,
My wonderful, wonderful Lord.

I have found a deep peace that I never had known
And a joy this world could not afford
Since I yielded control of my body and soul
To my wonderful, wonderful Lord.

Oh, what a wonderful Saviour is He!
Constant and true is Jesus.
More than I fancied He ever could be
Is Jesus, my wonderful Friend.

PASTOR: Thank you, choir, that is wonderful!

We want to recognize the special guests in a few moments, but now we will have a few announcements. Someone has written in this request: "Dear Brother Rice, will you sing, 'The Windows of Heaven Are Open?' This is a request." Here is a note that was placed on my desk: "Dear Dr. Rice, would you sing, 'The Windows of Heaven Are Open'?" So just forget your program for a minute, and by popular vote Dr. Rice is going to sing.

DR. RICE: Brother Terry, you come and sing it with me. I will sing the harmony.

DR. RICE AND MR. TERRY:

The windows of Heaven are open,
The blessings are falling tonight,
There's joy, joy, joy in my heart
Since Jesus made everything right.

I gave Him my old tattered garments.
He gave me a robe of pure white.
I'm feasting on manna from Heaven,
And that's why I'm happy tonight.

PASTOR: Oh, that is good. Thank you, thank you. I am glad that somebody thought of that. Now we would like to just say a word of greeting to our visiting friends and express to you our sincere appreciation because you are here. It has been a real joy for me to walk through the building this afternoon and meet people whom I have not seen for a long time and to see others who refreshed my own heart by their presence.

Let us have every person tonight who is not a member of First Baptist to honor us by standing. Would you stand, please. That is right. All over the house, there are many, many of you, and we want you to stand. I think that it is only fair to say that we have a great crowd of visitors tonight. Take one of our visitors' cards. One half of it is for you for a souvenir. Deposit the other half in the collection plate after awhile, please.

Tonight we do have honored guests. Mrs. John R. Rice is here. Mrs. Rice, would you stand, please. It is always a joy to have you, Mrs. Rice. God bless you. We are glad that you could come this week. Fairy Shappard is here. Fairy, would you stand. Fairy has been employed by the Sword of the Lord for thirty-two years. It is always a joy to have Fairy with us.

Leroy Troyer is here. He works with Bob Foltz and has made a real contribution to this building and the new building. Leroy, will you and your lovely family stand, please. Here he is with his wife, twin boys, and another little fellow. Leroy, it is so nice to have you.

Presentation of the Building

Now we come to the dedication part of this service, and we start off with the presentation of the building. Mr. Harry Edwards (the building superintendent), would you come, please, and present the building. Bless his heart. We have had the finest, most congenial people working on this job that I have ever worked with in my life. One of the most congenial is Harry Edwards. He has done a tremendous job. He has heard me say only one word. He doesn't think that I have but a one-word vocabulary. That is "Hurry!"

MR. EDWARDS: Hurry, Harry.

PASTOR: Hurry, Harry. That is right.

MR. EDWARDS: Thank you. Well, we made it. First of all, I wish to extend, on behalf of our contractor, Mr. Reuth, who could not be here this evening, our sincere thanks to you, your staff, and Bob Foltz for his complete cooperation. We thank you for the understanding that we have had from you people throughout the construction period, which has been approximately a year. It has always amazed me how that during the planning of a new structure the architect can visualize in his mind what the new building will look like and then transfer these dreams on paper line by line, which would make up the construction drawings for the new building. In the hands of the builder these lines become concrete, brick, glass, and wood as the structure rises out of the ground. Mr. Foltz, I sincerely hope that you can recognize this as your dream building as I offer it to you for your acceptance in offering you the keys in behalf of Leo Reuth and Sons.

PASTOR: Mr. Foltz, will you come, please. Actually, I told the fellows a while ago that Mr. Edwards presents the keys to Mr. Foltz, Mr. Foltz presents them to Mr. Rausch, Mr. Rausch gives them to me, and then we are going to give them back to Mr. Edwards so that he can finish the building. (Laughter from the congregation)

Mrs. Edwards is here tonight. Mrs. Edwards, would you stand, please. We are delighted that you could come. May I just say again to you and your husband how much we appreciate your contribution. I have a letter to read while these men are here. I have a letter to read from Mr. Reuth of the Reuth Construction Company:

Dear Dr. Hyles:

I am very sorry that I cannot be with you on this happy occasion of the completion of another milestone in your growth. I had promised to take my wife and children on a vacation which is the first in fourteen years. Our reservations for Expo '67 came last week after a month's wait, and I could not change the date.

Congratulations on the dedication of this new building. I am sure that it will be more than a new building. It will be a place of learning, where people of all ages can learn of Christ. To know Christ is to love Him. If truly we become Christians with love and charity for all, we will not only improve the world but insure our own eternal salvation.

May God Almighty bless your efforts. Smile! God loves you.

Harold Reuth

This is from the Reuth Construction Company. We do appreciate so much your coming, Harry. God bless you. We do appreciate you.

Presentation of Keys

Mr. Bob Foltz is our architect. Bob is an artist. He is the one who conceived in his mind this lovely auditorium. Preachers from all over the world have commented on the loveliness of this building, and, in fact, it is probably one of the most copied buildings in America today. Numbers of churches are being built much like this one. Then the Lord seemed to lead us to Bob Foltz again for the new Sunday school building. The many, many little niceties on which you commented today are largely attributed to Bob Foltz and his ideas. We are glad that he could be here. Bob, is your family with you?

MR. FOLTZ: I have been winking at them right up there in the balcony.

PASTOR: All right, will you stand, please, Mrs. Foltz and the Foltz children. We are so glad that you could come tonight. We appreciate it so much. Bob Foltz is a born-again Christian man. He works with churches and has a love for the Lord. We are glad that he could come. Bob Foltz will present the keys.

MR. FOLTZ: Thank you. Destroying Adams Chapel by arson was a dastardly act. Many people of many places have agonized with you of First Baptist over the loss of that old structure. I have personally shown many times the pictures I took on that Friday morning, and, without exception, there are always oh's and ah's and groans as they see the flames still burning on the remains over there.

We know that all things work together for good for those that love God. Rising in the place of Adams Chapel is a new building (of course, I may be accused of being prejudiced) that is not only beautiful, but one that is utterly functional. We thank the Lord for the privilege of being able to participate in this program with you. I too have congratulated Harry on the work that Leo Reuth and Sons, and Harry Edwards in particular, has done here. Publicly I would like to say that in my experience the cooperation and the caliber of employees and subcontractors, etc., that go to make the program have been without equal. We realize that this building is just a tool, but it is a tool that can be used for good, measured not only in time but eternity. We trust that you might use this new tool well. It is a great pleasure to pass these keys to Brother Rausch. Do, by God's leading, use this tool well and effectively for Him.

PASTOR: Thank you, Bob. Let's give Mr. Foltz and Mr. Edwards and their companies a big hand, shall we? (Applause)

Acceptance by the Church

Now, God's good man and my good friend—Mr. Ed Rausch. I don't know what I would do without him. I don't know what I would have done these eight years without him. Ed Rausch will accept the building and give the words from the board of deacons, our building committee. Let us have all of the deacons to stand before he does this. Will all of the deacons please stand. God bless these men. I don't know how many meetings we have had in the last five years just for buildings, etc. It has been a wonderful picture of God's grace and cooperation together. How these men have worked! Thank you, fellows. God bless you. Now Brother Rausch will accept the keys for the church.

MR. RAUSCH: On behalf of the church congregation, it is with the very deepest of appreciation that I accept these keys to the beautiful building that you have already seen. Certainly, in a building of this nature, there has to be good planning, and we had good planning by Mr. Foltz and his staff. Then there has to be a building made from those plans, and for Mr. Edwards' following of those plans and for Mr. Reuth, certainly we are deeply appreciative of that which we are able to use and see this day.

As I think of this building, I realize that it is made of brick, of stone, of wood, and it is constructed in a way that it will probably last for scores of years. That fades in the thought that in this building there is a facility where the lives of people will be changed for all eternity. So we are thankful today and deeply appreciative to accept this fine building which will be used solely for the glory of Christ. We praise Him for this opportunity and this occasion, for surely the blessings of God have been on this congregation, this ministry, Brother Jack Hyles, and his good staff. Certainly we would have Christ have all of the glory and all of the honor. We praise Him for it.

PASTOR: Thank you, Ed. God bless you.

Dedication Prayer

What I am about to do is going to be a little bit emotional for me. There is a lot involved here. Nobody knows the hours that C. W. Fisk has worked. He has been the man from the church's standpoint that has kept things going. I have asked him to lead our prayer of dedication. Last night at 2:30 he started to leave the building and, as he has been doing for these weeks, he does much of the work himself. He got a broom and went down to the corner to sweep off the sidewalk. Three men came up and hit him in the face (as you can see) and knocked him nearly unconscious. He couldn't move. They rolled him over, got his billfold, and left him lying on the sidewalk. But for the grace of God he could have been killed. We are so thankful that God spared him. He is a good man. He was saved in this church and called to preach in this church. The work he has done on this building absolutely has been phenomenal.

Brother Fisk, would you come, please, and we are going to award this check of $300.00 as a token of our appreciation. I appreciate so much what he has done. God has given us here the greatest staff in America and only God knows how much credit these deserve. When everyone around the country says, "Dr. Hyles is doing a great work in Hammond," I say, No, no. God is doing a great work in Hammond and is using people like Fisk and others to get the job done. This is to you from grateful people. If you can compose yourself, we want you to lead our dedication prayer.

MR. FISK: Let's pray. Our Father, Thou hast said in Psalm 127:1, "Except the Lord build the house, they labour in vain that build it." Now Father, we know that the Lord has been the One who has built this building. We thank Thee, O God, for the wisdom Thou hast given these men to plan the building—Mr. Edwards, Mr. Foltz, and all of these contractors who have worked together on it. We thank Thee, O God, for our board of deacons and for our pastor. We thank Thee that Thou hast blessed. There has been much work and much prayer, but Father, we have something for which to be grateful. We just pray, Father, that in the days to come we will be faithful to preach and teach the Word of God in this building. Father, I pray if the day would ever come that we cease to preach and teach the Word of God in this building and see people saved in this building, that it be razed to the ground. Father, we thank Thee for the building. We thank Thee for all of these who have worked to make it possible. Bless now in the days to come and may we see many souls saved. In Jesus' name, Amen.

PASTOR: Brother Fisk leaves a week from tomorrow on a well-deserved vacation. Maybe the check will help him to stay in a little higher-class motel as he goes. Nobody ever took a $300.00 check that deserved it any more than Brother Fisk. Let's give him a hand. (Applause)

Pastor's Message

The Apostle Paul said in Romans 8:28, "And we know that all things work together for good to them that love God, to them who are the called according to his purpose." It is awfully easy for us to say that. It is easy to learn it, and it is easy to quote it, but sometimes it is not easy to believe it. When you stand beside a casket, as I will do tomorrow morning, and look into the face of one who has served faithfully through the years in the church, sometimes it is difficult to believe. When you look in the face of a little baby who has been taken before an opportunity to live was granted, and you try to tell the parents why, sometimes you wonder if Romans 8:28 is really true. Oh, yes, you believe it, but it is hard to explain.

Three years ago this month we stood across the street as a congregation. From the wee hours of the morning until noontime of the next day, most of us stood across the street. Many watched a lifetime of memories go up in smoke. People wept openly and unashamedly, for the building was more than a building. In 1913 God gave to our church the building that we had known then as the Adams Chapel. The auditorium was used as a place to preach the Gospel for a half a century. Many of you were born with your family attending this building. How many of you were born and reared in this church and grew up in the other auditorium? Would you raise your hands, please. Oh, many of you were, and you stood across the street, and mingled our tears. We thought that "all things work together for good to them that love God, to them who are the called according to his purpose." I confess it wasn't easy to see. I stood alone on the street corner over at the Firestone Store weeping. Brother Jim Lyons came over and put his arms around me. I did not know he was there.

He said, "Preacher, we have seen an awful lot together."

And I said, "That is true, Jim."

We stood and watched the dome, which was a landmark in the city of Hammond, when it fell and crushed to pieces. The Associated Press got the story and all across the world it went. Television stations, radio stations, and newspapers told of the fire at the First Baptist Church of Hammond. We said to ourselves with tears in our eyes that "we know that all things work together for good to them that love God, to them who are the called according to his purpose." It was hard to see.

We still have lingering in our minds the memories of walking through the halls of our lovely new building, and tonight we not only believe Romans 8:28, but we can see how it is true. As a church tonight we can say with the Apostle Paul, "And we know ...." That word "know" in the original language is an interesting word. It means that we know something that no one else knows. We have a little private, secret order of people who love God and who live in His will. There is something we know. What is that something? "...that all things work together for good to them that love God, to them who are the called according to his purpose."

My heart fills with gratitude tonight as I look at our people, realizing that many of you have sacrificed. Numbers of you had planned to buy a car this year. You have not bought the car. Many of you have foregone vacations this summer because of your sacrificial gift. This is not Hyles' building. This is not the deacons' building; it is *our* building—yours and mine. We thank God for it, for His blessings, and yes, even for the fire. "And we know that all things work together for good to them that love God, to them who are the called according to his purpose."

MUSIC DIRECTOR: We have a special song by Mrs. Jack Hyles, Mrs. Vic Nischik, and Mrs. Johnny Colsten. This trio of ladies shall sing a song of testimony called, "Now I Am Saved."

Lost in my sins, in the darkness I wandered,
Banished from God, knowing not of His grace,
Seeking by merit to gain my salvation,
Ever despairing of winning the race.

Now I am saved, I can shout, "Hallelujah!"
Saved from my sins and my pathway made right;
No more in darkness and fears shall I wander;
Jesus has scattered my gloom and my night.

Oh, how I grasped at God's offer of mercy
When by His grace He revealed it to me,
Showing me Christ, who had purchased my pardon
When for my sins He was judged on the tree.

MUSIC DIRECTOR: Now then, turn to number 52 in your hymnals. "Praise Him! Praise Him! Jesus Our Blessed Redeemer!" Number 52.

CONGREGATION:

Praise Him! Praise Him! Jesus, our blessed Redeemer!
Sing, O earth, His wonderful love proclaim!
Hail Him! Hail Him! Highest archangels in glory;
Strength and honor give to His holy name!
Like a shepherd, Jesus will guard His children,
In His arms He carries them all day long:

Praise Him! Praise Him! Tell of His excellent greatness;
Praise Him! Praise Him! ever in joyful song!

MUSIC DIRECTOR: Now for the last stanza.

CONGREGATION:

Praise Him! Praise Him! Jesus, our blessed Redeemer!
Heavenly portals loud with hosannas ring!
Jesus, Saviour, reigneth forever and ever;
Crown Him! Crown Him! Prophet, and Priest, and King!
Christ is coming! Over the world victorious,
Power and glory unto the Lord belong:
Praise Him! Praise Him! Tell of His excellent greatness;
Praise Him! Praise Him! ever in joyful song!

Special Offering

PASTOR: Now we come to the offering time. We want all to make a
final offering to the building fund. The envelopes are before you in the
pews. We decided to raise $82,000.00. This much money has been
spent. As of now, so said the financial secretary a few moments ago,
we have $79,609.62. Isn't that wonderful! Tonight we would like to
raise that other $2,400.00. Most of you have but a few dollars any-
way. Let us just go ahead and see this through. My billfold has
$11.00 in it. I have already given quite a bit, and I am going to put
$11.00 in the building fund offering. Take one of the envelopes and
make a final contribution to the building fund tonight. We had a meeting of some of the newer members of our church, and they plan to
give some in the next thirty days. Wouldn't it be wonderful if I could
announce tomorrow night in the service that the $82,000.00 was all
in? Make some offering to the building fund tonight. Are there any
envelopes in the choir? Bring some to the choir. This is one of the
wealthiest choirs in America. (Laughter)
Here is an interesting thing. A man came to me who had met me
one time. I sat across from him at a banquet in Indianapolis. I would
not have known him if I had seen him. He came to me this afternoon.
He said that he wanted this church to have this envelope. In the envelope is a check for $500.00. That man does not even belong to our
church. He is just a friend. He just loves the First Baptist Church of
Hammond. I thought you would be glad to hear that. Mr. Sinning is
his name. You will want to make your offering tonight as the final
building fund offering. Brother Johnny Colsten, would you come tonight and lead us in prayer. Johnny Colsten is on our staff. Johnny,
would you come, please, and lead us in our offertory prayer.

MR. COLSTEN: Shall we please pray. Our Father, we are grateful
for Your goodness. You have been good beyond any deserving on our
part and yet we are so grateful. We are grateful for Your hand of

blessing, grateful for Your evidence of power and might as shown in not only the raising of this building but the people who have been behind it. You have guided and led every step of the way. You have laid it upon the hearts of many people not only to give, but to sacrifice. We are thankful for it and we ask now Your blessing upon this building-fund offering. We pray, Lord, that You would put it upon our hearts to do what is right and what You would have us to do concerning this offering. Bless it and use it to the building, not only of buildings, but to the building of souls of men, women, boys and girls, and for the exaltation of our Lord and Saviour, Jesus Christ, in whose name we ask it. Amen.

(The Dedication Message was then preached by Dr. John R. Rice.)

6. The Deacon Board

Our discussion centers around the Bible office of the deacon. The Word of God has a divine message. It also contains divine methods. It is not enough to preach the message unless we also use the methods of the Word of God. Our discussion for this chapter is the Bible deacon.

Not long ago a very fine family moved from our church and our city to another area and another state. The man was a medical doctor, and he and his wife had a lovely little daughter. The daughter loved our church dearly (for that matter, so did the mother and father), and she missed us so much. She was particularly impressed by the fact that the pastor preached behind the pulpit and the deacons sat around on the front—many on the front rows and others near the front. When she attended the church in the other city, she came home the first morning and said, "Mommy and Daddy, I didn't like that church at all."

"Why didn't you like that church?" asked her mother and father.

"Well," she said, "at First Baptist Church in Hammond, Brother Hyles stands behind the pulpit and all the 'demons' sit on the front."

She was talking about deacons, of course, and she was disappointed because the "demons" (deacons) did not sit on the front at the new church they were attending.

Now in many cases I am afraid "demons" would be a more appropriate term than deacons for the leaders of many of our churches. These men of God who hold this Bible office can be deacons or demons, depending upon whether or not they take the Word of God as their authority and their plan. I hope in the next few pages to show you the Bible plan for deacons in a New Testament church. If we do not follow the Bible plan, deacons may become demons and may do more harm than good.

How I thank God for those men through the years whom God has given me to hold up my hands in prayer and to work with me in the work of the church and the Lord Jesus Christ.

When Moses' arms were heavy in days of old, God gave to him Aaron and Hur to hold his hands high. Aaron got on one side; Hur, on the other. Each lifted one of Moses' arms high. When his arms were lifted, the battle was won. When his arms were lowered, the battle was lost (Exod. 17:12). God has, in His wisdom, given to pastors today in the New Testament church men of God called deacons who lift the hands of the pastor, work with him, and serve God with him in loyal, sacrificial service to the church and to the Saviour.

It is said of Saul, the first king of Israel, shortly after he was anointed, "And Saul also went home to Gibeah; and there went with him a band of men, whose hearts God had touched" (I Sam. 10:26). How much easier it is for a pastor to serve the Lord Jesus Christ when it can be said of him that there went with him a band of men—deacons, if you please—whose hearts God had touched. Even our Saviour, the Lord Jesus Christ, chose twelve men to work with Him, or stand beside Him, walk with Him, and learn from Him in His work of redemption.

How I thank God for the men whom God has given me in the First Baptist Church of Hammond, Indiana; in the Miller Road Baptist Church of Garland, Texas; in the Southside Baptist Church of Henderson, Texas; in the Grange Hall Baptist Church of Marshall, Texas; and even in the Marris Chapel Baptist Church near Bogata, Texas, a little country church where I served my first pastorate, I had a godly deacon.

In this chapter I hope to help deacons and pastors properly fulfill God's plan and purpose for church organization and help them realize the qualifications, duties, responsibilities, etc., of this great Bible office.

ELECTION OF THE DEACONS

We turn our attention first to this subject: How are the deacons elected? In the First Baptist Church of Hammond we use the following procedure:

The Deacons Form the Nominating Committee

Each deacon is asked to bring a list of ten men in the church whom he feels would make good deacon material. These ten men are listed and brought to the deacons' meeting early in the calendar year. The pastor writes the name of each man that is recommended by the deacons on the blackboard. Oftentimes we have as many as seventy-five or one hundred names listed on the blackboard. Then, the name is called orally. The deacons bow their heads, pray about whether they feel that man should run for deacon or not, and then we vote. Unless a man received a unanimous vote from our present deacons, he cannot run for the office of deacon for that year. In other words, the pastor and each deacon have veto power. We presently have sixty-six men serving as deacons in the First Baptist Church of Hammond. For a man to run for the office of deacon he has to have sixty-seven affirmative votes—sixty-six from the deacons and one from the pastor.

With heads bowed and eyes closed, the pastor says, "Is any person here ready to veto this particular man?"

If a deacon lifts his hand, the man is vetoed and does not run for deacon.

We do not ask the man why he vetoes this prospect. He simply lifts his hand. At this meeting we do not discuss the merit or demerit of men of our church. No word of criticism is given. He simply is accepted or vetoed.

The Pastor Meets with Prospective Deacons

When the list is completed and the names that have been vetoed have been scratched from the list, the remaining names on the list are asked to run for deacons for the next year. The pastor meets with these men and tells them of the honor that the present deacons have bestowed upon them. The pastor talks with them frankly. He explains to them the qualifications of a deacon. He explains the responsibilities and duties of a deacon. He explains what is expected of deacons of our church. Then the pastor simply says, "If for any reason you do not meet the qualifications or would not fulfill the responsibilities, would you please not run."

The pastor then gives a card to each of these men who have been approved by the deacons to run for deacon. The pastor simply asks each to write his name on a card and "yes" or "no." If he wants to run, the answer is "yes." If he refuses to run, the answer is "no." Once again, the pastor does not ask them why they will not run. He does, however, explain to them that if they do not meet all the qualifications or if they will not fulfill each responsibility, they should not run for deacon.

The Church Approves Those Who Run

When the men have been passed unanimously by our present deacons and have agreed themselves to run for the office of deacon, then their names are presented to the church at a regular monthly business meeting. The church approves them as candidates for deacons. Bear in mind, this does not elect them as deacons but simply approves them to run for the office of deacon. We usually have several more running than we have offices to fill. For example, if we have twenty vacancies, we may have twenty-five or thirty men running. This gives the people a choice.

Shortly after the church approves these men to run, a ballot is made and an election is held. We keep the polls open between six o'clock and seven-thirty on a particular Wednesday night. The people come between six and seven-thirty, receive their ballots and cast their votes at the polls. If we have twenty offices available, and if twenty-five names are listed, each person is asked to put a check beside twenty of the twenty-five names. These represent the men they feel should be deacons for the new year. Those with the highest number of votes, of course, become deacons in our church.

A Dedication Service Is Held

Shortly after the election we have a dedication service and we set aside these new men to be deacons in the First Baptist Church of Hammond. You may want to call it an ordination service, if you please. Some would prefer this; some would not. We call it a dedication service. At this service we honor the deacons who have served the previous years. We welcome the deacons who have been chosen to serve for the new year. We have the biblical service of the laying on of hands and of offering prayer to God that He may give wisdom and leadership to these men who shall lead our church for the coming year.

After this, the pastor writes a letter of appreciation and thanks to those who were not elected, thanking them for running for deacon and assuring them of his love and appreciation to and for them. This is how we elect deacons at the First Baptist Church of Hammond.

QUALIFICATIONS OF DEACONS

Our second thought for this discussion shall be the qualification of deacons. Of course the first thing that we have to remember is the Scripture. In I Timothy, chapters 2, 3, and 4, God gives the divine order for a local church—pastor and deacons. In chapter 3, verses 8-13 read:

"Likewise must the deacons be grave, not doubletongued, not given to much wine, not greedy of filthy lucre; Holding the mystery of the faith in a pure conscience. And let these also first be proved; then let them use the office of a deacon, being found blameless. Even so must their wives be grave, not slanderers, sober, faithful in all things. Let the deacons be the husbands of one wife, ruling their children and their own houses well. For they that have used the office of a deacon well purchase to themselves a good degree, and great boldness in the faith which is in Christ Jesus."

Now we require that every man who becomes a deacon or even runs for the office of deacon in the First Baptist Church, meet these qualifications. If you notice very carefully, you will notice not only are the qualifications listed for the men but also for their wives. A man should not be a deacon unless he meets the qualifications laid out in I Timothy 3:8-13. A man should not be a deacon unless his wife meets the qualifications laid out in I Timothy 3:11-13.

There are other qualifications, however, that our church requires. For example, we require that the man be a member of the First Baptist Church for at least one year before he can run for the office of a deacon. We do not accept a man from another church as a deacon just because he was a deacon in the other church. We accept each man on an equal basis according to his qualifications, his devotion and service for the Lord Jesus Christ.

Let me pause to say this word of warning: We do not choose a man to be a deacon because of his financial standing. That is not even taken into consideration. We do not take into consideration a man's social standing in the community. He might be the head of the school board, the mayor of the town, the president of the bank, or the richest man in the whole city. That does not give him one bit of preference over the poorest man in the city. We use only Bible and spiritual qualifications. Pastor friend, you will rue the day, and my Christian friend, your church will rue the day that deacons were chosen because of talent, social standing, financial standing, prestige, or educational background. The Bible says nothing of this. We choose them because of spiritual qualifications only!

Let us list some others. A deacon must be a soul winner to fill this office in the First Baptist Church of Hammond. No one can run for the office of deacon unless he actively participates in the soul-winning ministry of this church.

Then, we require a deacon to be separate from the world. No man can be a deacon in our church if he drinks alcohol in any form. No man can be a deacon in our church if he uses tobacco in any form. No man can be a deacon in our church if he dances or if he would transgress against any of the convictions that we have here at the First Baptist Church. We believe that the leaders of the church ought to be above reproach. We believe that the leaders who fill the Bible offices for a church ought to be men who walk straight, whose lives are clean, who are peculiar people, a chosen generation, a royal priesthood, an holy nation, men who walk with God, avoid the appearance of evil, and whose lives are clean. Consequently, we expect and demand separation from the world and from worldly practices by those who fill this Bible office.

There is still another qualification. We expect and demand faithfulness to the public services of our church. No man can run for the office of deacon in the First Baptist Church of Hammond unless he is faithful to the Sunday school, faithful to the Sunday morning service, faithful to the Sunday evening service, and faithful to the Wednesday evening service. The men who fill the office of deacon in the First Baptist Church are required to be faithful! Just because a man has money, prestige, power, influence, or leadership ability does not give him any preference over the others. I know church after church that has such men serving as leaders in the church who do not even attend the midweek service on Wednesday night, and oftentimes not even the Sunday evening service, when the preacher pours his heart out before sinners and before God. What a pity! What a shame! How we need to reexamine ourselves concerning the qualifications of our deacons.

Another qualification is the trait of loyalty. We demand and expect that our deacons be loyal—loyal to the church, loyal to the pastor, loyal to the program of the church, and loyal to what God is doing through the church and through the pastor. Don't you see? The deacons were originally chosen by God (if the men chosen in the sixth chapter of Acts were, for a fact, deacons—and I think they were) to help the pastor, to lift up his hands, to help serve him, to be a boost to him, and to be a help to him. When a deacon ceases to be loyal to the church program and the pastor whom God has called, then he ceases to fulfill one of the main purposes for a deacon and the original purpose for the office.

In Acts 6:3 we read, "Wherefore, brethren, look ye out among you seven men of honest report, full of the Holy Ghost and wisdom, whom we may appoint over this business."

With these Bible qualifications, I believe that God can make your church and mine a spiritual lighthouse and a soul-winning center for the Gospel of the Lord Jesus Christ.

Someone would ask, "Pastor, what happens if you elect a man to be a deacon in your church and find out that he smokes or drinks?" Immediately he is dismissed by the board of deacons. Immediately we call a special meeting of our board and this man is asked to resign. If he does not resign as requested, then, of course, we will excuse him from the board of deacons. This is important.

Let me make this word of warning, however. If enough pressure, earnestness, and frankness is exerted in the meeting *before* the deacons run and *before* the men are presented to the church, explaining to these men that if they run for deacon they must meet the qualifications, and if they do not meet the qualifications after they are elected, they will be excused from the board, this will avoid some problems and heartaches later on. Make the front door small and the back door will not have to be large either.

DUTIES OF THE DEACONS

Now we think not only of the election of the deacons and the qualifications of the deacons, but let us notice the duties of the deacons. May I list them for you.

1. The deacons help in the work with the shut-ins of the church.

2. The deacons form an advisory board. The board has no authority whatsoever. A simple, organized church has pastor, deacons, and

people—this is the scriptural plan. There are only two offices mentioned in the Bible—pastor and deacon. The deacons have no authority whatsoever. They are simply a board of advisory, a board of recommendation.

These men seek out plans for the future of our church. They prayerfully consider what direction we ought to go. They prayerfully consider the future of our church. They consider the buying of property, the drawing up of the budget, and the planning of the church's future. They consider the building of buildings, etc. These men find what they feel are the best plans for the First Baptist Church. Then they come before the church body and recommend to the church body what they think should be done. The final authority rests, not with the pastor, not with the deacons, but with the church. Hence, these men can not spend one dime on their own. They cannot make one decision on their own. The decisions are made with the approval, yea, with the vote of the church. We believe that a church in business matters should be a democracy. Our deacons only advise.

I do think that it is only fair to say, however, that in almost every case our church accepts the recommendations of the deacons. I cannot recall a single recommendation that our deacons have made to our church that was not heartily, enthusiastically, and even unanimously accepted by the church. In spite of this fact, the final authority rests with the congregation and not with the deacons. They are simply an advisory board.

3. The deacons are the pastor's helpers. Let us never forget this. In the book of Acts, this was the purpose of their existence. You will notice in Acts, chapter 6, verses 1-3:

"And in those days, when the number of the disciples was multiplied, there arose a murmuring of the Grecians against the Hebrews, because their widows were neglected in the daily ministration. Then the twelve called the multitude of the disciples unto them, and said, It is not reason that we should leave the word of God, and serve tables. Wherefore, brethren, look ye out among you seven men of honest report, full of the Holy Ghost and wisdom, whom we may appoint over this business."

The purpose of the choosing of these men in the first place was that the pastor might be helped. The deacons in the First Baptist Church of Hammond, thanks be to God, are the pastor's helpers.

4. From the board of deacons is chosen all elected officers of the church. Every committee of our church is composed of men on the board of deacons, and the deacons form every committee of our church. Our church treasurer must be a deacon. Our church clerk must be a deacon. Our head usher must be a deacon. All of our committees must be chosen from the deacons. Now there is a reason for this.

This means that when the deacons meet, every committee is present, and every church officer is present. Most pastors, I am afraid, are busier than a one-arm paperhanger running from one committee meeting to another. Why not enlarge the deacon board and why not choose from these men the men who hold offices in the church and form committees in the church, thereby having every committee and every church officer present every time the deacons are called together. Many a pastor would have been saved a nervous breakdown and ten ulcers if he had followed this simple procedure.

By the way, I think I should say this: We have no standing committees. We appoint a committee of deacons to do a job. When that job is done, the committee disbands.

5. There is another duty that our deacons fulfill which we list as number five. The deacons elect five of their own to serve as trustees in the church. We do not have a double board, or a dual board in our church. We simply have the one board—the board of deacons. Since, however, we are a corporation under the laws of our state, we must have trustees. These trustees are elected from the deacon board. By virtue of the fact that our chairman is also the president of the corporation, he is a trustee. Four other men are elected from the other deacons to fill the office of trustee. These five trustees have no authority. They have no meetings. They simply fill an honorary position fulfilling the laws required by the State of Indiana. Why have two boards when the board of deacons can care for the needs of the church?

6. Our deacons do the personal work at the altar. On Sunday morning when the invitation is given, the deacons come to the front and as the people come receiving Jesus Christ as Saviour, a deacon takes his Bible, kneels at the altar, opens the Word of God and leads the man or woman to the Lord Jesus Christ. All of the personal work is done by the board of deacons.

7. Our deacons count the money on Sunday afternoon. We divide our men into four different groups. Each group counts the money one Sunday afternoon a month. The money is counted in the afternoon and deposited by the deacons. No one else touches the money. For that matter, when the offering is taken in a public service, the deacons (several of them) must go together and carry the offering to the safe. The money is handled only by deacons.

8. The deacons take care of baptism and the Lord's Supper. The deacons prepare the Lord's Supper and work in the men's dressing rooms preparing the new converts for the ordinance of baptism. The deacons serve the Lord's Supper. We have men from our deacon board chosen to do these jobs.

9. Our deacons oversee the entire program of the church. With no authority, only as a board of recommendation or board of advisory,

these men guide the church, stand out in front, sit up in the tower, and look toward the future, trying to suggest the best way the First Baptist Church should go.

HOW MANY DEACONS?

We leave the responsibilities and duties now and discuss how many deacons a church should have. We feel it is best to have many deacons. I think there is strength in numbers. We have sixty-six deacons. We try to have one deacon for each one hundred members of our church. At the present time we have more than 6600 members but we do have only sixty-six deacons.

One-third of the deacon board goes off annually. Each man is elected for a three-year term. He must run again if he is to succeed himself, and by the way, he can succeed himself, which means that twenty-two of our men go off each year. They can run again, others run against them, and from these men we have another twenty-two men elected for a three-year term.

OFFICERS OF THE BOARD

What are the officers of the deacon board? We have these officers: a chairman, a first vice chairman, a second vice chairman, a secretary, an assistant secretary, and five trustees. These men are elected by the deacon board at the first deacons' meeting after the starting of our new church year.

In conclusion, may I simply make this observation. The main relationship of a deacon is to be a pal and an encouragement to his pastor.

Have we demons or deacons? I say deacons. I have not known what it is to pastor demons. How I thank God for those men who have labored with me through these years filling the Bible office of deacon, helping the pastor, praying for the pastor, and serving with the pastor.

God bless these good men and increase their tribe.

.

7. A Dedication Service for New Deacons

(Wednesday, May 18, 1967—7:30 p.m.)

Of the thirty-four deacons elected in the 1967 election of deacons, ten had not served on the deacon board previously. For these ten men a special dedication service was held in the auditorium on a Wednesday evening, which is annually set aside for this purpose.

PASTOR: Once again we come to the annual Deacon Dedication Service here at First Baptist Church. It has been our policy now for many years to set aside one Wednesday evening service a year for the consecration, dedication, and ordination of our new deacons. It is a real joy this year to have ten new deacons, nine of whom are here tonight. One is on vacation. We present them to you for ordination this evening.

The type service we have this evening is certainly a biblical one. I read for you, Acts, chapter 6, starting with verse 1:

"And in those days, when the number of the disciples was multiplied, there arose a murmuring of the Grecians against the Hebrews, because their widows were neglected in the daily ministration. Then the twelve called the multitude of the disciples unto them, and said, It is not reason that we should leave the word of God, and serve tables. Wherefore, brethren, look ye out among you seven men of honest report, full of the Holy Ghost and wisdom, whom we may appoint over this business. But we will give ourselves continually to prayer, and to the ministry of the word."

Verse 6, please.

"Whom they set before the apostles: and when they had prayed, they laid their hands on them. And the word of God increased; and the number of the disciples multiplied in Jerusalem greatly; and a great company of the priests were obedient to the faith."

The service about which we just read is the type service we plan to have this evening. I think it is one of the sweetest services of the year, and certainly I have occasion to rejoice and feel gratitude in my own heart for the privilege of welcoming these fine new men who are on the front row of our auditorium tonight.

I think first, however, I should, as pastor, on behalf of our people, once again express our sincere appreciation for these men who served for the past year. I do not see how any pastor could have more faithful, loyal, loving, spiritual deacons than I. How I thank God for the deacons of our church. It has been this way from the first until now. Our deacons have stood the test; they have proven their loyalty to the pastor through thick and thin. Much has been thick and some has been thin. I appreciate these men personally, and I know that you appreciate their ministry and their labor of love for the past year.

Introduction of New Deacons

Now we come to the introduction of the new deacons—those whom you have elected to join our deacon board for 1967-68. We introduce them one at a time to acquaint you with them. Deacon Rausch will come and introduce the first one.

MR. RAUSCH: I would like to have Brother Thomas Bennett to come up. I have known Brother Bennett for several years now. In fact, he came into the Men's Bible Class, which I teach, and there it was a joy for me to see him grow in grace and service for the Lord. He became an officer for the class. I believe about a little over a year ago Brother Tom became a teacher in our Sunday school. I think this always gives evidence of a man's growth in the Lord. It is a joy tonight to introduce him to you as one of our new deacons. Certainly he has proven himself. A man must be proven to be a deacon. He has, without doubt, all of the qualifications set apart in Scripture for a deacon. It is a joy to welcome you, Brother Bennett.

MR. BENNETT: Thank you, Brother Rausch.

PASTOR: As I look at these men tonight many memories come to my mind as I recall experiences we have enjoyed together. I would like to take time to say much about Tom Bennett, his growth, and the things that have led to this occasion, but time would not permit.

Deacon Parr will come and introduce to us another of our new deacons.

MR. PARR: I would like to take this opportunity to present to you Mr. Terry Wright. I have known Terry for quite a few years. A few years ago—not last year but a few years ago—we played a little softball together. I haven't played too much lately—too old, I guess. It has been a joy knowing Terry. Brother Rausch has said that when these men are approved, they are approved by the board of deacons, talked to by the pastor, presented to you, approved by the church to run as a deacon, and then they are elected by the church.

We trust that being a deacon will be a blessing not only to Terry, Wright, but that he might in turn be a blessing to each one of you. We trust that the church as a whole will support him and help him as a deacon, realizing that he is a new deacon. We who have been on the board and serving with these men know that it will be a challenge to Terry, as it has been to each one of us, and that he will grow in the Lord as we serve with these men in the position that they hold and the seniority that many of them have on the board, helping us when we need it. Brother Terry will be able to receive help from each one of the older deacons when he needs it, and we trust that you folks will stand behind him as a new deacon and that he will grow in the Lord.

PASTOR: Terry, how long have you been in this church?

MR. WRIGHT: All of my life—twenty-eight years.

PASTOR: Twenty-eight years. Isn't that something! They tell me you were a real corker in the nursery when you were a baby!
Deacon Fields, will you come please, and introduce another of our new deacons.

MR. FIELDS: It is a great pleasure to introduce to you Brother Bob Stooksbury. He has been a Christian for six years. I've watched Brother Bob, and he has been very faithful and diligent. Just last night I talked to a person he works with, and he was telling what a good witness Bob had been on the job. He works with him and he said he talked his salvation and tried to get other people saved. It gives me great pleasure to introduce to you Brother Bob Stooksbury.

PASTOR: I was just noticing that of these nine men five of them were here when I came eight years ago, and four have come since I came. So it is a good representative group.
Cal Streeter, come, please, and introduce another of our new deacons.

MR. STREETER: Ken Ball, would you come up, please. It is my privilege tonight to introduce to you Ken Ball. I have known Ken for several years now. I have gone soul winning with him and have won souls with him. I believe it was three years ago when he started working on the bus route with Brother Nischik. I remember the first time that Brother Ball came up to me one Sunday in the alley. This was the first impression I had of him. He said, "I won my first soul this week."
So I know that Ken is a soul winner. I have been with him in the mission services. We have been to missions together. I have watched

him want to see men saved, cry over men, and plead with men to get them saved. It is my privilege to introduce him to you tonight. I know he will be an asset to the deacon board.

PASTOR: Of course, I have an added blessing here because I led Ken to the Lord, and because I appreciate Ken's loud "Amen" from the choir. That gives me real encouragement from time to time.

Deacon Graves, would you come, please sir, and introduce another one of our new deacons.

MR. GRAVES: Richard Barr, come forward. Brother Jack referred a little while ago to the almost eight years that he had been here. It was through the Lord's direction that my wife and I brought our family here the same Sunday that he became pastor here at this church. I can't recall a service or activity that I haven't seen this fellow's face. He has been here. He has been faithful. He and his wife are both very active in the Sunday school work and I am sure have been to a great extent responsible for bringing down part of the blessings of the Lord on the work here.

PASTOR: Thank you, Mel. Welcome to you, Dick.

John Olsen, would you come, please sir, and introduce to us another one of our men.

MR. OLSEN: Will Mr. John Vaprezsan come to the front, please. My first recognition of Johnny Vaprezsan was when my own son began going out with the fellows such as Jim Ruskowski, Terry Smith, Terry Duff, Larry Loser and Johnny Vaprezsan. My first impressionable recognition of Johnny Vaprezsan was when I was here at the church one Saturday evening (I believe it was just before the Christmas vacation) and two fellows had come back from college—Jim Ruskowski and Johnny Vaprezsan. I was here doing some work in the Pioneer Classroom with some of the other folks and they came bursting through the door. I was just amazed! These two had left as boys and came back as mature, poised, young men. Johnny was chosen as a deacon candidate because he expressed maturity, poise, intelligence, a love of the Lord, and a support of this church and its program. It gives me great pleasure tonight to present to you Mr. John Vaprezsan.

PASTOR: Thank you. Mr. Nischik, would you come, please, and introduce still another of our new deacons.

MR. NISCHIK: Terry Duff, would you come, please. It is a real honor for me this evening to introduce this young fellow. He is my friend, my buddy, and he is almost too young really to be a deacon. He is newly married, and he is still in college. I told Brother Blandford Duff, Terry's father, a few years ago that if the Lord ever gave me a son (and I am praying) that he will have many of the qualities and qualifications that Terry Duff has. I am really honored and pleased to have him on the board with me. Lord bless you, Terry.

PASTOR: Brother Fisk, would you come, please, and introduce another.

MR. FISK: Brother Dave Hammers, would you come, please. I do not know how long Brother Dave Hammers has been in this church but I have watched, especially the last three or four years, and I have seen Dave Hammers grow in grace. I have heard it said that at one time Dave could not even stand before a congregation and speak, much less sing. Many times our hearts have been blessed by his beautiful singing. He is now one of our Sunday school teachers. I have had the privilege of winning souls with Dave. I have watched his burden for souls grow and of course, this is the greatest requirement, I suppose, for being a deacon. So, of course, it is an honor for me to introduce to you tonight our Brother Dave Hammers.

PASTOR: Thank you and God bless you, Dave.
Brother Charles Hand will come and introduce the last of the nine men presented to you this evening.

MR. HAND: Brother Dave Sharp, come, please. It is a privilege for me to present Brother Sharp, for he and I have several things in common. We have worked together on the buses. I have enlisted Brother Sharp to teach in the Sunday school. In the first Sunday of April, 1963, when Mrs. Hand, the boys, and I came to the First Baptist Church, Brother Dave made his profession. He and his wife were the first two that we met after we became a part of the First Baptist Church. I know of no one that I am any more pleased to see as part of the great group of deacons here. I guess the greatest thing that I could tell you about Dave Sharp is that I know he gave up a most lucrative job because there were some things that in that job he could not do and still be what he felt a Christian should be. Dave, I am pleased to see you.

MR. SHARP: Thank you.

Message

PASTOR: Thank you, brethren. Now I would like to address the words for the next few minutes to these men. Of course, you will be listening to hear the admonition that I give to them. It will not be long, but I want to speak to you for a few minutes on the subject, "The Laying on of Hands." In a few moments these men will kneel here at the altar, and these men behind me will lay on hands. I could not help but think tonight of how Mr. Gifford introduced his son Dave to our deacon board. Mr. Gifford was, of course, always ready with a bit of humor and always wanting to brighten up the meeting a bit. He stood and said, "I am about to lay hands on my son. Many times I have laid hands on him and other times I have wanted to lay hands on him."

The laying on of hands is a Bible custom. At least seven times the laying on of hands is mentioned in the Word of God. Many of these times it has to do with the laying on of hands for the ordination of preachers. However, on at least one of these occasions it deals with laying hands on the deacons. It is something to be a deacon. This is because it is one of the two Bible offices.

For many years now I have filled the office of pastor, which is the other of the two church offices found in the Word of God. I have never gotten used to it. I have never gotten accustomed to it—being a pastor, filling an office that Jesus Christ started Himself.

Now we come to the second office of the church. You are about to fill a Bible office. What an honor! It is an added honor, however, to become a deacon in the First Baptist Church of Hammond. Those of us who are members here think of this church as probably the greatest church in all the world, and you have become a deacon here. Tonight we set you aside to this office.

You folks in this church may be interested to know that to become a deacon in the First Baptist Church you must have the unanimous approval of the deacon board. That means a man ordained here is approved by each of these men that you see on the platform and every other deacon in our church. Not only is that true, but these men are screened carefully. We, of course, choose them realizing their wives are godly ladies. After awhile we will say a word about the deacons' wives.

Along with the honor of being a deacon comes a tremendous responsibility. Men, you were not chosen because of your financial position. You were not chosen because of your educational background. You were not chosen because of your social standing. You were chosen because we believe that you are godly men who fulfill the biblical requirements for being a deacon.

Now in our deacons' meetings we laugh a great deal, as you know already. We have a big time. We discuss the King's business oftentimes with a little bit of frivolity, but behind all of it there is that sobriety and seriousness of the work of God. I knew one time of a family who had a child that could not live. Those people had the most fun. They laughed a lot. They told funny stories. They enjoyed life. Yet, behind all of that there was a seriousness because of a baby that could not live. Behind all of the fun and even frivolity that we have in our deacons' meetings there is the burden for the church. Many victories have been won that would not have been won had it not been for these men on the platform. The truth of the matter is, I would not be pastor of the First Baptist Church of Hammond tonight were it not for these men on the platform.

So you join a godly group of men. I mean this when I say it. YOU are highly honored tonight. One reason it is an honor is that godly men are about to lay hands on you. In Deuteronomy 34:9 we find the first mention of laying on of hands in the Bible. "And Joshua the son of Nun was full of the spirit of wisdom; for Moses had laid his hands upon him: and the children of Israel hearkened unto him, and did as the Lord commanded Moses." When Joshua took the place of Moses, Moses laid his hands upon Joshua. You think that is something wonderful. It is not any more wonderful than that which we do tonight. Moses was a man like we are. Joshua was a man like I am. Just as one man laid his hands upon another thousands of years ago, we follow the same procedure tonight. When Moses laid his hands on Joshua, Joshua received wisdom. Who needs wisdom more than a deacon? The business matters that have to be discussed, the decisions we will have to make, the budgets we will have to figure, the financial program of the church we will have to steer, the properties of the church we will have to care for, and the program of the church we will have to lead, are some of the many things we on the deacon board must do. We do not have human talent nor wisdom enough to do these matters, so we ask the Lord for wisdom.

Another mention we find in the Bible concerning the laying on of hands is found in Acts 19:6. "And when Paul had laid his hands upon them, the Holy Ghost came on them...." Now the Bible says in Acts, chapter 6, that a deacon is to be full of the Holy Ghost. So tonight as we lay our hands on you, may you, as did Joshua, receive wisdom and may you, as did the disciples of Ephesus, receive the anointing of the Holy Spirit.

The third time we find the laying on of hands mentioned in the Bible is in Acts 8:17. "Then laid they their hands on them, and they received the Holy Ghost."

Then in Acts 6:6 we find that they chose seven deacons in the early church. This office was created as a pastor's helper. Did you know the word "deacon" in the original language comes from the same root word as the word "servant"? The root word means "to crawl in the dust." It means that the deacon is a servant. He is one who humbles himself to serve the people and help the pastor. So it was in the early church.

One day the church in Jerusalem gathered together just as the church in Hammond is doing tonight. They called the names of the men. (We are reading between the lines.) "Philip, would you stand up, please." Peter said, "I am glad to introduce to you Philip. I have known him all of his life." Then John said, "I am glad to introduce to you Stephen, one of the finest men that ever lived." They did much as we are doing tonight. They were human like we are. They had a church like we do. They had problems and weaknesses and burdens just like we do. They were just common people. We are prone to deify people and experiences in the Bible. No, some preachers just got together and set aside some godly men. That is what we are doing tonight.

The fifth time that we find the laying on of hands mentioned in the Bible is in Acts 13:3. "And when they had fasted and prayed, and laid their hands on them, they sent them away." Paul and Barnabas were being sent out from the church to the mission field. The church gathered around them and laid their hands on them.

The sixth reference is I Timothy 4:14. The Apostle Paul said to Timothy, "Neglect not the gift that is in thee, which was given thee by prophecy, with the laying on of the hands...." It is a very serious matter. George Whitefield said one time that he was filled with the Spirit when Bishop Benson laid hands on him in the ordination. This is Bible ground, brethren. This is a Bible practice. You are about to enter into a Bible position and about to follow Bible procedures. So do not leave the altar tonight without receiving something. Whitefield received the anointing of the Holy Spirit. Barnabas and Saul received a commission from the church. Joshua received wisdom from Moses. I trust when our hands are laid on you tonight that God will give you that which you will need to fulfill this task.

The seventh and last time we find the laying on of hands is in II Timothy 1:6.

"Wherefore I put thee in remembrance that thou stir up the gift of God, which is in thee by the putting on of my hands."

The Apostle Paul said, "Timothy, do you recall that night when I laid hands on you?"

Timothy said, "Yes."

Paul said, "Do not ever forget it."

Do not think of this ceremony tonight as some sort of ritual. It is more than that. Do not think of it as some kind of official decoration of becoming a deacon. It is more than that. It is godly men praying for you. It is God the Holy Spirit giving you wisdom and power for the job that is before you.

I have been pastoring for almost a quarter of a century. I have had scores of men on my deacon boards. I do not know what I would have done without them. I owe my life, my ministry, and much of my success (what little I have had) to godly deacons.

Now, brethren, the reason that deacons were chosen in the sixth chapter of Acts was that the preacher needed some help. I need some help, and that is why you have been chosen.

I trust that God will help us to be buddies, pals, co-laborers and co-workers. I hope that we will be able to say that we love each other as much in a few years as these fellows and I can say tonight about our relationship.

Bob, you painted the inside of my house. We live in a house which you painted.

Terry, you were reared in this church. What a privilege to serve here as a deacon.

John, were you reared here too? All of your life just about, I guess. You are one of our products.

Terry, you are one of the products too. If Brother Nischik ever has a boy, he wants him to be like you.

Dave, you and I have some memories we share that are quite sacred and precious.

Dick, you were here when I came. You were one of the first people I met when I came.

Of course, Ken, I recall the day that you were saved as I prayed with you.

The same is true with Dave Sharp. It was my joy to lead you to Christ, Dave.

Then, of course, Tom, if I had time, I would tell a lot of things about you. I remember the night that you first came into the church with that tremendous smile and winsome personality God has given you. You were just a visitor. You encouraged my own heart when you sat on the back row, near the center, in the other building. I count it a real joy to welcome you to our deacon board and to the group of pastor's helpers here at First Baptist Church.

Laying on of Hands

I am going to ask at this time for the five men on this side to kneel, starting at the corner here and about two feet apart, please, if you would. You four on my right, would you kneel starting at the corner and about two feet apart over here, please. Verlie Fields will lead us in a prayer of ordination and then we will have the laying on of hands. I will ask you to bow your heads during the prayer. Then after Brother Fields has prayed, you may observe the laying on of hands. This is the annual occasion where you see it done just as it was done in the early church in Jerusalem. Brother Fields, would you lead us in prayer, please.

MR. FIELDS: Father in Heaven, we thank Thee for this wonderful

privilege that we have of coming together to lay hands on these deacons, realizing, dear God, that this is one of the two offices mentioned
in the Bible. We realize, dear God, that we lay the hands on them, but
You do the ordaining, dear God. We believe that You have chosen
these men. We pray that You will just bless them. We realize, dear
God, that there is many a task to be done in this church, a church as
large as this. The most important one is to go out and win souls—to
be soul winners. We pray that You will just help each and every one
of them. We pray for the wives and the families and that You will
bless them that they will be faithful. We pray, dear God, for Brother
Earl. He is absent from us tonight. Wherever he is, bless him, and
You, Yourself, lay hands on him and bless him that he will continue to
be a soul winner. Now bless us as we continue in this service. In Jesus' name we pray.

(The pastors and deacons lay hands on those being ordained.)

Presentation of Certificates

PASTOR: Would you fellows stand, please, right where you are. Ed
Rausch will come, as chairman of our deacons, and present to each of
you your certificate of ordination.

(Brother Rausch gives each one individually his certificate.)

PASTOR: Few churches have been blessed with any more capable
leadership than our deacon board has. Ed, will you come beside me.
How we thank God for Ed Rausch. Words would fail me when I try to
tell you how I appreciate this good man. On behalf of our church and
our deacon board, Ed, give an official welcome to these men.

MR. RAUSCH: It is always a joy to have new men on the board because it gives evidence of the growth in the lives of men of our church.
Truly it has been said, "It is not easy to become a deacon at First
Baptist Church." In fact, when the Pastors' School was here I said, "It
almost takes an act of Congress to become a deacon of the First Baptist Church."

I say, fellows, to you particularly tonight, that we have the greatest
pastor that any church has ever been blessed with. We have a great
congregation, and you represent this congregation. We trust that your
faithfulness in the Lord's work will produce even greater things at
First Baptist Church. It is our privilege, men, to serve the living
Christ, to uphold His name, and to uphold our pastor as he upholds
Him here in the pulpit, and the fine staff that we have. Truly, we are
privileged men to be on the board of deacons of this church. We
praise God for you all.

Pastor's Welcome

PASTOR: Thank you, Brother Rausch. Now I would like to give you the right hand of welcome. (Each new deacon leaves his seat, comes to the platform, receives a handshake from the pastor, and takes his place with the board.)

Brother Stooksbury, would you come, please, and as you leave the front row you will take your place here. We welcome you to our deacon board and welcome you to join our group tonight.

Terry Wright, will you come, please. Terry, on behalf of our church and our deacon board, we welcome you and count you as one of us as you have your seat with us here on the front.

John Vaprezsan. John, we are pleased to welcome you to our deacon board. It is a real joy to have you to serve with us. Will you take your place with us here on the front row.

Terry Duff. We had suggested tonight that Terry's dad introduce him, but I am afraid that he would have broken down and we would never have finished the service. Terry, we welcome you to our deacon board and pray God's blessings on you as you join us here on the front.

Dave Hammers. Dave, on behalf of our church, we welcome you to our deacon board as you join us here on the front row.

Dick Barr, we welcome you to our group. On behalf of our deacon board and our church we welcome you, Dick, as you join us here on the front.

Then, Ken Ball. Ken, we do welcome you to our deacon board. Officially as pastor, deacons, and church, we wish God's blessings upon you as you join us here.

Dave Sharp. Dave, it is a real joy for me to welcome you, on behalf of our church and our board of deacons, to our board. God bless you as you have your seat.

Tom Bennett, last but not least. Tom, welcome and God bless you as we serve together. Would you have a seat with us, please.

Let us give both the deacons who have served previously and these new deacons a hearty round of applause, shall we? (Applause)

Now to close this ordination service I think it is fitting that one of our own from our board of deacons, Brother Ed Wolber, will sing for us, "I Wonder, Have I Done My Best for Jesus?" This is our desire. This is our goal. This is our promise, dedicated to the deacons who have done their best and to these who shall do their best. Each of us vows to God to do his best for Christ in the coming year.

MR. ED WOLBER SINGS:

I wonder, have I done my best for Jesus

Who died upon the cruel tree?
To think of His great sacrifice at Calvary,
I know my Lord expects the best from me.

Chorus:

How many are the lost that I have lifted?
How many are the chained I've helped to free?
I wonder, have I done my best for Jesus,
When He has done so much for me?

No longer will I stay within the valley;
I'll climb to mountain heights above.
The world is crying now for want of someone
To tell them of the Saviour's matchless love.

CONGREGATION: Amen.

PASTOR: It has been our custom for many years for the new deacons to stand here at the front. So, fellows, would you come down and stand at the front, please. Would each of the nine wives find her respective husband and come and stand beside him, please. This is interesting. Here comes a mother and daughter—each has a deacon husband. Are they all here?

Ladies, it has been our custom at every deacon ordination service for the wife to kiss her husband. Be sure you know on which side of you he is standing! Be sure you kiss the one that you have a license to kiss! At this time, you will greet your husband with a holy kiss of congratulations. Don't take this too far now! (Laughter)

After we have the dismissal, come by and shake their hands. Congratulate them and tell them how happy we are to have them. I know that you will want to do so. It will be a time of joy for them and for you.

Our Heavenly Father, we come to the close of this important service—important because many churches languish in failure and mediocrity because of poor decisions in choosing deacons. We thank Thee that Thou hast led us every step of the way as we have chosen deacons. Truly they have been the pastor's helpers, the servants of the people, and winners of souls for Jesus Christ. We dedicate them to Thee and thank Thee for them. In Jesus' name. Amen.

8. The Church Records

It is vitally important that an adequate record system be kept of the membership of the church. In this chapter we plan to take a person from his first visit to the church and, step by step, show the records that are kept on him.

1. He receives a visitor's card in the public services. This card is divided into two sections. One section is a souvenir for him. The other section is to be filled out and deposited in the collection plate.

2. *On Monday, the following letter is sent to each visitor:*

First Baptist Church

523 SIBLEY STREET   TELEPHONE: WE 2-0711   HAMMOND, INDIANA 46320

Charles Hand *Associate Pastor*	C. W. Fisk *Assistant Pastor*	Johnny Colsten *Pastor's Assistant*
Sandra Plopper *Pastor's Secretary*	Lindsay Terry *Music Director*	Maxine Jeffries *Deaf Interpreter*
Meredith Plopper *Financial Secretary*		Erma McKinney *Director of Literature*
Jennie Nischik *Membership Secretary*	Elaine Colsten *Music Secretary*	Rose O'Brien *Church Secretary*

JACK HYLES, *Pastor*

Dear Friend,

It was a real joy to have you as our guest at First Baptist Church. We sincerely trust that you received a blessing from the service and that you will visit with us as often as possible.

If you do not have a church home, we trust that you will prayerfully consider First Baptist.

May the Lord bless you in your service for Him. If I can be of help to you, feel free to call the church office. It would be a joy to be of service to you.

Sincerely,

Jack Hyles

Jack Hyles, Pastor

jn

INDIANA'S LARGEST SUNDAY SCHOOL

3. The visitor's card is then given to the pastor to be used for visitation teams and pastor's visitation.

4. The visitor is reached for Christ, if at all possible, before the next Sunday. Let us suppose that the pastor or a soul winner wins this one to Christ and the next Sunday he comes forward in the public services. After the person is received at the altar, a secretary or clerk fills out the following decision card:

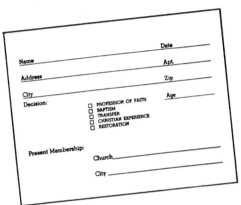

This decision card is in triplicate: a white copy, a green copy, and an ivory copy. The white copy is torn off and given to the pastor to be read publicly. He keeps this one. The green card is put in the visitation files for follow-up work, and the ivory card is given to the records secretary for the processing of the convert and his records.

5. On Monday, the following decision letter is sent to him:

We praise the Lord for your decision Sunday and want to assure you that our prayers and personal interest are with you. Your decision was the beginning of great things for you and for us as we do His will together.

Please fill in the enclosed questionnaire and return it to the church office so that our records will be correct. Do not hesitate to call the church office, 932-0711, for further information.

May the Lord bless you as you serve Him.

Sincerely,

Jack Hyles, Pastor

JH:jn

6. *The card below is enclosed in the decision letter.*

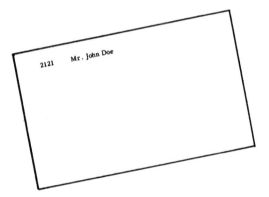

7. *The convert is then voted into the church after baptism and is given a vote-in number and a financial number.* Then a permanent record card is made on the new member as shown below:

2121   Mr. John Doe

8. *As soon as the member is received a financial card such as seen below is made for him:*

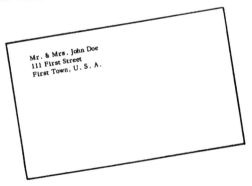

9. *The birthday card is made for him.*

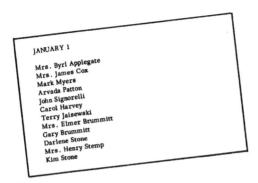

10. *A cardex card is made for our cardex file.* This is also illustrated below:

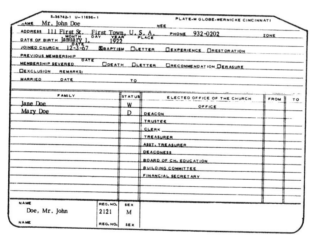

11. *A financial plate for use on the addressograph machine is then made out.*

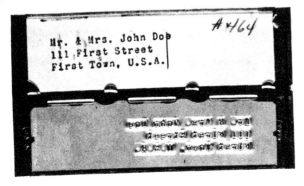

12. *A flash plate is made for the new member.*

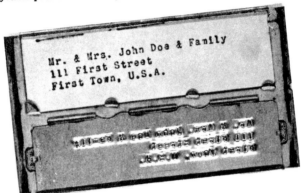

13. *The person's name is placed in the permanent record book as seen below:*

Chronological Register

Page No. _____

Vote In Num.	Vote Out Num.	Names	How Received How Dismissed	Date	

14. Periodically a reception is held in honor of all of the new members of the church. A letter is sent to each person who is a new member of the church. Following is a copy of such a letter:

First Baptist Church

523 SIBLEY STREET TELEPHONE: WE 2-0711 HAMMOND, INDIANA 46320

Charles Hand *Associate Pastor*	**C. W. Fisk** *Assistant Pastor*	**Johnny Colsten** *Pastor's Assistant*
Sandra Plopper *Pastor's Secretary*	**Lindsay Terry** *Music Director*	**Maxine Jeffries** *Deaf Interpreter*
Meredith Plopper *Financial Secretary*		**Erma McKinney** *Director of Literature*
Jennie Nischik *Membership Secretary*	**Elaine Colsten** *Music Secretary*	**Rose O'Brien** *Church Secretary*

JACK HYLES, *Pastor*

Dear Friend:

This week, in the monthly business meeting of our church, you were officially voted into our fellowship. We want to take this opportunity to welcome you into our church family and wish the blessings of the Lord upon your life as we serve Him together here at First Baptist. We trust that your stay here will be a long, fruitful, and happy one and that we will mutually be a blessing to each other.

In order to get better acquainted with you, we are having a special reception in your honor in Horton Hall, Room 106, at 5:30 p.m. this Sunday, JAN 7 1968 . Here you will be able to meet our church staff, the deacons and the trustees, and their families.

We will also acquaint you with your church program by showing you colored slides concerning the various ministries of First Baptist Church.

At this meeting you will receive your offering envelopes for the year, a copy of the church constitution, the church budget, a copy of the articles of faith and a certificate of baptism.

If for any reason you cannot attend, please call the church office (932-0711) as soon as possible.

I am looking forward to a good time of fellowship with you this Sunday evening at 5:30 p.m. and trusting God's blessings upon your life.

Sincerely,

Jack Hyles

Jack Hyles

JH:jn

INDIANA'S LARGEST SUNDAY SCHOOL

At this new members' reception the pastor, staff and deacons meet to welcome the new people into the church. The pastor first gives a brief word of welcome. Then he introduces each staff member and tells the responsibilities of each. He then introduces the chairman of the board of deacons, the officers of the deacon board and the deacons present. Then he introduces the deacons' wives.

Following this, some slides are shown portraying the life of the church. Slides concerning the buildings, the youth program, the musical program, the financial program and various phases of the church program are shown. This usually takes about fifteen minutes.

Following the showing of the slides, the new member receives several things. He receives a packet of envelopes as shown below:

He then receives a copy of the pastor's book, *Let's Go Soul Winning*, which will enable him to win others to the Lord Jesus Christ. He then receives a baptismal certificate as a remembrance of this high occasion.

The new member is then given a copy of the articles of faith and the church covenant as well as a copy of the church budget.

Each new member is requested to fill out the form below. This will enable us to locate potential workers for the church program.

WORKERS' SURVEY
First Baptist Church
523 Sibley
Hammond, Indiana 46320

Below are listed some aspects of our church program. Please indicate the areas in which you would like to work. Experience is not a prerequisite.

BUS MINISTRY:

_____ Bus route.

_____ Assist someone who already has a bus route.

_____ Drive a bus.

Work schedule:

_____ Days.

_____ Afternoons.

_____ Midnights.

_____ Shift work.

SUNDAY SCHOOL:

_____ Secretary for a department or a class.

_____ Pianist for a department or a class.

_____ Teach a class.

_____ List experience in Sunday School teaching:

Church_____

City and State_____

Age of pupils taught_____

STORY HOURS: (These take place during the Sunday morning service. Workers rotate and are obligated only one Sunday each month.)

_____ Worker.

_____ Pianist.

Age preferred:

_____ Nursery Story Hour (2-3 years).

_____ Beginner Story Hour (4-5 years).

_____ Primary Church (6-7 years).

NAME_____ AGE_____ PHONE_____

STREET ADDRESS_____

CITY_____ STATE_____ ZIP_____

Following the receipt of these important items, there is a time of refreshment and fellowship. The new members are invited to go to a table filled with refreshments such as cookies, finger sandwiches, punch, etc. They enjoy refreshments as the deacons and their families come by, shake their hands, and welcome them into the church.

15. *A three-week new members' course is then conducted for the convert.* One Sunday night he is taught soul winning. Another Sunday night he is taught the doctrines of the church and how to grow in grace. Another Sunday night he is taken on a tour of the church properties. He is encouraged to be faithful to all the services of the church. He is encouraged to have family devotions, to say grace at the table. He is told about the need for a daily devotional time.

Many other things are done for the new member; but as you can see, we have taken the convert from his first visit to the church through his conversion, his joining the church and his being integrated into the life of the church.

16. *We use our own forms in granting and receiving of letters of transfer.* When a person unites with the First Baptist Church by transfer from a church of like faith, we send to that church the following request for a letter.

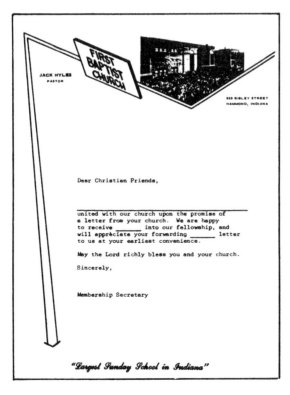

When a member of a church which is not of like faith is converted and joins our church by baptism, the following notice is sent to the church where he formally held membership. This simply notifies the church to make adjustment on their church records.

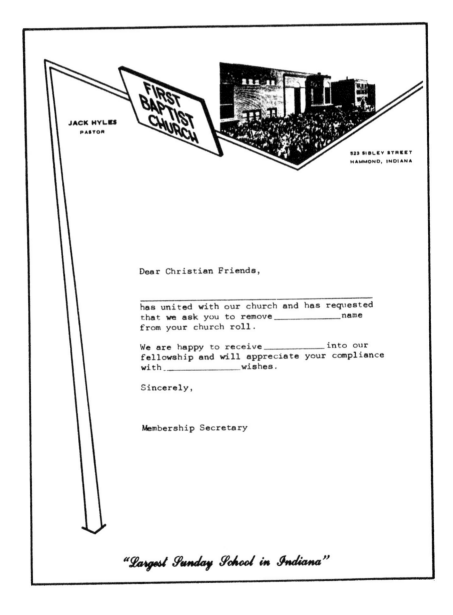

JACK HYLES
PASTOR

FIRST BAPTIST CHURCH

523 SIBLEY STREET
HAMMOND, INDIANA

Dear Christian Friends,

_____
has united with our church and has requested
that we ask you to remove _____ name
from your church roll.

We are happy to receive _____ into our
fellowship and will appreciate your compliance
with _____ wishes.

Sincerely,

Membership Secretary

"Largest Sunday School in Indiana"

When a person transfers from our church to a church of like faith, we vote to grant his letter and use the following form to notify his new church.

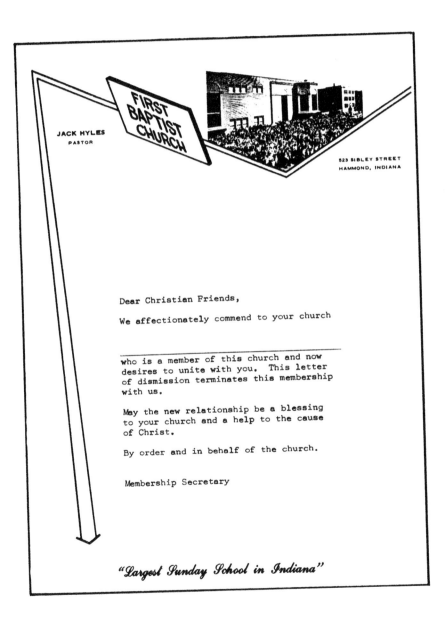

JACK HYLES
PASTOR

FIRST BAPTIST CHURCH

523 SIBLEY STREET
HAMMOND, INDIANA

Dear Christian Friends,

We affectionately commend to your church

_____
who is a member of this church and now desires to unite with you. This letter of dismission terminates this membership with us.

May the new relationship be a blessing to your church and a help to the cause of Christ.

By order and in behalf of the church.

Membership Secretary

"Largest Sunday School in Indiana"

9. An Ordination Service for Preachers

On October 19, 1966, at 6:45 p.m. the First Baptist Church witnessed the ordination service of Mr. Johnny Colsten, Mr. Larry Loser, and Mr. David Loser. This service was recorded and transcribed as follows:

PASTOR: As you know we are here this evening to set apart three of our finest to the gospel ministry. We certainly thank God for His blessings upon our church as He continues to reach down and call our young men to preach the Gospel. Many of our young men are now pastoring. Many of our young men are now preparing for the ministry in colleges and seminaries around the nation.

Tonight we shall ordain three of our own. Two of them are pastors and one is on our staff, directing the work of our rescue mission. I am going to ask Brother Fisk, our assistant pastor, to come and introduce these three candidates to you.

Presentation of Candidates

MR. FISK: I am going to ask Brother Johnny Colsten if he will come to the platform, please. I would like to ask Mrs. Colsten if she would do us the honor of standing so that you folks might know Mrs. Colsten. All right, thank you so much.

For the past year and a half I have had the privilege of working hand-in-hand with Brother Johnny Colsten. He has been a blessing to me personally. We have cried together and have rejoiced together. We have worked together and we've played together. I know that Johnny has a real concern for souls. I know that, needless to say, God knew what He was doing when He called this man to preach the Gospel. We heard so much about Johnny Colsten before he ever came to this church. Everything we heard was true and more so. I certainly count it a privilege tonight to be able to introduce to you Johnny Colsten. Brother Johnny, would you be seated right here.

PASTOR: Would Mrs. Colsten stand. One of our secretaries would like to present you with a lovely corsage.

MR. FISK: All right, I would like to ask Brother Larry Loser if he would make his way to the platform, please. I was talking with Brother Larry before the service, and he tells me that he was practically born and raised in this church. He comes from a godly Christian family. Now that he is grown into a fine young man God called him to preach. He is pastoring the Jump Off Baptist Church in Jump Off, Tennessee. That is just sixty-five miles north of Chattanooga. I have known Larry personally for the six years that I have spent here at First Baptist Church, and I count his friendship a blessing. I know Larry also has the desire to win souls. I know the kind of ministry that he will have and I certainly count it a privilege tonight to introduce to you folks our Brother Larry Loser. God bless you, Larry.

PASTOR: Mrs. Loser is here. We have a flower for her, too. Pat, will you stand, please. It seems as though you were just married yesterday because you have been gone ever since you got married. It is nice to see you, Pat.

MR. FISK: I would like to ask Brother David Loser (I know him as Dave) to make his way to the platform. I would like to ask Mr. and Mrs. Loser if they would do us the honor of standing so that the folks might know the parents of these two fine young men.

PASTOR: Ladies, would you come, please, and pin a corsage on Mrs. Loser.

MR. FISK: Thank you so much. As was the case with Brother Larry Loser, Brother David also was raised in this church, saved here, baptized here, called to preach here, and now, thank the Lord, he is going to be ordained tonight. I have been soul winning with our Brother Loser. I have heard him preach at our rescue mission. I have heard good reports about his supply preaching in other churches. Just recently he was called to pastor a Baptist church in Georgia.

The report is that just about every Sunday since he has been there now they have seen someone saved. Just this past Sunday God gave them four souls down the aisle for Christ. It is certainly evidence of God's blessings already on this young man, and I count it a privilege tonight to introduce to you Brother David Loser.

PASTOR: I want the three fellows to stand, please. Let's give them all a hand. (Applause)

Brother Colsten's mother and father are here, I understand. Where are they? Would you stand, please. All right, we have a corsage for you too, Mrs. Colsten. We are glad that you are here.

Public Questioning

(The following, of course, does not include the lengthy private questioning.)

PASTOR: I would like to have the three brethren to stand to my left, please.

David, do you believe in the doctrines of the Articles of Faith and practice of the First Baptist Church of Hammond?

DAVID LOSER: Yes, sir.

PASTOR: If there ever comes a day when you do not believe in the Articles of Faith of our church and the inspiration of the Scriptures, would you be willing to surrender your ordination certificate to the First Baptist Church?

DAVID LOSER: Yes, sir.

PASTOR: Larry, do you believe the Articles of Faith adopted by the First Baptist Church of Hammond?

LARRY LOSER: Yes.

PASTOR: If the day would ever come and you did not, would you surrender willingly your ordination papers?

LARRY LOSER: Yes.

PASTOR: Mr. Colsten, do you believe the Articles of Faith adopted by the First Baptist Church of Hammond?

MR. COLSTEN: Yes, I do.

PASTOR: If the day would ever come that you did not, would you surrender your papers?

MR. COLSTEN: Yes, sir.

PASTOR: Do each of you understand this? I say this seriously because oftentimes men are ordained to preach the Gospel who later change their doctrinal stand. It could happen. It has happened to many. The Apostle Paul recognized the possibility that it could happen even to him.

Now you may be seated, please.

I am going to ask each one of you to say a word about your conversion and your call to preach. We will start with David.

DAVID LOSER: Well, I praise the Lord, first of all, that I am saved. I had been going to First Baptist for a number of years and I had walked the aisle when I was just about eleven or twelve years old. I had thought I was saved, but after Brother Jack came to our church and preached one evening on Hell and how that if you didn't know Christ as Saviour and didn't know for sure that if you died, you would go to Heaven, you would spend an eternity in Hell, it shook me up, and I had to make sure of my salvation. On November 19, 1961, I made sure that I was born again. I was baptized that evening.

On July 23, 1963, I was called to preach the Gospel. Ever since then I have been preaching every chance I get. I would just like to say that there is nothing any better, and there is no bigger joy in life than being in the center of God's will and doing what He wants you to do.

PASTOR: Larry, it has been a long time since we have had you here full time. You have been to college and seminary, and it is a real joy to have you back with us this evening. Come and tell us about your conversion and call to preach.

LARRY LOSER: I have attended the First Baptist Church since I was very young. When I was six years old, I went forward with my parents and joined First Baptist. I was baptized, but like David, I wasn't saved. I didn't know Christ as my personal Saviour. It wasn't until later after Brother Jack came to First Baptist. I was singing in the choir. He preached a sermon on the tares among the wheat, and it struck home. Even though I didn't go forward in the service, there in the choir I trusted Christ as my Saviour. I was later baptized in Springfield, Missouri, because I got under conviction about it and I realized that my baptism wasn't scriptural. Even before that, God had called me to preach. The summer after I got out of high school I went away to school to prepare to serve Him the best way I could. I praise the Lord for every opportunity He has given me to serve Him and for the chance He has given me now to pastor a church. I just pray that He will be able to use me to win people to the Lord Jesus Christ.

PASTOR HYLES: Of course, all of us know the Colstens and know Brother Johnny. We have had the opportunity of having Brother Johnny with us from week to week. For many months he was simply an unknown quotient to us. We did not know anything about him. We had heard a lot about him. His wife, being a woman, talked a great deal about him, and we waited until he came, and of course, now that he is with us we are glad. We certainly have learned to love him and appreciate him and the family and the fact that God has called him to preach. So Brother Johnny, would you come and tell us briefly about your conversion and your call to preach.

JOHNNY COLSTEN: Dr. Falls preached an old-fashioned revival meeting in Whitely Methodist Church back in Muncie, Indiana. I was twelve years of age and at that time opened my heart to the Lord Jesus Christ. There were periods of time when I was not sure about my salvation, but the Lord so graciously gave me assurance through the years. He has brought me now to this time.

The call to preach was something that was real to me, and yet there was a period of time involved in which I felt that I was called to preach but I just wanted Him to prove it to me. He very graciously did after a period of time. It just became so bottled up it just had to come out, and I surrendered my life to preach then not too long ago back in June. So very sincerely I know that Jesus is my Saviour and that He has called this unworthy servant to preach.

PASTOR HYLES: The presbytery will vote to recommend to the church that we do ordain these men. Then the church will vote to give the presbytery the authority of laying on of hands.

Vote of the Presbytery

PASTOR HYLES: I now entertain a motion from the presbytery that we recommend to the church that we ordain these three men to the gospel ministry. Do I hear a motion? Brother Streeter makes the motion. Is there a second? Brother Wolber seconds the motion. Is there any discussion or any question that you would like to ask any of these?

If there are no questions, if you are in favor, would you say "Aye."

PRESBYTERY: Aye.

PASTOR: If opposed, like sign...and it is so ordered.

Vote of the Church

PASTOR: You have heard the motion and second and unanimous vote that we recommend to you the ordination of these three men. Now would someone in the church like to move that the church invest the authority in these men to lay the hands on these brethren. Brother Bell makes the motion. Brother Townson seconds the motion. Is there any discussion? Those in favor of proceeding with the ordination and in-vesting in the presbytery the authority to proceed with the laying on the hands, would you say "Aye."

CONGREGATION: Aye.

PASTOR: If you oppose, "No." And it is so ordered.

Ordination Prayer and Laying on of Hands

PASTOR: That brings us to the laying on of hands and the ordination prayer. I am going to ask Brother Colsten if he would kneel to my left. I am going to ask Brother Larry if he will kneel in the center, please, and I am going to ask Brother David if he will kneel on the right.

After we have the ordination prayer, you may observe the laying on of hands. As we lay on the hands, pray, and wish a word of encourage-ment, wouldn't it be a wonderful thing if God could hear the unvoiced prayers of the hundreds of people in this auditorium praying for God's blessing upon the ministry of these, three of our choicest.

Brother Terry will come and lead us in our ordination prayer. After the prayer we will have the laying on of hands and you may observe this service.

MR. TERRY: Our Father, we thank You truly for each of these men. We thank Thee that in Your great wisdom You did choose to save them. We thank Thee for our own salvation. We thank Thee for the Christian training they have had in their homes. We pray that You would help them now as they continue their study, that You would guide them. As they go into their work deeper and deeper we pray that You would give them wisdom for the decisions that must be made. We pray that You would help them. We pray that You would help them in their churches and in their work and as people come to them with problems that they will have the wisdom that only God can give. We pray that You would help each of them to be the kind of soul winner that You would have them to be. We thank Thee that they are and have been becoming real soul winners for Thee. Help us all to be more of this as we ought to be. We pray now that You would bless their families. We pray that You would be with them and that we may be an encouragement to them. Help us all that we might remember them from time to time in our prayers, for we pray in Jesus' name. Amen.

(Laying on of hands of the presbytery)

PASTOR HYLES: With every head bowed and eyes closed, I am going to close the service of the laying on of hands by laying my hands on these men. As I lead in prayer audibly, I want each of us to pray for each of them as we are led by the pastor. Let each of us pray for God's blessings upon them.

Our Heavenly Father, we join, as pastor and people, in prayer for Johnny. We thank Thee for a sweet spirit and his love for Thee. We thank Thee for his diligence, his sincerity. We pray Thy blessings upon him. We pray that the Holy Spirit will give him power for service. We know not where the ministry will take him. We know not of his future. We pray that wherever it be, whatever it be, You will guide and bless him, his wife, and his children.

Our Heavenly Father, we come to pray for Larry, thanking Thee for his family, his childhood, and teen-age years. Many scores of people in this room this evening remember joys, experiences, and blessings of the past. We pray Thy blessings will continue upon him. Bless his ministry. Bless his wife as they labor together, and may their lives always count for Christ. May the laying on of our hands only symbolize the laying on of the Holy Spirit. May he be able to point back to this hour, as Timothy did when Paul reminded him of the gift that was given him at the laying on of hands. In Jesus' name.

Our Heavenly Father, we come to the laying on of hands for Dave. We thank You for him, for his spiritual growth, and for the fact that Thou hast given him maturity above his years already. Thou hast called him to a church. We pray that Thy hand of blessing will rest upon him as our hands rest upon his head. We pray that the power of God will be upon him. Bless his life. Crown his ministry with Thy power. Let many be saved because of his labors. In Jesus' name. Amen.

Presentation of Bibles

PASTOR HYLES: Brethren, you may stand and come to the platform, please. Brother Hand will come and present a gift from our church to each of you. You will treasure this gift more and more with the passing of the years.

MR. HAND: Every trade has its tools. If I owned a business and you became a part of my business, I think that the proper thing to do would be to furnish you with tools. In a real sense we cannot give you anything tonight except a leather back and some exceptionally fine India paper. That which is printed on the paper does not belong to us. It is not ours to give to you. It is a tool that God has furnished us. When we say it is God's Word, rightfully, it is possessive. It is God's Word. It belongs to Him. As such, He has the right to determine how it is used. Remember always as you use it, it is God's Word. He gave it to us that we might know how to serve Him properly. He gave it to us that we might do that which is exactly pleasing to Him. He gave us the most powerful force in all the world. Dynamite is in these pages. There is no dynamite under Heaven that is as powerful as the dynamite of the Word of God. Remember it. Written on the flyleaf of each of these: "Presented to David Loser as he is ordained to the gospel ministry, October 19, 1966, First Baptist Church of Hammond." Brother David Loser, Brother Larry Loser, and Brother Johnny Colsten, you have the greatest tool in all the world. May God bless you as you use it.

Presentation of Certificates

PASTOR HYLES: Now as they remain standing, the chairman of our board of deacons, Brother Ed Rausch, will come and present the official certificates from the First Baptist Church to these men.

MR. RAUSCH: Brother David, Brother Larry, and Brother Johnny, this Certificate of Ordination which I will present to each of you represents an expression of the church family as a matter of confidence and faith in the high calling that God has given you. It not only represents this expression of faith and confidence but it also represents the fact that many people have made an investment in your lives. I am sure that each who has made an investment would have only Christ get the dividend.

So we pray tonight as we give you this certificate, Brother Johnny, Brother David, and Brother Larry, that you will fulfill the faith of our people and be diligent to fulfill also the high calling, the highest calling that can come to man—to preach God's Word. May God's blessings rest upon your ministry, each one.

Charge

PASTOR HYLES: I am going to ask the brethren to stand here facing me, please. I would like to talk to you a few minutes. Of course this is for every person, but there are seven things that I would like to say to you brethren as we talk together just personally for a few minutes while the others look on. I am going to wrap these things around the number three. I am going to give some important "three's" for you as preachers.

I have been preaching for many years. I hope that I have learned some things in these years. Some of the things I have learned I hope you can learn faster than I learned them.

   1. Three Books You Should Know Well.

The first thing that I would like to suggest is that there are three books in the Bible that you ought to know better than any of the other books if you are going to pastor. There are three books in the Bible that I have found to be the most needful books. All of this service is being taped and you will each receive a tape recording of the service so you need not write them down as you can hear them again and again as you listen to them in the future.

If you know these three books well, you will know more about all the rest of the Bible, and each book will be easier for you to understand. Every preacher should know well the book of Genesis. There is no excuse or substitute. The book of Genesis is certainly a key book. Every preacher should know well the book of Romans. Every preacher should know well the book of Revelation. If you know these books well, liberalism will never darken the doorstep of your ministry. Study carefully the books of Genesis, Romans and Revelation.

2. Three Books You Should Read Daily.

Then there are three books that I would exhort you to read daily for your own personal edification. I would exhort you to read from the book of Psalms, Proverbs and Acts every day. No preacher can be successful unless he has the warmth and praise of the Psalms, the integrity and character of the Proverbs, and the zeal of the book of Acts. What combination could be more effective in the ministry than the love of David in the Psalms, the wisdom of Solomon in the Proverbs, and the zeal of the life and ministry of the apostles in the book of Acts.

3. Three Christian Privileges.

Then there are three Christian privileges that you ought to exercise constantly. The first one is Bible reading, the second is prayer, and the third one is soul winning. It is a tremendous temptation for a preacher to major on any one of these at the exclusion of the other two. I know many pastors who have become Bible students to the exclusion of their prayer life and their soul-winning time. I know many others who have spent hours and hours on their knees in prayer but not in learning the Bible and not in winning souls. I know others who have spent all of their time on the field witnessing to the exclusion of prayer and Bible study. No two of these will take the place of all three of them. To be a successful preacher or pastor, you must know the Book, you must know God, and you must know sinners. These three things are essential in the ministry.

4. Three Things for Which You Must Pray.

There are three things that as a preacher you must pray for more than any other single thing. The first thing you must pray for is the power of God. The second thing you must pray for is love, and the third thing for which you must pray is wisdom. Without the power of God, there can be no spiritual service. Without the love of God, the power of God is void. Without wisdom to use love and power oftentimes wrong decisions make void what we do for God.

For many years I have had on top of my prayer list the power of God.

Secondly, pray for love — love for lost sinners, love for your people, and love for everybody.

Then pray for wisdom. You will have to know how to advise people. You will have to counsel with people who need advice about their homes. You will need wisdom. You will have to know some things that only years can tell unless you get wisdom from God. People will come to you and ask you questions, and your answers will determine what they will do. You will hold in your counsel and your advice the destiny of homes, of children, and of souls. You will need wisdom. I exhort you to pray for the power of God, for love, and for wisdom.

   5. *Three Types of Preaching.*

In the fifth place, there are three types of preaching that you ought to do. Number one is evangelistic preaching. Number two is the exhorting of the saints. Number three is the teaching of the Word of God.

Evangelistic preaching without Bible study will build Christians but not strong Christians. Bible study without evangelism will build strong Christians without getting new Christians. Always stay after sinners. Never think it is shallow to be a soul-winning preacher or an evangelistic preacher, but never let it be said truthfully that you do not teach the Bible to your people, and that you do not exhort the Christians.

   6. *Three Temptations You Will Face.*

There are three big temptations that face a preacher. May I alert you to them tonight. Never, never forget what I am about to say. The first temptation that you will have as a preacher is laziness. I suspect that of all the sins of the ministry laziness is one of the greatest. There is no place for a lazy person in the ministry. Many talented men have failed because they did not work hard.

The second temptation you will find in the ministry is that you will find the temptress over and over again. Your relationship with the opposite sex will be scrutinized very carefully by all who hear you. They will watch how you behave yourself with women.

Yesterday morning I heard of a pastor who had misinterpreted someone's affection for him as a pastor to be romantic affection and had left the ministry because of an ugly story. Let me say this to you (I say this because I know preachers and I know them well): Never mistake the affection that a member has for a pastor and a man of God to be romantic affections. Men, stay in love with your wives. Let it be known that you are in love with your wife. Let the whole world know that you have the only woman you want. The Devil is after a fundamental preacher. Fundamental preachers are real men. They have to be men to stand the test. Be careful! Gird yourself now for the temptations that are to come.

The third temptation is a strange one but it does happen. Money oftentimes enters into a preacher's temptations. One reason is that things are given to preachers. People love to give things to their pastor. I think this is well and good but if you do not watch it, you will become expectant of things to be given to you. One of the cheapest things that will ever happen to a preacher is when he expects to be given monetary privileges that others do not have. Never expect a discount in a store. Never expect people to give you something. Just serve God and let God take care of all of the provisions. Never talk about how much the salary is going to be. Let others talk about that. You just stay busy for Christ. God will take care of you. He said, "But seek ye first the kingdom of God, and his righteousness; and all these things shall be added unto you." So keep your attention on His work, and He will take care of your needs.

   7. *Three Things You Must Be.*

There are three things that you ought to be as a preacher. You ought to be a leader. The ability to be a leader of men comes only from God. You should also be a pastor and an evangelist.

First and foremost, if you will notice your ordination paper, it says "ordained to preach." We are ordaining you to be preachers! This is the great work. If you fail in conducting funerals, that would be sad but not fatal. If you fail in performing weddings beautifully, that would be sad but not fatal. If you were to fail in your hospital visitation, that would be sad but not fatal. However, if you fail in preaching and do succeed in every other facet, it will be fatal! WE ORDAIN YOU TO PREACH! This means to herald the good tidings and tell the world something good has happened.

With this admonition, as pastor and people we ask God's blessings upon you and express to you our love and appreciation. Wrapped around this little service are thousands of memories. We wish the power of God upon your lives and the blessings of God upon your ministries. We pray these 'three's' shall be incorporated in your lives.

You may have a seat where you were, if you will, please. May I say to Mrs. and Mr. Loser my word of congratulations. Seldom does God bless a home by calling one of its boys to be a preacher. Even more seldom does God bless a home by calling all of its boys to be preachers. This is unusual. Night before last I had refreshments in a home and the pastor of the church said, "I want you to meet my son, who is my assistant pastor; my other son, who is an assistant pastor in Denver, Colorado; my brother, who is a pastor; and his two sons, who are also pastors." My, what a time we had. Each home had two preacher boys; you have three. Two of them are already pastors. May we commend you for it and wish God's blessings upon your boys. We know that each of you has a lion's share of the credit in making these boys what they are.

To Johnny's mother and father, we pray God bless you dear ones.

Young men like Johnny Colsten do not come accidentally. They come from a lot of toil, prayer, training, and teaching.

Of course, Elaine, our congratulations, our love, affections, and God's blessings to you.

Mrs. Larry Loser—Pat—we share a lot of memories together. We do wish God's blessings upon you and Larry.

Barbara, you are not Mrs. Loser yet but if I had kept my big nose out of it you would have been! (Laughter) Dave and Barbara came to me last summer and said, "Brother Hyles, we would like to get married this summer but we will do what you say because we would like to have your advice. What you and Dad and Mom say is what we will do. So Dad and Mom and Brother Hyles agreed that waiting another year would be better. Do we have a flower for Barbara? Yes, Barbara, if you will please stand, we would like to pin a flower on you. Of course if you do not go through with the marriage plans, you will have to return the flower. (Laughter)

The Bible says that a preacher should be the husband of one wife. Dave does not qualify, but I have talked with the Lord and received a special dispensation. If we can have the assurance that he will have a wife soon, we can proceed.

Thank you. God bless each of you. We trust that God will bless the lives and ministries of these young men. After the service we are going to ask you to come by and shake hands with them.

II. Church Program

10. The Sunday School

The greatest business in all of the world is the preaching of the Gospel of Jesus Christ and the teaching of the Word of God. One of the most effective methods and means of propagating this Gospel and teaching God's blessed Word is the Sunday school. In this chapter we are going to discuss methods and promotional material in the building of a great Sunday school.

Let us first be plainly understood by saying that nothing will take the place of the Word of God and consistent teaching of the Bible in the Sunday school. No amount of promotion, no amount of organization, no amount of methods can be substituted for the teaching of the Word of God. A consistent Bible-teaching program is necessary in the building of a great Sunday school.

Our discussion will be under three main topics: (1) the planning of the Sunday school program, (2) the preparing of this program, and (3) the promoting of the program of a great Sunday school.

PLANNING OF THE PROGRAM

Choosing the Worker

Let us look in the first place to the planning of the program. We could not begin such a discussion without first discussing the choosing of the worker. There are many qualifications that we present here at First Baptist Church of Hammond to our prospective Sunday school teachers, workers, and superintendents. These are as follows:

(1.) Every worker in our Sunday school must be a converted, born-again person.

(2.) Every person who teaches in our Sunday school must be an active member of the First Baptist Church of Hammond, Indiana.

(3.) We require faithfulness on the part of all of our Sunday school teachers and workers. By this we mean: faithfulness to the Sunday school hour, faithfulness to the morning preaching service on the Lord's Day, faithfulness to the Sunday evening service, faithfulness to the Wednesday evening service, as well as faithful attendance to the Sunday school teachers' and officers' meeting preceding the regular midweek service on Wednesday evening.

(4.) We expect loyalty from our Sunday school workers. Certainly no Sunday school, or any other organization for that matter, can be built successfully without loyal workers, loyal teachers and a loyal staff of helpers. The Sunday school teacher should be loyal to the church program, loyal to the ministry of the pastor, loyal to the Gospel of Jesus Christ and to the Word of God.

(5.) Every Sunday school worker is required to be doctrinally sound. By this we mean they should adhere to the doctrines of the church. They should certainly believe the Articles of Faith adopted by the church and be loyal to the teachings and doctrines of the Word of God.

(6.) We require that each of our Sunday school teachers and officers live a separated life. No one should open the Word of God to teach it to boys or girls or men or women in the Sunday school unless he is separate from the world. No teacher should participate in such questionable amusements as drinking any kind of alcoholic beverages, dancing, gambling, or other habits that would be detrimental to the testimony of Jesus Christ and the work of building a great Sunday school.

(7.) Last, but not least, is the important qualification of having a love for souls of men. Every Sunday school teacher should be burdened for souls and should be actively participating in reaching people for Jesus Christ.

Enlisting the Worker

Now that we have *chosen* the worker, let us *enlist* the worker. We turn to the enlistment of a Sunday school teacher. Probably one of the outstanding failures in Sunday schools today across America is the slipshod way in which we enlist our workers. Here at the First Baptist Church of Hammond we require that each worker be enlisted either in the privacy of his own home or the privacy of the office of the staff member. No one is enlisted casually; no one is enlisted walking down the hall of the church; no one is enlisted after the service at the altar or around the pulpit, but rather the person is enlisted privately. The work is laid upon his heart. The challenge of the work is presented to him, and he realizes the tremendous challenge and opportunity that is being presented to him as he assumes the responsibility of teaching the Word of God in a great Sunday school.

We give to the worker at this conference the qualifications. We alert him to what we expect him to do and what God expects him to do. We assure him that this job will occupy much of his time. We assure him that we expect faithfulness, and present to him the aforementioned qualifications for being a Sunday school teacher in the First Baptist Church. Then, we offer him time to pray about it—maybe a week or less. He then calls or stops by the church to give us his answer and to inform us as to his decision. Nothing could be said to magnify too much the importance of enlisting the worker properly.

Choosing the Material

Now that we have chosen and enlisted the worker, as we plan the program let us notice the choosing of the material. In the First Baptist Church of Hammond we use only the Bible as our literature. Children eight and over receive no quarterlies but only the Word of God. Though I am aware of the fact that there are many wonderful companies writing literature in our generation (I certainly admire good literature; and I am not opposed to Sunday school literature), we simply make a practice, however, in the First Baptist Church of using the Word of God and teaching only from the Bible in our Sunday school.

How, then, are our lessons chosen? Approximately in the month of September, our teachers and officers meet to discuss and pray about the lessons for the following year. Suggestions are presented, a discussion is conducted, and finally we vote upon what we think we should teach for the following year. Maybe we are in a building program, and we should have special lessons geared to our building program. Perhaps we plan to have a great enlargement campaign, and we plan our lessons around the program of the year. After we have discussed and prayed concerning the material for the new year, then we vote and decide concerning what subjects, Bible lessons, etc., we shall teach in our Bible Sunday school for the new year.

We have taught in our Sunday school the book of Romans verse by verse. We have taught the book of Acts chapter by chapter. We have taught famous people in the Bible person by person. We have taught the little books of the Bible and the insignificant characters of the Bible. We have taught Bible separation, Bible stewardship, and other important doctrines, subjects and books from the Word of God. This is how we choose our material.

Finding Space

Once we have chosen the worker, enlisted the worker, and chosen the material, we turn our attention toward finding space for the class and the department. Of course all of us would love to have adequate space. Each of us would love to have a beautiful educational building with Sunday school facilities that are first class. Most of us, however, simply dream about this kind of a Utopian situation, and have to do the best we can with what we have.

The first thing I would like to say about the finding of the space is this: a Sunday school does not have to have adequate space to grow. The church at Jerusalem had, it is said, over twenty thousand members and no church building. To be sure, it is an asset and an advantage to have proper space for our classes and departments. Once again may I emphasize, though it is an advantage, it is not a necessity. A great Sunday school can be built under adverse conditions and with limited space and improper lighting and building facilities. The only thing that stops the work of God is the lack of faith in the people of God. When people have a mind to work, have faith in God and stay busy at the main task of reaching people for Jesus Christ, I believe that Sunday schools can be built even without proper space.

Here in the city of Hammond we had a tragic fire in 1964. Six hundred nineteen thousand dollars of our property was swept away overnight. In spite of this fact (minus $619,000.00 of our Sunday school facilities) we continued to grow. And today we are averaging one thousand more in Sunday school than we were at the time of the fire. At the time of this discussion we are utilizing a furniture store, a Knights of Columbus Hall, an apartment house and other inadequate facilities; and, through it all, the work is going forward. God is blessing and the Sunday school is growing by leaps and bounds.

Dividing the Classes

As we consider the planning of the program, we turn our attention to the division of the classes. I have read many books about class divisions. Some say that the beginners should have five per class, the primaries should have seven, the juniors between ten and fifteen, and the older young people no more than twenty per class. Much discussion has been presented concerning the division of classes. I advance to you that I think the size of the class should be determined by the number of qualified workers. I had rather have a consecrated, dedicated worker teaching fifty than divide into small classes or small units and have inferior teachers teaching the Word of God to boys and girls. I do, however, advocate departmentalizing the Sunday school. I think it is certainly advantageous to have the beginners together. The breakdown in our Sunday school is as follows:

> The Nursery Department — age three and under
> Beginners — ages four and five
> Primaries — first and second grade
> Juniors — third grade through sixth grade
> Junior High — seventh and eighth grade
> High School — ninth grade through twelfth grade

The Junior High Department and High School Department are followed by the adult classes. Certainly departmentalization is important in the building of a great Sunday school.

As we think about the division of classes and departments, our attention is turned toward the adults' division of classes. We have found it necessary to have many types of adult classes. I teach a large auditorium Bible class. Last Sunday we had 583. We have had as high as 1,100 in this class on a special Sunday. This class is the largest in our Sunday school. However, we have many other large adult classes. We have a young couples' class, a couples' class for middle-aged friends. We have a class for unmarried adults, a class for college-age adults, a men's Bible class, and several ladies' classes. These classes each perform an unusual and unique purpose in the building of our Sunday school. We have found it helpful also to have classes for the deaf, the retarded children and many, many other groups that oftentimes are overlooked in the building of a Sunday school.

PREPARING OF THE PROGRAM

We turn our attention now to the preparing of the program. We have been discussing the planning of the program. Certainly the first and foremost thing should be the planning of the proper program—the right kind of teachers, the right kind of lesson, the right kind of facilities, the right kind of division. These are certainly important things in the building of a great Sunday school; but we turn now to a discussion of the preparing of the program.

The Annual Training Course

In the First Baptist Church of Hammond we have two great preparation meetings. The first one is an annual course for our teachers and officers. Once each year we conduct this course. It may be for five nights the same week, or it may be for five consecutive Wednesday evenings prior to our midweek service. It may be for three of these Wednesday evenings prior to our midweek service. We have found it advantageous for the pastor to teach such a class and have such a course annually. At this course we teach forty things. I list them one at a time for you:
1. Have a separated life.
2. Have a daily private devotion.
3. Have a daily, clean and pure thought life.
4. Start studying the lesson on Monday.
5. Have proper motives in the teaching of the Word of God.
6. Prepare yourself physically to teach.
7. Prepare yourself mentally to teach.
8. Prepare yourself spiritually to teach.
9. Pray daily for each pupil of your class.
10. Visit in the home of each pupil every quarter or every three months.
11. Visit all of the absentees.

12. Be a pastor to your pupils.

13. Attend the teachers' meeting on Wednesday evening.

14. Support the entire church program.

15. Be faithful to every public service of the church.

16. When absent, contact the superintendent at least three days before the Sunday on which you are to be absent.

17. Have a monthly class meeting.

18. Organize the class properly.

19. Get up early enough on Sunday morning not to be rushed before teaching the Word of God.

20. Brush over the lesson again on Sunday morning.

21. Make the classroom attractive.

22. Greet the class members as they come in.

23. Meet all visitors before the starting of the class.

24. Properly introduce the visitors, making them feel at home in the class.

25. Enlist every new member possible.

26. Spend the maximum time of five minutes on announcements and business so you can get down quickly to the teaching of the Word of God.

27. Ask all visitors to fill out visitors' slips.

28. Each teacher should tithe.

29. Leave the quarterly at home. I could not say enough about this. The cardinal sin in a Sunday school class would be for a person not to teach from an open Bible.

30. Teach only from the Bible.

31. Do not make any pupil read or talk.

32. Have an interest getter or a point of contact for the lesson.

33. Have a written aim for the lesson.

34. Stay on the subject of the lesson. Do not allow anyone to get you off of the subject at hand.

35. Be the age of the pupils as you teach.

36. Teach until the bell rings or until it is time to dismiss the class and prepare for the morning service.

37. Take your class directly to the auditorium.

38. If you have lost people in your class, sit with them in the morning service.

39. Keep the Lord's Day holy.

40. Make the work of the Lord the most important thing in your life.

These forty things are presented to our teachers and officers at the opening of each Sunday school year. This is one way in which we prepare the program. We dwell on separation at these meetings. For example, we teach our teachers how to prepare the lesson. We teach them to prepare themselves, to prepare the pupils, to prepare the classroom, and to prepare the lesson. In the preparing of the lesson we teach them to start studying the lesson on Monday afternoon. We suggest that every teacher read the lesson material from the Bible at least seven times before he begins to prepare his outline. We suggest they read it one time for content, one time looking for types of Jesus Christ, another time looking for thoughts, another time with helps, another time with a classbook beside the Bible (so as to be able to apply the lesson to each pupil in the class), another time to outline the lesson and prepare it for the Sunday school class on the Lord's Day.

Then we discuss at this annual course how to present a lesson. We teach our teachers to present the lesson only from the Bible. We teach them to seek limited participation from the pupil. For example, we never say, "What do you think about verse 2?" Why, they may think ten minutes about verse 2. Consequently, we seek limited participation. Ask questions that demand only a one-word answer or a very brief answer — a fill in the blank, a multiple choice, or some other question, or some other type presentation that will require participation, yet on a limited scale.

There are many other things that we offer in this annual course. Time would not permit us to discuss each of these.

Weekly Teachers' and Officers' Meeting

As we discuss the preparing of the program, we come to a very important subject — probably the most important single subject that we will discuss on the subject of building a great Sunday school. This is the Teachers' and Officers' Meeting. Here, at the First Baptist Church, we have found it helpful to have a meeting prior to our Wednesday evening midweek service. Our meeting starts at 6:00 and ends at 7:30. The teachers and officers are required to attend this meeting. We have the following schedule: From 6:00 to 6:30 we have a meal. From 6:30 until 6:50 we have a twenty-minute time of promotion. At this time we have a pep rally. We present the plan. We challenge the teachers. We compliment, rebuke, scold, and promote the work of the Sunday school. We compliment classes doing a good job and exhort the classes doing a poor job to accelerate their work in the building of the class and department. It is somewhat a pep rally — a time of enthusiasm, zeal and pledging God to do better in the work of the Lord Jesus Christ. At this meeting we present what we call the *Echoes*. The *Echoes* is a little paper (one sheet, mimeographed, but neatly done) given to each of our teachers at the midweek Teachers' and Officers' Meeting.

(Illustration on next page)

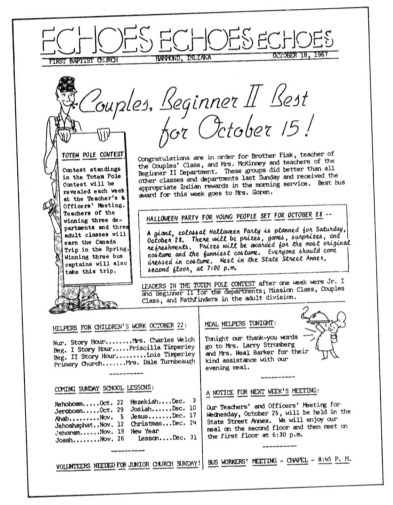

ECHOES ECHOES ECHOES

FIRST BAPTIST CHURCH   HAMMOND, INDIANA   OCTOBER 18, 1967

Couples, Beginner II Best for October 15!

TOTEM POLE CONTEST

Contest standings in the Totem Pole Contest will be revealed each week at the Teacher's & Officers' Meeting. Teachers of the winning three departments and three adult classes will earn the Canada Trip in the Spring. Winning three bus captains will also take this trip.

Congratulations are in order for Brother Fisk, teacher of the Couples' Class, and Mrs. McKinney and teachers of the Beginner II Department. These groups did better than all other classes and departments last Sunday and received the appropriate Indian rewards in the morning service. Best bus award for this week goes to Mrs. Goren.

HALLOWEEN PARTY FOR YOUNG PEOPLE SET FOR OCTOBER 28 --

A giant, colossal Halloween Party is planned for Saturday, October 28. There will be prizes, games, surprizes, and refreshments. Prizes will be awarded for the most original costume and the funniest costume. Everyone should come dressed in costume. Meet in the State Street Annex, second floor, at 7:00 p.m.

LEADERS IN THE TOTEM POLE CONTEST after one week were Jr. I and Beginner II for the departments; Mission Class, Couples Class, and Pathfinders in the adult division.

HELPERS FOR CHILDREN'S WORK OCTOBER 22:

Nur. Story Hour........Mrs. Charles Welch
Beg. I Story Hour.....Priscilla Timperley
Beg. II Story Hour........Lois Timperley
Primary Church.......Mrs. Dale Turnbeaugh

COMING SUNDAY SCHOOL LESSONS:

Rehoboam.....Oct. 22   Hezekiah....Dec. 3
Jeroboam.....Oct. 29   Josiah......Dec. 10
Ahab.........Nov. 5   Jesus.......Dec. 17
Jehoshaphat..Nov. 12   Christmas...Dec. 24
Jehoram......Nov. 19   New Year
Joash........Nov. 26   Lesson....Dec. 31

VOLUNTEERS NEEDED FOR JUNIOR CHURCH SUNDAY!

MEAL HELPERS TONIGHT:

Tonight our thank-you words go to Mrs. Larry Stromberg and Mrs. Neal Barker for their kind assistance with our evening meal.

A NOTICE FOR NEXT WEEK'S MEETING:

Our Teachers' and Officers' Meeting for Wednesday, October 25, will be held in the State Street Annex. We will enjoy our meal on the second floor and then meet on the first floor at 6:30 p.m.

BUS WORKERS' MEETING - CHAPEL - 8:45 P. M.

This is passed out as they come in for the meal at 6:00. This will discuss such things as the program for the future, activities for next Sunday, announcements to make in the departments, introduction of workers and other important facts concerning the growth and work of the Sunday school.

At this Teachers' and Officers' Meeting, during this time from 6:30 until 6:50, we also introduce new workers. We do it like this: "It is a real joy to have Mrs. Jones teaching with us in the Primary Department. Mrs. Jones, would you stand, please. Mrs. Jones, on behalf of the many workers, teachers, superintendents and officers of the Sunday School of the First Baptist Church of Hammond, Indiana, we welcome you to our faculty. We trust that God will bless you in your new class and make your stay with us a happy and profitable one as we serve the Lord together. Let us all give Mrs. Jones a hand." (All of the workers join in giving an applause to Mrs. Jones, welcoming her to the faculty and staff of the Sunday School of the First Baptist Church.)

From 6:50 until 7:10 we teach the Sunday school lesson to our teachers. The pastor has made a three-page outline prior to the meeting. This outline consists of an aim, a point of contact, an introduction, a body and a conclusion to the lesson. An example would be as follows: *the aim:* to teach my pupils the truth concerning the keeping of the inside clean as well as the outside; *the point of contact:* Teacher, bring a cup or a platter to the class on the Lord's Day. Shine to a high gloss the outside of the cup but leave the inside dirty. Ask your pupils if they would like to have a drink of water from the cup. Of course the answer would be negative. Ask them why. They will reply that the cup is dirty. Immediately, you have their attention. You are about to teach them the story of Jesus' rebuking the scribes and Pharisees for having external cleanliness but internal filth. Do you see the point of contact? The interest getter has gotten their attention directed toward the lesson. This outline also consists of a memory verse and questions and answers concerning the lesson. Some of these may be true and false questions; some, multiple choice; others, underline the right answer; others, fill in the blanks; but these questions are the close of the lesson outline as presented each Wednesday evening.

Sunday School Lesson
February 15, 1967

By Jack Hyles, Pastor
First Baptist Church
Hammond, Indiana

THE FIRST EPISTLE TO THE THESSALONIANS

Aim: to teach my pupils the basic teachings and the story in I Thessalonians.
Point of Contact: Read carefully Acts 17:1-9. You will be able to understand this letter far better if you have this foundation first. As a point of contact, explain that Paul went to the synagogue of a city if at all possible. There, it was his custom to preach on the Hebrew Messiah and how that this Messiah had to suffer and rise from the dead. He then showed that Jesus fulfilled these conditions and was the long-awaited Messiah of the Jews. Since Paul, we think, was a member of the Sanhedrin, he usually had an open door into the synagogues. It was their practice to stand up to read the Scriptures and then sit down to expound them. Some little child in the class can be the one in charge. He can stand up to read the Scriptures, sit down to expound the Scriptures, etc.

Still another point of contact would be to have the pupils learn the order of the epistles. The Apostle Paul wrote at least thirteen books of the New Testament and perhaps another. We should know the order of their writing. Why not list them as follows, then scramble them and have the class put them back in order.

Proper Order:	Example of Scrambled Order:
I Thessalonians	Romans
II Thessalonians	I Timothy
Galatians	Galatians
I Corinthians	Titus
Romans	I Thessalonians
II Corinthians	II Corinthians
Colossians	Philemon
Ephesians	Ephesians
Philippians	II Timothy
Philemon	II Thessalonians
I Timothy	Philippians
Titus	I Corinthians
II Timothy	Colossians

(There may be some difference of opinion as to the exact order. It is important, however, to remember this: I and II Thessalonians are his earliest epistles. Then come the four doctrinal books--Romans, I and II Corinthians, and Galatians. Then come four prison epistles--Colossians, Ephesians, Philippians, and Philemon. Then come three pastoral epistles--I and II Timothy and Titus. This is the most important grouping.)

Introduction: Thessalonica is a seaport town situated on what was called the Thermaic Gulf and was anciently the capital of Macedonia. It was first visited by Paul about A. D. 52. It had many Jews at that time; they had a synagogue where Paul preached the Gospel to them.

1. THE FOUNDING -- On Paul's second missionary journey he established this church. He reasoned in the synagogue three Sabbath days with them (Acts 17:2). Maybe he stayed a few days later; we do not know, but from Acts 17:5-10 we know that he was not there long. We do know, however, that in his brief visit he did a tremendous job of indoctrinating the saints concerning the doctrines and the work of God. We find glimpses of this in I Thessalonians 4:2; 5:2, 4; II Thessalonains 2:5, 15; and 3:10. When Paul preached, the Scriptures say that some believed (Acts 17:4). Some of these were Jews, some were Greeks, some were women, and a church was started. However, the Jews became envious. Those who rejected Paul's message started a riot and charged Paul with some base things (Acts 17:5-9). This led to the brevity of his visit. Shortly after he left he wrote them back to try to strengthen them in the things of God.

(General Questions)

1. How long will the Christians be in the air?
2. Where do we go from there?
3. How long will we be on the earth?
4. What great judgment takes place at the end of this one thousand year period?
5. Where do we go then?
6. How long will we be there?

MEMORY VERSE: I Thess. 4:13 -- "But I would not have you to be ignorant, brethren, concerning them which are asleep. . ."

2. A LEADER'S RELATIONSHIP TO HIS FOLLOWERS -- We find this in I Thessalonians 1:1-4. This could be applied to a pastor and his church, a superintendent to her department, a teacher to her class, officers to followers, etc. Let us notice some of these characteristics of a leader:
    1 - Kindliness (verse 1)
    2 - Recognition of other leaders (verse 1) He mentions Silvanus, who is probably Silas, and Timotheus, who no doubt is Timothy. These brethren had accompanied Paul on many of his journeys.
    3 - Thanking God for followers (verse 3)
    4 - Praying for followers (verse 2b)
    5 - Remembering followers (verse 3)
    6 - One can hardly go through these verses without finding the heartbeat of love that Paul had for his people. This, of course, is a necessary characteristic for leadership.

3. THINGS ABOUT THE CHURCH AT THESSALONICA
    1 - They received the Word of God with much affliction (I Thess. 1:6). In spite of their affliction, however, they had joy. This persecution was, no doubt, continued after Paul left; and their suffering was caused by the opposition that Paul experienced.
    2 - They turned from idols (I Thess. 1:9). The pagan culture of Thessalonica was bathed in idolatry. They had idols of all colors and designs. These believers deserted the heathen temples, idols, etc. and left the heathen rites.
    3 - They were examples (I Thess. 1:7). Their lives were changed, and they were certainly a good testimony for Jesus Christ. This is always a good sign of one's sincerity.
    4 - They had a testimony (I Thess. 1:8). Notice the words, "from you sounded out the Word of the Lord." These words, "sounded out" are very interesting. They imply an audible impact of musical instruments. The same root word is used in I Corinthians 13:1 when it speaks of the "sounding brass and tinkling cymbal." In other words, these people made noise about the Gospel. Their lives were changed first, however; then the noise was made. They certainly were not timid. They advertised the Gospel; they announced the Gospel; they demonstrated the Gospel; they declared the Gospel. What a church!
    5 - They served (I Thess. 1:9). Notice the words, "to serve the living and true God." They held their positions and filled them properly. They did their jobs. They worked hard.
    6 - They were looking for Jesus to come (I Thess. 1:10). They had a hope, and they waited for this hope.

4. EXPLANATION OF THE SECOND COMING -- Perhaps this is the main purpose of the writing of the book. Paul had mentioned the coming of the Lord while he was with them. How interesting this is. He was only there a few weeks, and yet he was careful to tell them of the coming of the Lord. This hope began to beat in their bosoms.

They became disturbed regarding those who had died. They were afraid that those who had died would have no part in the Second Coming or the Rapture. They supposed it to be near and were wondering about those who had fallen asleep or had died in Christ. Paul writes them to assure them that the Rapture is not only for those who are alive but also those who have died in Christ. Notice the order here:

1 - The Lord's descent from Heaven.
2 - The resurrection of the dead in Christ.
3 - The changing of the bodies of the living saved and their rising to meet the Lord in the air.
4 - The whole company, living and dead, are raised to meet the Lord in the air.
5 - From then on, we are ever with the Lord.

(TEACHERS, it might be wise here to give a little outline of the future of the believer after the Rapture. Teach them about the Rapture, the seven years we are in the air, the Marriage of the Lamb, the Judgment Seat, our coming back to the earth at the end of the seven years with Christ, our reigning with Him for a thousand years, our helping Him judge the unsaved dead at the Great White Throne, and then our entrance into the New Jerusalem. Even a little child in our Sunday School should know these basic things.)

5. SOME SUGGESTIONS AS TO HOW TO LIVE IN VIEW OF HIS IMMINENT RETURN -- The last chapter is a list of things a Christian should do because Jesus' coming is imminent.
1 - Be sober (verse 8).
2 - Learn to comfort each other (verse 11).
3 - We are to edify each other (verse 11b). The word "edify" means to "build up." Paul said that this church was already doing it, but to continue to do so.
4 - To know their spiritual leaders and to esteem them highly (verses 12 and 13), to love them and be in peace with them.
5 - Verse 14 gives several things we are to do as we look for the Lord's coming. He says, "warn them that are unruly." What this means is to "admonish the disorderly." Then he says to "comfort the feeble-minded," which means to "encourage the weak." Then he tells us to be longsuffering and "patient toward all men."
6 - We are not to be vindicative or retaliatory (verse 15).
7 - We are to rejoice all the time (verse 16).
8 - We are always to be praying (verse 17).
9 - We are to give thanks (verse 18).
10 - We are never to quench the Spirit; we are always to follow His leadership (verse 19).
11 - There are other things listed one after the other such as abstaining from the appearance of evil, etc. The coming of the Lord Jesus Christ should find us doing all the above-mentioned things. May we be that kind of Christians.

- -

QUESTIONS: (Scrambled words)

1. This man joined Paul as a youth to accompany him on many of his journeys, and he was with Paul at this writing. M Y T T I O H
2. Another one of Paul's fellow travellers. L A S S I
3. The first epistle that Paul wrote. I E H L N A A S I S T S O N
4. What Paul did daily for the Thessalonian people. Y R A D E P
5. Where Paul preached first in Thessalonica. G U Y S N O E A G
6. Position of the person who read the Scripture. I T A S N G D N
7. Position of the person who expounded the Scriptures. N I T S G I T

(True or False)

T F   1. Paul's earliest and main opposition in Thessalonica came from the Greeks.
T F   2. After Paul left, the church at Thessalonica had persecution from the same group.
T F   3. Paul was in Thessalonica a long time.
T F   4. The Christians at Thessalonica did not turn from their idols.

(Fill in the Blanks)

1. The Christians in Thessalonica were not only believers but they were such good believers that they became good E _ _ _ _ _ _.'
2. They S _ _ _ _ _ out the Word of God. _ _ _ _.'
3. They were looking for the R _ _ _ _ of the Lord.
4. They were concerned, however, about the Christians who had D _ _ _.
5. Paul told them that the dead in Christ would rise _ _ _ _ _.
6. Then he said, "Those who are alive and remain unto the _ _ _ _ _ _ of the Lord shall rise."
7. He said, "They shall together be caught up into the _ _ _ _ _ _."

From 7:10 until 7:30 a different staff member takes each department and applies the lesson to this particular age level. For example, one of our staff members will take the Junior teachers. With the information that I have given in teaching the lesson from 6:50 to 7:10, the worker takes the lesson and shows the teacher how to break it down and apply it to the Junior level or the level of each departmental age group. This is certainly an important time.

Let us review. From 6:30 until 6:50 we promote. From 6:50 until 7:10 we teach the lesson and present the outline. From 7:10 until 7:30 we present methods, plans, and ways to apply the lesson to the particular age level involved. I could not emphasize too strongly the importance of the weekly Teachers' and Officers' Meeting.

PROMOTING OF THE PROGRAM

We have discussed the planning of the program; we have discussed the preparing of the program, and now we come to discuss the promoting of the program. Let us remind you once again that the program itself is the most important part of the Sunday school. Consistent week-by-week teaching of the Word of God and the preparation of the teacher, the pupil and the worker is tremendously important. However, it matters not how *much* we teach the Bible and how *well* we teach the Bible if no one is there to hear us teach the Bible. Then we have become as sounding brass and tinkling cymbal. Consequently, we must spend much time, energy and effort in the promoting of the program.

Visitation

Of course the first and most important phase in the promoting of the program would have to be the visitation. Every Sunday school and church should have, and *must* have to be a great Sunday school and church, an active visitation program. We call our visitation program here at First Baptist "trotline fishing."

When I was a little boy I fished in the creek near our house. I fished for crappie. I would get one hook, one line, one pole and fish. One day I noticed a fellow beside me who had two hooks and two minnows on one line. I thought that was a tremendous idea. Perhaps that would even double the amount of fish that I would catch. So I put another hook on my line. Later, I added the third hook to the same line. It wasn't long that the tremendous idea dawned upon me that I had two hands; consequently, I made two poles. When I say I made two poles, I mean I *made* two poles. We used a limb of a tree and I put three hooks and three minnows on each pole. Finally, I decided to make a third pole. Consequently, I had three hooks on three different poles, giving me nine chances to catch the fish instead of the previous one chance.

One day I saw some men coming out on the creek in a boat. They went down the creek a bit and pulled up a big line, and there was a big twelve-pound catfish on one hook and another big catfish on another. I said, "Fellows, what kind of fishing do you call that?"

They said, "It is trotline fishing."

"That is for me," I said. "Never again will I fish with one hook and one minnow and one pole. I want to put many hooks in the water."

Now the average church fishes with one hook, one minnow, one line and one pole. This is the preaching of the Gospel from the pulpit. We at First Baptist Church have many hooks in the water. We throw our trotline in the water after the Sunday evening service ends. Then all week long we keep the hooks out in the water. On Sunday morning during the invitation we simply pull the hooks out of the water and see how many fish we find on each hook.

The first six months of 1966 my secretary gave me the report that 1,400 people had walked the aisle — either receiving Christ as Saviour or joining the First Baptist Church. That is in six months. In the first six months of the year, 721 of these had followed Christ in believers' baptism and had been baptized in the baptistry in the First Baptist Church of Hammond. These people were not preached down the aisle. Oh, maybe a few came in response to the preaching, but 85% of these people had been dealt with or won to Christ in the home prior to their walking the aisle. This is what we call trotline fishing.

Jesus said to go into the streets, the lanes, the highways and hedges, and bring the halt, poor, sick, the blind to Himself. And so, we go where they are.

Let us notice for a few moments the hooks that we keep in the water in our visitation program: The first hook is the pastor's personal soul winning. No one can build a great soul-winning church unless the pastor is a soul winner. The pastor himself should lead in soul winning. Every Sunday he should have someone prepared to walk the aisle professing publicly his faith in the Lord Jesus Christ.

The second hook we throw in the water is the staff. Each member of our staff is required to witness for Jesus Christ. My assistant pastors, yes, even the secretaries are required to spend at least four hours a week witnessing to unsaved people. Our staff last year brought over six hundred people down the aisles of the First Baptist Church professing faith in Jesus Christ.

The third hook that we put in the water is the hook of our Sunday school teachers. Last year our Sunday school teachers led 411 people to Jesus Christ. We constantly put before our teachers and officers the importance of soul winning. Every Sunday of the year some teacher or officer brings someone down the aisle professing faith in Jesus Christ.

The fourth hook we put in the water is the deacon hook. We have sixty-six deacons here at First Baptist (one for each 100 members of the church). These are dedicated men, not chosen because of their financial position or social standing or eminence in the community, but rather chosen because of their love for Jesus Christ and their love for the souls of men. These deacons bring souls to Jesus Christ. Every Sunday of the world some deacon brings someone down the aisle receiving Christ as Saviour.

A little girl who moved away with her family from our city and visited another church said she didn't like the church. Someone asked her why. "Well," she said, "at the First Baptist Church at Hammond, the pastor stands behind the pulpit and the demons sit on the front. At this church the demons don't sit on the front." I am sure she was a little mixed up. She meant deacons, but she said demons. I am afraid that in far too many cases the word demons is more descriptive than the word deacons, for God did not intend for the deacons to be somewhat of a Wall Street financier, but rather God intended for deacons to be men of compassion and burdened for souls. And so our deacons lead people to Jesus Christ.

The fifth hook we have in the water is the work with the handicapped. Our church has one person who uses several others to help in work with the handicapped constantly. The shut-ins receive periodical visits with a tape recording of the services and a personal tape from the pastor. It is nothing unusual for someone to roll down the aisle in a wheelchair. It has happened that some have been rolled down the aisle in hospital beds. We have a constant agreement that any handicapped person who is won to Christ can have a wheelchair, a hospital bed and ambulance service to come to our services.

A few weeks ago, in fact in the last four weeks, we had two people roll down the aisle in wheelchairs the same Sunday professing faith in Christ or being added to the church.

Our sixth hook in the water is the work with the deaf. On a recent Sunday we had fifty-one deaf people in our deaf section. Our deaf and hard-of-hearing work brings about fifty people to Jesus Christ every year. Last year sixty-one people came down these aisles professing Jesus Christ who were deaf and hard-of-hearing. This is a tremendous ministry of our church.

Another hook we have in the water is the rescue mission hook. Our church owns and operates a full-time rescue mission. We will average about two men per Sunday walking the aisles in our church for believers' baptism who were saved in our rescue mission. Hundreds of others are saved each year in the rescue mission who do not actually stay for the Sunday services and come forward in our church.

Another hook we have in the water is our visitation committee. We have divided our city into fifteen different sections. Two fine, well-trained people are chosen to visit in each section of the city. For example, let's suppose that you and I are chosen to visit in section one. It would be our job to visit every new person who moves into section one. It will be our job to visit every person who visits our services from section one. We also will contact every hot prospect who lives in section one. These two people are chosen like Sunday school teachers and officers. They are trained like Sunday school teachers and officers, and they are responsible for making a good visit in section one or their particular section of the city. We call this our visitation committee. Week by week people are brought down the aisles professing faith in Christ by these people.

Another hook we have in the water is our bus ministry. The First Baptist Church operates forty-five bus routes. We bring as many as 1,500 people to Sunday school and to preaching service every Sunday. Yes, I said to preaching service! These people stay for the preaching of the Word of God. We have, I suspect, sixty or seventy people in our church who do nothing but go from house to house in certain neighborhoods and communities inviting people to come to church and Sunday school on our buses. We will secure a bus, enlist two or three workers, give them a certain section of our area, and they will simply work their section filling up their bus. Our buses will average through the year, I suspect, eleven hundred to twelve hundred people per Sunday, and many are saved who ride the buses to Sunday school and to the preaching service.

Another hook we have in the water is the hook with the Spanish-speaking people. In the Calumet region we have many Spanish-speaking people; consequently, we provide for them a Sunday school lesson in Spanish. Many Sundays we have Spanish-speaking people who come down the aisle professing faith publicly in the Lord Jesus Christ.

Another hook we have in the water is our work with the retarded children. There are literally hundreds of thousands of children in our great metropolitan area who are retarded. We provide for them a Sunday school class with trained workers. Many of the parents, unable ever to attend Sunday school and church, now find it possible to attend the Sunday school hour and stay for the preaching service because we have a work for their children. Numbers of these have professed faith in Christ and have been saved in our services.

Another hook we have in the water is the hook we call the obituary column. A committee of people in our church reads the obituary column every day in the local newspaper. The family of every person who passes away receives a letter of sympathy and a gospel witness from the First Baptist Church. Still another group is the hospital group.

We have a group of people who visit hospitals and win people to Christ in the hospitals.

Then, we have another hook in the water. We call it our honors team. Someone checks the newspaper daily and sends a letter of congratulation to every person who wins an honor. Let's suppose that you have been selected citizen of the month. You will receive a letter of congratulations from the First Baptist Church along with a gospel tract and a card to fill out if you are interested in a visit from our church or one of our soul winners. Let's suppose that your hog won a contest in the County Fair, the Future Farmers' Association, etc. You would receive a letter from our church congratulating you. Of course we may even send one to the hog, but we want the people in our area who receive some mark of distinction to know the First Baptist Church congratulates them and thereby they receive a gospel witness from our church.

Another committee checks tragedies that take place. For example, if a person has a fire, he receives a letter of sympathy from the First Baptist Church and a gospel witness and a card to fill out. If someone has a car accident, a letter from the First Baptist Church, a gospel tract and a card to fill out.

Every person who marries in our area receives a letter of congratulation from the First Baptist Church, a tract and a card to fill out.

Every couple who has a new baby receives a letter of congratulation from our church, a gospel tract and a card to fill out.

So you see these hooks are thrown into the water after the services on Sunday. The visitation team, the pastor's visitation, the staff's visitation, the Sunday school teacher, the rescue mission, the bus ministry, the retarded children's class, the Spanish-speaking class— all of these hooks are in the water all week long. On Sunday we simply pull up the trotline and find the hooks that have fish on them, and they come forward professing faith publicly in the services of our church.

There are other hooks we have in the water—our youth visitation. Just last evening one of our young men stood in the service and said, "We had fourteen saved last week." These were led to Christ by the teen-agers and young people of our church in youth visitation. We have a youth visitation night when the teen-agers go forth and win other teen-agers to Jesus Christ.

Another hook we have in the water is our ladies' visitation. Each Friday morning our ladies, several of them, go out to visit and witness to those who need Jesus Christ.

There are many, many other hooks we have in the water—enough for now. I trust you get the idea. The preaching of the Gospel from the pulpit is not enough. If one is going to build a great Sunday school and a great soul-winning church, he must have many, many different facets of this program, reaching every area and every type of person imaginable. This is what we call our trotline fishing.

Publicity and Promotion

Now, we turn from the visitation program as we discuss the promoting of the program to the promotion itself. I am a great believer in promotion. Our Lord has said that the children of this world are wiser in their generation than the children of light. What a sad commentary on the work of the Gospel! Far too many churches have shut themselves away in a corner of their city, not making the city realize that they even exist. I believe that every person in town ought to realize the work of the Sunday school marches on. We ought to keep everybody in town conscious of the growing of the great Sunday school.

We do this by newspaper advertising. Every week of the world a big advertisement, advertising the Sunday school of the church and the services of the church, is placed in our local newspaper.

We also do this by the radio ministry. We have a "Radio Bible Class" taught by the pastor on Sunday morning from the auditorium. We have a daily ministry. This daily ministry, called "The Pastor's Study," is used greatly to promote the work of the Sunday school. This, added to our nationwide radio ministry and other forms of publicity locally, adds to the promotion of the work of the Lord Jesus Christ in the Sunday school.

Now, as we think of promoting the program of the Sunday school, let me suggest a few things of planning a year's program for the Sunday school. In the first place, I would suggest that you plan the natural high days for the year. As the year begins, or sometime before the beginning of the year, the pastor and those interested in planning the program for the year should get down a calendar, look at the calendar, and plan the activities for the year.

The first thing we do is plan the natural high days. These days will include Easter, Promotion Day, revival Sundays, etc. We do *not* plan special activities on these days, for these days take care of themselves. People come to Sunday school on Easter just because it is Easter. Consequently, we save our big drive and our big push for other Sundays, realizing that Easter and other natural high days will take care of themselves.

The second thing we do is plan the natural low days. Now there are natural low days in the year. One is Memorial Day weekend. Another is Labor Day weekend, the Fourth of July weekend, etc. Especially when I was pastoring smaller churches would I plan something extra special for these natural low days.

Then we plan for the natural low season. The natural low season, of course, is the summertime. We have heard about the "summer slump."

We have heard about the attendance going down in the summertime, and, certainly, in our area especially is it true. Many of our people have four, five, six, seven, eight, nine and some even thirteen weeks' vacations, making the summertime a very difficult time of growing the Sunday school. Consequently, we plan something for the summer.

It has been our policy now for a number of years to have what we call the "Carry-the-Load Sunday." Each department is requested to "carry the load" one Sunday of the summer. Each department has a given Sunday when they promote a big, supercolossal Sunday. The first day, for example, is the Beginners' day. The Beginners promote a big Sunday. Now, when they have a big crowd, the adults have a larger crowd. We do not have a single beginner child (age four or five) in our Sunday school who knows how to drive; consequently, the parents have to drive them to Sunday school.

The next Sunday the Primaries have a big Sunday; and the next Sunday, Junior I; and the next Sunday, Junior II; and the next Sunday, Junior High. Each department has a big Sunday. Because of the bigness of one department's attendance, the entire Sunday school is helped because of the family coming with the person who has the big Sunday. So we plan for the summer season. In this time the pastor, or one of the pastors, goes to each department on their big day, preaches a gospel sermon and gives an invitation trying to get people saved in each department — an annual tour of the department. These people who are saved come forward in the public services.

The fourth thing we do in the planning of a year's program is plan for a special holiday. By this, we mean we plan something special for regular holidays. We plan something special for Mother's Day. Just this last year we gave a little ball-point pen with a flower on top of it (you have seen these artificial flowers on top of ball-point pens with the words "Happy Mother's Day-1966") to each mother who attended. We made of all of these flowers a beautiful, hugh corsage (I guess six feet high), and each mother received one of these ball-point pens with lovely flowers on the end. Mother's Day is planned.

Something is planned for Father's Day, for Thanksgiving Day, for Christmas and other special holidays. Some little something that will bring the people on these holidays certainly is advisable.

The fifth thing we do in planning the annual program is plan special seasonal days. Such things as "Back-to-School Day" when school starts, "Old-Fashioned Day" in the summertime, the fall "Kickoff Sunday" or "Round-Up Day," the church's anniversary, perhaps the pastor's anniversary and other anniversary occasions or special seasonal days are good to promote. These promote easily, by the way.

The sixth thing we do is to plan days for special activities. If you are going to have a vacation Bible school, why not have a "Vacation-Bible-School Sunday" and let it help your Sunday school attendance.

If you are going to have a big youth camp, maybe you could plan a "Youth-Camp Sunday," and the activities should be integrated into the Sunday school program and increase the attendance in the Sunday school.

Number seven, plan a ten-week spring program and a ten-week fall program. Beginning on the last Sunday of March and going through April and May and into the first Sunday of June, we have a tremendous spring program. Beginning with the last Sunday of September or the first Sunday of October, we have a fall program lasting through the early Sundays of December. These are the programs that become the life's blood of our church. These programs are built maybe around contests, special drives, awards for those who bring so many visitors, etc. During one program we had New Testaments engraved in gold given to every visitor or every person who brought as many as ten visitors during the ten weeks' program. On the front of this Testament engraved in gold was a picture of the First Baptist Church.

We have church contests and departmental contests. We give prizes. For example, we have an annual Bible conference near here at Cedar Lake, Indiana. We have a contest each spring. The top ten people in the contest bringing visitors receive some help in attending this Bible conference. The first prize, for example, would be motel rooms and meals for the family who brings the most visitors during the contest. The second prize would be the same thing. The third prize perhaps would be just a cabin with meals, and the fourth prize would be the same thing. The fifth prize would be maybe just the cabin for the week, and the sixth prize would be the same thing. This creates a tremendous interest in our spring program.

Let me make one suggestion. Never have a contest with only one prize. If someone gets far ahead, others will give up and only one person is working. I would suggest that several prizes be given in every contest making it possible for the ones who are behind not to give up.

I would also suggest that the prizes be of a spiritual nature. We never give a prize unless it has a spiritual connotation. For example, we give Bibles, Christian books, commentaries, or maybe a trip to a Bible conference. These prizes add to spiritual growth. Also we give prizes that publicize the church. We would give ball-point pens with the church's name on it, the pastor's name and a Scripture verse. Only things that advertise the church or give spiritual benefit are used as prizes in our promotional program. We also plan a similar program in the fall.

The eighth thing we do is plan four big, supercolossal days each year. We have one big day each quarter—the kind of a day that will double the attendance. I am of the conviction that a church that runs a hundred in Sunday school can come nearer having 300 on a big day than she can having 150. A big goal challenges people. A big goal instills in people a tremendous desire to do something big for God. Oh, we have played church long enough. We have played "little" long enough. It is time that we decided to do something big and launch out in the deep and build a great, growing Sunday school for the Lord Jesus Christ.

Let me share with you some of the big days and special occasions that we have used here at the First Baptist Church.

(1.) One is "Old-Fashioned Day." This is an annual occasion and is one of the most enjoyable days in our church. We do not set a specific attendance goal on this day but we do try to have it on a weekend that would normally have a lower attendance than usual. A good time for "Old-Fashioned Day" is the 4th of July weekend or the Labor Day weekend. We have on this day a collection of antiques that we show. Such items as old-fashioned churns, washpots, spinning wheels, clocks, Bibles, curling irons and smoothing irons are brought and displayed for this special day. Many people bring antiques that others are interested to see. We use on this day an old-fashioned organ. We pass hats instead of plates. We use a mourners' bench at the altar covered with old, worn-out quilts. We have a creek baptizing in the afternoon if weather permits or maybe in a pond nearby. In the evening service we have coal oil or kerosene lamps and lanterns lighting the building. The electric lights are all turned off. Our people wear old-fashioned costumes for this day, and so many wonderful things highlight "Old-Fashioned Day." We preach old-fashioned messages, and old-fashioned songs are sung. We may sing fifteen stanzas of the "Old-Time Religion." What a blessed day it is. It is not a novelty day, but rather normally the power of God comes and many are saved and people are brought back to the old-time religion of faith in Jesus Christ and remember the worship of yesteryear. This is "Old-Fashioned Day."

(2.) Then we have the church's birthday. On this day we could have a big birthday cake. We have had birthday cakes weighing as much as seven hundred pounds. We send out candles to each person in the Sunday school; he brings his candle for the birthday cake. A large candle is lighted for the department that reaches its goal on this particular Sunday. It is the "Church's Birthday Sunday."

(3.) Another day we have is "Back-to-School Day." Personal letters are sent to the school students. A lovely gift is given to every person going back to school. A corsage oftentimes is given to each of our lady schoolteachers, a boutonniere to each of our men schoolteachers. A prize is given to each child who gets his or her schoolteacher to come to "Back-to-School Day." We have a special prayer of dedication for the schoolteachers and for the school students as we promote "Back-to-School Day."

(4.) Another day is "Baby Day." On "Baby Day" we have a special letter sent to the parents of the babies. We give a little gift to each child—perhaps a blue Testament to the boy babies and a pink Testament to girl babies. Maybe a little corsage is given to each mother of the baby.

(5.) We have had an annual "Homecoming Day" in some of our churches.

(6.) "Picture-Taking Day" is a good day to have. Each class has its picture made. There are other days. On "Record-Breaking Day" a record is broken over the Sunday school superintendent's head if the department's record is broken. On "B One Sunday" we sent some vitamin B-1 pills out one time and asked everyone to "B One": "Absentee Sunday," "Good-Neighbor Sunday," "Christmas Sunday," "Ladies' Rally," "Men's Rally," "Round-Up Day," "Pack-the-Pew Day" and other days are used in promoting the Sunday School of the First Baptist Church.

The biggest business in all the world is the Sunday school and the reaching of people with the Gospel of Jesus Christ. Perhaps no other facet of our church organization reaches more people than the Sunday school. Would God that every church across America that believes the Bible would launch out into a great Sunday school drive reaching more people and more people and more people. Let us challenge our own people to reach more and more for Jesus Christ. Let us build our Sunday school to the glory of God and the salvation of those without Christ.

11. A Teachers' and Officers' Meeting

(Following is a transcription of an actual teachers' meeting as conducted by the First Baptist Church of Hammond on Wednesday, February 15, 1966.)

The teachers and officers of the Sunday School of the First Baptist Church meet each Wednesday evening from 6:00 to 7:30. From 6:00 to 6:30 we enjoy a meal together. The meat is provided by the church, and each teacher is requested to bring a covered dish. At the close of the meal an offering is taken to defray the cost of the meat.

From 6:30 until 6:50 I lead the entire teaching staff in promotion and inspiration to do a better job. During this twenty-minute period we recognize new workers, and we compliment classes and departments that have done good jobs. Oftentimes we scold, rebuke, inspire, congratulate, etc. Here we set our goals, make our plans, and vow to do a better job.

From 6:50 until 7:10 I teach the Sunday school lesson to all of the teachers who teach from the junior age and up. (The Primaries, Beginners, and Nursery Departments go to their own rooms to plan their work.) A three-page outline with an aim, point of contact, introduction, body, conclusion, questions and answers, and memory verse is given to each teacher. This outline is prepared by the pastor each week. We also give each worker a little paper called the *Echoes*. This is simply a little promotional sheet to inspire the workers to do a better job and to inform them concerning plans for the Sunday school.

Then from 7:10 until 7:30 the teachers go to their individual departmental levels where the teachers of the various age groups are taught how to apply the lesson to their particular age level.

PROMOTION: 6:30–6:50

PASTOR: Look at your *Echoes*, please. It might be wise to notice the interesting statistics just a little below the middle of the page in the left column, comparing last Sunday's attendance with that of the same Sunday for the past few years. Last Sunday it was 2,830. It would have been over 3,000 had it not been for six buses that froze because of sub-zero weather. One year ago—2,250. You can notice a 580 gain over last year. Two years ago—1,970; three years ago—

1,510. The corresponding Sundays give us a growth of 1,320 for three years, which is 440 for an average growth per year. I think that is wonderful. You may notice that the last year has been the best year. It has been this way all of the time. This past year has been the best in every case, and many Sundays we are running 600 or 700 more than we did a year ago.

Now, notice the balcony duty listing in the upper right-hand column. The Junior High School Departments will have it this coming Sunday. I think that last week we had twenty-five workers. Once again, be sure to instruct your workers that it is not their job to create more problems than they solve in the balcony. I often look up in the balcony and see four adults sitting together. That is not the purpose. The idea is for them to scatter so they can be in reach of every child that is misbehaving, rather than getting up and misbehaving to correct a child.

Now a few words about the attendance last Sunday. Some of the departments did very well and some did not do so well. The Nursery had 105. Beginners, you were way down last Sunday. Maybe it was because of the weather, but you had only 135, which is about eighty down. Primaries had 224, which is some down. Junior I, 256, which is some down. Junior II, 226. Down just a little bit? Junior High I, 77, down a little bit. Junior High II, 61; High School, 178. It looks like everyone was down about 15% except the adults. We can thank the Lord that the adults had 1,380. This gave us a grand total of 2,830. Now let me say this: Since everybody was down, I would suggest you do some thinking about contacting the absentees.

I know you are tired. I know you have worked hard, but now look! I also know that Sunday is the Lord's Day. Let's not slack up.

How many of you work on buses? Will you raise your hands, please. Let me suggest that you give some time Saturday working on the bus routes and doing the best you can to get the bus crowds up. Whose bus broke down Sunday? I would suggest very definitely that you contact the people and tell them that you are going to be by this Sunday. Tell them what happened, etc. I understand that it will be warmer next Sunday.

I am going to suggest that we make three visits per teacher between now and Saturday. If every class (we have about two hundred classes) increases by three we will have six hundred more people. We will not have 1,380 adults besides all of the other classes this coming Sunday. We were up this last Sunday because of the Building Program Rally. We normally have about 1,000 adults besides the teachers. We are not going to have 2,800 in Sunday school Sunday if you do not do better than you did last Sunday. I am asking every teacher in the Sunday school to visit three absentees that would have been here last Sunday had it not been for the weather. I would ask you to do more except for the fact that you have been busy this week. You have been teaching. You have been cooking. You have been entertaining preachers. You have been busy, and I know it. I also know why this is true. I know that most of the work in an endeavor like this falls on your shoulders because you are the church. You are the inner circle, and you are the finest folks we have or you wouldn't be teaching.

If the Sunday school has a "normal Sunday" this coming Sunday, we are going to have to get these absentees back. For example, we will not even have 2,500 Sunday if Beginners have only 135. Where are the Beginner workers? Lift your hands. Now you understand, if you have 135 Sunday, we won't have a normal 2,600 Sunday, which is our average during the winter months. Primary workers, lift your hands. If you have 224 and everybody else has corresponding attendances, we will not have 2,500 in Sunday school Sunday. Junior I, I hate to say this because you are usually up, but you were down Sunday too, and so were Junior II, Junior High, and High School. If everybody has what you had last Sunday, and the adults have a normal crowd, we are going to have about 2,300 in Sunday school, and that would be a catastrophe!

Remember, I am asking every teacher to contact three absentees this week. I do not want you to contact those who have not been here since 1932. I am not concerned this week, basically, about the fellow who has not been here in a year or six months. What I am concerned about mainly this week is the fellow who is normally here but was not here last Sunday.

Three Sundays ago we had the bad snow—27 inches! The next Sunday we had another bad snow—11 more inches! Then the attendance was 1,584, which was the smallest attendance we have had in years. Then last Sunday the adults were up and carried the load. That means the children who were absent last Sunday in your department haven't been here for three Sundays. You hear me! Three Sundays can make a habitual absentee. You can wreck your class in a couple of snows.

You say, "Well, they will come back."

Some of them won't. There are at least three in your class that if you will get them back Sunday, you will save them. What is our motto? Absentees are...what?

TEACHERS: People.

PASTOR: Say it again.

TEACHERS: Absentees are people.

PASTOR: Again.

TEACHERS: Absentees are people.

PASTOR: One more time.

TEACHERS: Absentees are people.

PASTOR: All right, that means these 600 that we need to get back are people who have problems. They have burdens. They have needs.

Somebody said the other day, "Where do you lose them?" We have five hundred Juniors but only a couple hundred Junior Highers and High Schoolers. You lose them when some teacher does not visit them when they are absent.

"Well," you say, "High Schoolers will be High Schoolers."

No, teachers will be teachers.

You say, "It is juvenile delinquency."

No, it is teacher delinquency. That is the problem.

You start a child when he is a Beginner or in the nursery, and if you will visit him every time he is absent, you will never lose him! Everyone who becomes a backslider missed one Sunday for the first time.

All right, let us visit three absentees this week. Now that is not too much. Ordinarily we ought to visit more than that. How many teachers will say, "I will pledge to the Lord that I will visit at least three absentees between now and the Lord's Day." I am very serious about this. Would you raise your hand up high, way up high. Keep them up. If you will do it, we will have 2,600 in Sunday school.

Look, this is not my work. This is God's work and it ought to be done right. We ought to do it in season and out of season. I know you will.

Now I want to say a few words about one or two other things. You will notice in the upper left-hand column of the *Echoes* that the dates of the spring program have been set. The dates will be April 2 through June 11. That is eleven Sundays. Plans for the spring will be presented to the teachers and officers in the March 8 meeting. Of course I want you definitely to be in the March 8 meeting.

This is the lull before the storm. This is the inner period between the fall program and the spring program. Until the weather hit us we were having a wonderful winter. Last winter we tried so hard to top 2,000. If we had 2,000 or 2,100, we were very pleased. Until the big snow came we were averaging over 2,600 for this winter.

Let me give you some interesting statistics. Do you recall a year ago when we decided to be "number six in sixty-six" and everyone got a pennant? We had 2,400 and something, and we thought we were off to a tremendous start. That was a big-drive day. I mean, that was one of the biggest days that we had ever had. Do you recall that? We gave everybody a pennant. We had, I think, 2,442. We thought we were off to a big start—2,400! Now then, the next winter, without any push at all, we have averaged over 2,600. We can have 3,000 a

Sunday this spring if we don't drop too far in the wintertime.

Introduction of New Teachers

This evening we have some teachers who have joined us recently and have not been officially welcomed. These are the new teachers, and we would like to have you stand. Mrs. John Vaperzsan in Junior II. Mrs. Maxine Clark, would you stand, please? Mr. Lyle Kerr, would you stand, please. Mrs. Earl Reeves, will you stand, please. We welcome you. We congratulate you because of your new challenge. We welcome you and we are glad you are with us. Let's give them a hand, shall we? (Applause) Thank you, you may be seated.

Please notice that the lessons for the new quarter are listed in the lower left-hand corner. A new series of lessons will begin the first Sunday of April. For twelve weeks we will study the twelve apostles.

Next, notice the calendar of coming events. May 21st is Promotion Day. By the way, we have changed Promotion Day from the last of September to the last of May. May 28 will be the first day in the new classes.

March 13-15 will be the Canada trip for Primary and Junior I teachers.

All right, that concludes the first part of this meeting.

TEACHING OF THE LESSON BY PASTOR: 6:50–7:10

Now we come to the teaching of the lesson and we will open our Bibles to I Thessalonians, please, and prepare our minds for the lesson on the Lord's Day. This quarter we are studying Paul's epistles. Let us go through them. The first we studied was...?

TEACHERS: Romans.

PASTOR: Why did Paul write the book of Romans? He was...?

TEACHERS: Going to visit Rome.

PASTOR: He was soon going to visit Rome, and he was writing them telling them of his coming visit. He was also telling them what he would preach, what doctrines he believed, and what would be taught while he was in Rome.

The second of the epistles was what?

TEACHERS: First Corinthians.

PASTOR: Okay. First Corinthians was written to the church at

Corinth. They had one big problem and the book of I Corinthians was written to solve that problem. They were what kind of Christians?

TEACHERS: Baby Christians.

PASTOR: Some said, "I am of..." whom?

TEACHERS: Paul.

PASTOR: Some said, "I am of..." whom?

TEACHERS: Apollos.

PASTOR: Some said, "I am of..." whom?

TEACHERS: Peter.

PASTOR: Yes, they were divided. Paul was writing and telling them not to be babies in the Lord.

The third epistle was the epistle to the church at Corinth. As soon as Paul left Corinth (now think hard) somebody came in and spread something. They spread the fact that Paul really did not have the right to be a what?

TEACHERS: An apostle.

PASTOR: So the book of II Corinthians is written to the church at Corinth. Paul is vindicating his apostleship. There are also three wonderful chapters here about the Christian grace of what?

TEACHERS: Giving.

PASTOR: That is right, giving.

All right, we come to the fourth epistle, Paul's epistle to the Galatians. Now the Galatian people were guilty of doing some sewing. What was it that they sewed?

TEACHERS: The veil.

PASTOR: Yes, they sewed the veil that had been rent in twain from the top to the bottom. This meant now that the days of what were over?

TEACHERS: Legalism.

PASTOR: Yes, the law, ritualism, ceremony, etc. The Galatian people had some legalizers to come to lead them back to Judaism. Paul said, "You observe days and seasons, and I am afraid lest I have bestowed labour upon you in vain."
Then we come to what letter?

TEACHERS: Ephesians.

PASTOR: What do you know about the church at Ephesus?

TEACHERS: It was big.

PASTOR: It was probably the largest church in the group and it was also a very influential church. Ephesians is a beautiful doctrinal book telling about the heavenly life in Jesus Christ. Now think hard. Who carried the book of Ephesians from Paul to Ephesus?

TEACHERS: Tychicus.

PASTOR: Right. Tychicus carried it. He also carried another one. What was it?

TEACHERS: Colossians.

PASTOR: Right. Now that leads us to the book of Philippians. The book of Philippians is a what?

TEACHERS: A thank-you note.

PASTOR: Yes, someone had come to Paul and brought him a gift. Who was it?

TEACHERS: Epaphroditus.

PASTOR: Yes, Epaphroditus brought Paul a gift from the church of Philippi. Epaphroditus also visited Paul when he was in jail in Rome. Epaphroditus got sick and almost died, but he got well. He was the messenger that Paul used.
Now, Romans is a reminder of Paul's coming. First Corinthians is a letter to baby Christians. Second Corinthians is a letter vindicating Paul's apostleship. In Galatians, Paul is rending the veil again. Ephesians is the heavenly letter to the great church, and Philippians is a thank-you note from Paul to the church at Philippi.
Now let us review Colossians. The book of Colossians was written

because somebody came to Paul and told him about an error in the church at Colosse. What was the fellow's name?

TEACHERS: Epaphras.

PASTOR: Epaphras came. What kind of false doctrine did he say had crept in?

TEACHERS: Angel worship.

PASTOR: Right. Paul is writing telling about the preeminence of Christ and the danger of angel worship.

That leads us to the book of I Thessalonians. Get your outlines, please, and look at I Thessalonians.

The first thing I would like for you to do is to get something that is made of metal like a fountain pen, spoon or knife and hold it in your hands, please. All right, if you have it, raise it up. Now I want you to beat it on the table very loudly. Keep doing it. Everybody keep doing it. Okay, you may stop. I will tell you in a minute why I had everybody beat on the table. This is the point of contact for Sunday. Have all of the kids make noise.

Now I want to show you why I gave you that for a point of contact. Look in I Thessalonians 1:8. "For from you sounded out the word of the Lord." Those two words, "sounded out," come from the same Greek root word that Paul used in I Corinthians 13:1 where he said, "I am become as sounding brass, or a tinkling cymbal." With a noise like that of sounding brass and tinkling cymbals the church at Thessalonica sounded out the Word of God.

Now beat on the table again. With that much racket you are supposed to get out the Gospel.

Take your Bibles and place a marker at I Thessalonians 1. Then turn to Acts 17. To me the church at Thessalonica was a very unusual church and a striking one in one respect. Look at verse 1 of Acts 17. "Now when they had passed through Amphipolis and Apollonia, they came to Thessalonica, where was a synagogue of the Jews." Hold it! "A synagogue of the Jews"—what do we already know? When Paul was in Philippi, did he go to the synagogue?

TEACHERS: No.

PASTOR: Notice that here he went to the synagogue. Because of the fact that he went to the synagogue here we know one thing about the city of Thessalonica. What is that?

TEACHERS: They had at least ten responsible Jewish men in the city.

PASTOR: Yes, if they had not had ten responsible Jewish men in the city, somebody raise your hand and tell me what they would not have had.

TEACHER: A synagogue.

PASTOR: Right. What would they have had instead?

TEACHERS: A place of prayer.

PASTOR: Yes.

"And Paul, as his manner was, went in unto them, and three sabbath days reasoned with them out of the scriptures." Paul was not here long. He was in Ephesus three years, but he was here only three Sabbaths. Look at verses 5-10 of Acts 17 and see why: *"But the Jews which believed not, moved with envy* [that is usually why folks oppose any work of God], *took unto them certain lewd fellows of the baser sort, and gathered a company, and set all the city on an uproar, and assaulted the house of Jason, and sought to bring them out to the people. And when they found them not, they drew Jason and certain brethren unto the rulers of the city, crying* [Note this is a great statement], *These that have turned the world upside down have come hither also; Whom Jason hath received: and these all do contrary to the decrees of Caesar, saying that there is another king, one Jesus. And they troubled the people and the rulers of the city, when they heard these things. And when they had taken security of Jason, and of the other, they let them go. And the brethren immediately sent away Paul and Silas by night unto Berea: who coming thither went into the synagogue of the Jews."*

So Paul was not at Thessalonica long. He reasoned at least how many Sabbaths in the synagogue?

TEACHERS: Three.

PASTOR: It is absolutely amazing what he did. Notice if you would, please, in I Thessalonians 4:2 what he did in three Sabbath days. "For ye know what commandments we gave you by the Lord Jesus." We know on those three Sabbaths he gave them the commandments. Now look in chapter 5 and verse 2: "For yourselves know perfectly that the day of the Lord so cometh as a thief in the night." Hold it! How long was he here?

TEACHERS: Three Sabbaths.

PASTOR: Yes, he said they knew perfectly about the Day of the Lord. You have probably heard some folks say, "We do not know much about the coming of the Lord. We haven't been saved but about five years. You see, we are just baby Christians." Paul said that they knew perfectly about it, yet had been saved only three weeks.

Turn, if you would please, to verse 4 of chapter 5: "But ye, brethren, are not in darkness, that that day should overtake you as a thief." He also taught more about that, for in II Thessalonians 2:5 he reminds them, "Remember ye not, that, when I was yet with you, I told you these things?"

Wait a minute. What "things" does he mean? Look back up to verse 3: "Let no man deceive you by any means: for that day shall not come, except there come a falling away first, and that man of sin be revealed, the son of perdition; Who opposeth and exalteth himself above all that is called God, or that is worshipped; so that he as God sitteth in the temple of God, shewing himself that he is God."

Perhaps you have said, "I am just like Paul. I am just going to preach Christ and Him crucified."

No, you are not like Paul. Paul was here three Sabbath days and told them about the Antichrist, the day of the Lord, the rapture, the falling away, the son of perdition, the Man of Sin, and the Lord's coming as a thief in the night.

Look to verse 15, please, of chapter 2 of II Thessalonians: "Therefore, brethren, stand fast, and hold the traditions which ye have been taught." He taught them how to serve God. He taught them the doctrine. He taught them the traditions of serving Christ, etc., and he was there just three weeks.

Now please notice your outlines. I think it might be wise if you would give your class the proper order of these epistles. We have the chronological order here for you, and on the other side we have the example of scrambled order. I would suggest that you give your class the scrambled order and ask them to unscramble it, you see. You could write them all on the board scrambled up and ask someone to come up to the front of the class to the blackboard and put a "1" by the first one that was written and a "2" by the second and so on. See how close to the proper order they can get.

I want you to look at I Thessalonians again and notice the opening of it. I want you to notice Paul's relationship to his people. "Paul and Silvanus...." Whom do you think Silvanus is?

TEACHERS: Silas.

PASTOR: Right. "...unto the church of the Thessalonians which is in God the Father and in the Lord Jesus Christ."

Now notice Paul's tender expression in verse 2: "We give thanks to God always for you all, making mention of you in our prayers." It is amazing how quickly Paul could fall in love with God's people. In this area he spent only about three weeks. Yet he said that he thanked God for them and that he prayed for them. "Remembering without ceasing your work of faith, and labour of love, and patience of hope in our Lord Jesus Christ, and in the sight of God and our Father." Notice he said, "I thank God for you. I pray for you, and I remember you." Although he was there but a little while he fell in love with them.

"For our gospel came not unto you in word only, but also in power, and in the Holy Ghost, and in much assurance; as ye know what manner of men we were among you for your sake. And ye became followers of us, and of the Lord." I like that. A preacher ought to be able to say that if you are following me, you are following the Lord. "... having received the word in much affliction, with joy of the Holy Ghost: So that ye were ensamples to all that believed in Macedonia and Achaia."

Now notice what kind of church it was. "For from you sounded out the word of the Lord not only in Macedonia and Achaia, but also in every place your faith to God-ward is spread abroad; so that we need not to speak anything." Again we find the words, "sounded out." He said they were sounding out the Gospel. Like sounding brass and tinkling cymbal they were noisy in getting out the Gospel.

"For they themselves shew of us what manner of entering in we had unto you, and how ye turned to God from idols to serve the living and true God; And to wait for his Son from heaven." Now I want to give you the real reason why Paul wrote the book of I Thessalonians. This is what I want you to remember about the book when we review in the coming weeks. Paul had talked to them very much about the coming of the Lord. You cannot read I Thessalonians without reading a lot about this great truth. The people in Thessalonica fell in love with the coming of the Lord, but after Paul left they got worried. They said, "We know that we are going to be raptured. The Lord is going to come, but Paul didn't tell us much about the dead people. What is going to happen to the dead?" So they sent word to Paul that they were concerned about the dead folks (those that had died in Christ). What would happen to them? The book of I Thessalonians was written to explain this matter to them. The key verse is in chapter 4, verse 13: "But I would not have you to be ignorant, brethren, concerning them which are asleep." Hence he wrote the book to dispel their fear about those who were asleep.

Perhaps somebody who was saved had just died and they couldn't understand what would happen. They knew that the Lord was going to come back, but they did not understand what would happen to the brother who had died. Paul wrote the entire book to explain to them about the dead in Christ, and the events accompanying the rapture.

I think if I were you I would go over the future events with my class this Sunday. I would go through the rapture, judgment seat, marriage of the Lamb, tribulation, revelation (coming of Christ back to the earth), the millennium, the great white throne, and Heaven and Hell. Every child in our Sunday school ought to know what the rapture is. The word "rapture" ought to be a household word. "Millennium" and "great white throne" ought to be household words also.

Because the Lord is going to come, Paul speaks about what the Christians ought to be. The last few verses of I Thessalonians tells us how we ought to live. Look at I Thessalonians 5:10-22: "Who died for us, that, whether we wake or sleep, we should live together with him. Wherefore...."

Anytime you see the word "wherefore," that means something has gone what?

TEACHERS: Before.

PASTOR: "Wherefore comfort yourselves together, and edify one another, even as also ye do." Because He is coming, comfort yourselves together. "Edify one another" means build up each other. Why? The Lord is coming! He may come any minute. Hence, comfort and edify each other.

"And we beseech you, brethren, to know them which labour among you, and are over you in the Lord, and admonish you; And to esteem them very highly in love for their work's sake. And be at peace among yourselves." He said you ought to respect your pastors. Pray for them and esteem them very highly.

Not very long ago a little lad ran to me and said, "Hello, Jack."

I picked him up and held his face in front of mine and said, "What did you call me?"

He said, "B-B-B-Brother Hyles."

We don't allow that "Jack" business at our church. The children ought to be taught to respect the pastor, not because he is a man but because he holds an office. Paul said that the leader should be respected because the Lord is coming.

"Now we exhort you, brethren [all of this is because the Lord is coming any minute], warn them that are unruly, comfort the feeble-minded, support the weak, be patient toward all men."

Now see verse 16: "Rejoice evermore." Why? The Lord is coming! "Pray without ceasing." Why? The Lord is coming! "In everything

give thanks: for this is the will of God in Christ Jesus concerning you."
Why? The Lord is coming! "Quench not the Spirit." Why? The Lord
is coming! "Despise not prophesyings." Why? The Lord is coming!
All of these things we are supposed to do because the Lord could come
at any minute.

Now look at the questions at the close of your outlines. Close your
Bibles and let's see how well you do.

First we have scrambled words.

(1) *Mitoyht*—This man joined Paul as a youth to accompany him on
many of his journeys, and he was with Paul at the time of his writing
this book.

TEACHERS: Timothy.

PASTOR: That's amazing. That word doesn't look like Timothy,
does it?

(2) Another one of Paul's fellow travelers was—*lassi*. (Laughter)
This could only happen at First Baptist Church. Well, who is it?

TEACHERS: Silas.

PASTOR: (3) *Strif Salasostnhien*—the first epistle Paul wrote.

TEACHERS: First Thessalonians.

PASTOR: (4) *Radpey*—What did Paul do daily?

TEACHERS: Prayed.

PASTOR: (5) *Gognuesya*—Where did Paul preach first in Thessalonica?

TEACHERS: Synagogue.

PASTOR: (6) *Tingdasn*—The position of the person who read the
Scripture.

TEACHERS: Standing.

PASTOR: Now we have the true or false questions.

(1) Paul's earliest and main opposition in Thessalonica came from
the Greeks.

TEACHERS: False.

PASTOR: (2) Paul was in Thessalonica for a long time.

TEACHERS: False.

PASTOR: Now fill in the blanks.
The Christians in Thessalonica were not only believers but they *sounded* out the Word of God. They were looking for *the return of the Lord.* They were concerned, however, about the Christians who had *died.* Paul told them that the dead in Christ would rise *first.* Then he said that those which are alive and remain unto the *coming of the Lord* shall rise. He said, "They shall be caught up in the *air.*
Now the general questions: How long will the Christians be in the air?

TEACHERS: Seven years.

PASTOR: Where do we go from there?

TEACHERS: To the earth.

PASTOR: How long will we be on the earth?

TEACHERS: One thousand years.

PASTOR: What great judgment takes place at the end of this thousand-year period?

TEACHERS: Great white throne.

PASTOR: Where do we go then?

TEACHERS: New Jerusalem.

PASTOR: How long will we be there?

TEACHERS: Forever.

PASTOR: Right. Forever and forever.
Now note the memory verse:

"But I would not have you to be ignorant, brethren, concerning them which are asleep."

That is the lesson for Sunday.

AUTHOR'S NOTE: After I have taught the lesson, the teachers then go to their own departmental level meeting where a member of the staff takes the lesson that I have taught and shows the teacher how to apply it to his own particular age level. The one below is for junior teachers and deals with the lesson taught above.

MRS. SANDRA PLOPPER: First of all, get your lesson and a pencil just as you do every week. Make this little outline.

(1) Review. Here is our review board that we have been using every week. You will notice today's letter is here with a date on it as it is every week. To review this, what do we do? Take these off, mix them up, and ask the class which identification belongs with which book of the Bible, or we can do it by turning the identifications up, etc. Then we can ask the class, "What did we learn in the book of Romans?" The Gospel is the word we chose to use. "First Corinthians was about what?" Baby Christians. Review the class about each one. We also take down the names of the books, mix these up, and ask the class to place them back in order.

All right, this is the first point—review.

(2) Give your introduction to the book as you have in the lesson, and open today's "letter." February 19 we are going to study I Thessalonians. Inside of our envelope we have a letter. Now, of course, we want our class to learn that the epistles were letters, so that is why we have a letter here. It is from Paul. Do you see his return address in the corner? It is written to the Christians at Thessalonica. Let's see what Paul said. We suggest to our teachers that they read the letter briefly and make the reading of the letter the main part of the lesson, stopping to illustrate the different points. We rewrite the letter very simply to fit fifth grade boys and girls. We might say:

Dear Loved Ones:

I thank God for you and I pray for you. I remember that even though I was there for only a little while, you were so nice to me. You have been a good example to everyone around you. You have really sounded out the Gospel in a wonderful way.

In this way you rewrite the letter very simply and have it printed here in the envelope.

(3) After you introduce the book of I Thessalonians tell your class that you are going to teach them something about the Thessalonian Christians. Here are the points. I have them all written out to show you. Here are the things about the Thessalonian Christians. I have covered up the key word, you see. The reason we do this is to make the class curious. When you uncover each word as you make each point, you will have their attention. If you should happen to lose their

attention between points, you will surely have it when you uncover the next card because fifth and sixth graders will want to know what is underneath. We reveal just enough to make them curious. We also use different colors. That creates interest, doesn't it?

So we will teach: The Thessalonian Christians suffered PERSECU-TION. We will teach about this. They turned from their IDOLS. They were good EXAMPLES. We will teach about the fact that they were good examples. They had a wonderful TESTIMONY. They looked for .... For Whom did they look? JESUS. They served GOD.

Now I can cover these words again and review my class by asking them to tell me what was under each one.

All right, that will be the next point on your outline. The first point was review. The second was the introduction. The third was to teach the general things about the church of Thessalonica.

(4) Teach about the rapture. After teaching about the church at Thessalonica go back to the reading of your "letter" and read:

I know that you are very concerned because some Christians have died already, and you are very concerned about what is going to happen to them. Let me explain to you what will happen.

Now I will explain by using another illustration. I have some very pretty colored balls. They are wooden. I am going to put them in this dish to represent unsaved people who are living. Now I have some other wooden objects that are going to represent unsaved people who have died. I have some paper clips which will represent saved people who are living. Last of all, I have some little nuts. (Are these nuts or bolts? I always get mixed up. Nuts? Okay.) These will represent saved people who have died and gone to the grave. Now all four arti-cles are here in my plate, which represents the earth. The Lord is represented by this magnet.

"For the Lord himself shall descend from heaven."

I see that the paper clips and the nuts have come up, but the wooden objects, which represented the lost people, both alive and dead, did not come up. The paper clips and the nuts, which represented the living and dead saved people did come up. The saved not only shall go up, but they shall be *with* the Lord. When the Lord goes, they go. Now the reason the wooden objects did not go up is that they had nothing in them to take them up. The metal objects did. They were attracted to the magnet because they had that one thing in them that made them go up. The Christians have the Holy Spirit that makes them go whether they are alive or dead. You can teach your class about the rapture with this.

At the end of your lesson where you have the scrambled words you could play a game and have the class participate in this manner. I am going to show you in scrambled letters the name of the young man who went with Paul on many of his missionary trips. Now if you know the answer, don't say it aloud. Raise your hand, and I will let you come up and arrange the letters in the proper order. Are you ready? Raise your hand if you know. All right, Mrs. Hand, come up and see if you can show us the proper way this name should be. This is a heavy piece of paper with one edge folded over and stapled to make a little pocket, and the letters are written on cards. We use this quite a bit at the junior age. She says it is T-I-M-O-T-H-Y. Is she right? Right. Very good.

This is the name of another young man who was with Paul. Who knows the answer to this one? Meredith, would you come up, please, and see if you can show us the right name here. Is that right? S-I-L-A-S. Very good.

Okay, this is something that Paul did for the Thessalonian people every day. What did he do for them every day? Will you come and fix this for us, Verlie.

You can do this with the fill-in-the-blank words as well as the scrambled words on the outline.

With all of these different illustrations, of course, you could not fail on your lesson. We have used class participation. We have aroused their curiosity by covering up the words. We have used review. We have used printed things and, Junior II teachers, why do we use printed things? It is because you learn better when you see and hear than when you just hear. Right? We reinforce learning by seeing and hearing, and we also have something to use for our review from week to week.

Thank you.

AUTHOR'S NOTE: Once again I will give you the outline. The first twenty-minutes is promotion and discussion about Sunday—bring three visitors, make three visits before Sunday, get back up, and get your departments on the ball! The next twenty minutes is the teaching of the facts of the lesson. The third twenty minutes is how to apply the facts to the particular age level so that they will remember and understand the lesson and the truth concerning the lesson.

12. The Bus Ministry

One of the fastest and surest ways to increase Sunday school atten-dance is through the operation of buses. At this writing, the author's church has an attendance in Sunday school of approximately 3,500. Nearly 1,500 of these ride on buses. They, of course, stay for the preaching hour and provide for a large percentage of the attendance in both Sunday school and preaching. Of these 1,500 approximately 200 are bus workers and their families, and about 300 others would attend Sunday school if there were no bus routes but simply ride the buses for convenience or financial savings. This means that approximately 1,000 people attend Sunday school because of the bus ministry. These people, of course, would not attend our Sunday school were it not for this means of transportation provided for them. Hundreds of churches are finding the bus ministry a very profitable way to reach people for the Lord Jesus Christ. Following is a list of suggestions and pointers concerning this vital phase of the Lord's work:

Choosing an Area

This is the first and most important phase of the bus ministry.

1. *A housing project.* All over America there are government housing projects where thousands of people live. Many such projects form a little town located in just one building or perhaps a few build-ings. In such a case the bus would have to make only one stop or, at most, a few stops. Then, too, most of the children in such a project know each other and would consider it a privilege and a delight to have a weekly trip with their friends. Such a project makes it easy for the worker to contact his absentees and saves time that normally would be spent in the driving of a lengthy route. A church should comb the area for such projects in the beginning of a bus ministry.

2. *An apartment house area.* This is very similar to the above and offers the same advantages.

3. *A trailer court.* Once again we have a concentration of popula-tion which makes it easy to work the area and easy to pick up the pas-sengers. This also means just a few stops at the beginning of the route followed by a trip straight to the church.

4. *An area cut off from the community.* It is unbelievable what an expressway can do to a church's area. The same is true concerning a

busy railroad, or an industrial area. Psychologically people may feel
they are much farther from a certain church than they really are. In
our area there are two states involved. Though the state line is only
five blocks from our church, it is considered by some as a geographi-
cal barrier which means we have to work harder across the state line
even though it is less than half a mile away. When there is a community isolated for any purpose, it becomes a good area for a bus
route, and it certainly needs concentrated attention from the church.

5. *A poor area.* There are still people in this world, believe it or
not, who cannot afford the luxuries of life and to whom a bus trip to the
church would seem a big thing. It could well be the highlight of their
week. Slum areas, poor areas, and housing developments should be
seriously considered in the starting of bus routes.

6. *Schools or homes.* These are exceptionally good places to start
routes. A church may be located within ten or fifteen miles of a college where many of the students, no doubt, would appreciate a free
ride to church. The same could be said about a home for the aged,
homes for juvenile delinquents, or any other institution which provides
dormitories and living quarters for its constituents. These are excellent places to send buses and, once again, we find a concentrated
population.

7. *Another town.* There are churches located within ten or fifteen
miles of small towns who have no evangelistic, Bible-preaching work.
In many instances these churches send workers to the nearby towns
informing the citizens of a bus ministry. In thirty minutes a bus could
cover the little town and bring the interested people to the services.

8. *Country roads.* Many years ago in a rural pastorate we found
this a very beneficial way to reach people. Since people who live in
rural areas have no street addresses they are oftentimes overlooked
in the church's evangelistic program. A route beginning approximately
fifteen miles from town and covering every rural home into the town
can reach many people for Jesus Christ. As I dictate this chapter, I
think of scores of people whom we have reached through this method.
Many of them are now in the ministry or in full-time service for the
Lord.

Locating Buses

Once the area has been chosen, we must turn our attention to the
securing of buses. Of course the best way is to purchase them. Presently, an adequate bus would cost approximately $6,500. If a church
can afford such an investment, she should begin with new buses. Most
churches, however, will find it impossible to purchase new buses. If
care is taken in selecting a usable bus, one can be purchased for
$1,000 to $1,500. It is always a good idea for a church to purchase at

least a few buses. These can be used for youth trips, trips to camp, etc., as well as the regular Sunday morning bus routes.

Perhaps an even better way is to locate a private leaser of buses. Such a company can make a profit by leasing buses at $10 to $15 a trip. The company who owns the buses takes care of all of the upkeep, insurance, etc. The total church outlay is the rental fee.

In some areas city buses can be leased at a reasonable price. In such cases the City Transit Company provides not only the bus but the driver. This is, of course, the best way to lease buses.

It is our conviction that when the church really gets into the bus business and reaches hundreds of people for Christ, God intervenes and supplies their needs. We have had many miraculous answers to prayer in our bus ministry. It is unbelievable how God has provided. When God looks down and sees a church interested in reaching sinners, He desires to help them do so.

Recruiting the Workers

In the operation of a successful bus ministry many workers are needed.

1. The director. Someone should oversee the entire bus program. This can be the pastor, another staff member, or an energetic, creative layman. This person should be a real "live wire."

2. Bus captains. These are the key people. They are responsible for house-to-house visitation to obtain new riders and to reclaim absentees. Normally such a captain would spend from two to four hours a week just going from house to house lining up people to come to Sunday school on buses.

3. The bus driver. In some cases the bus captain drives his own bus, but usually there is a driver in addition to the captain. The driver, of course, drives the bus, is properly licensed, and sees that the route begins on time. He must be faithful to his work. The captain rides the bus but oftentimes must go to the door to get the riders, etc.

4. The parkers. As a bus ministry grows so does the need for space to park the buses. Each bus should have a designated place to be parked on or near the church property. It should be met by a person specifically chosen to park the buses. This person should have a clipboard with a list of the buses. He should write down the number of people on the bus, the number of the bus, and the arrival time of the bus. Below is such a form:

(Illustration on next page)

```
┌─────────────────────────────────────────────────────────────────────┐
│                      BUS ATTENDANCE REPORT                            │
│                                                                       │
│      AREA: East Chicago      CAPTAIN: Dennis Streeter    STREETER, DENNIS │
│      BUS: ENS1 55 Chev.                                  Passengers: _____ │
│                                                            Arrival: _____ │
│                                                               Date: _____ │
│                                                                       │
│                                                                       │
│                                                                       │
└─────────────────────────────────────────────────────────────────────┘
```

Then as the buses depart after the services he should see that every-thing is done decently and in order so as to avoid chaos and danger as the buses depart.

How then are these workers recruited? The pastor and the director of the bus ministry should be on the lookout for those in the church who make many trips with their cars to bring people. These people should be contacted and offered a bus.

Many fine bus captains develop from people who live a great distance from the church. These people could save money by starting a bus route in their neighborhood. Such people oftentimes find it difficult to visit for the church since they are strangers to the community. Using a bus, however, provides them with the opportunity to visit in their own neighborhood, to provide transportation for their own family, and to help tremendously in the evangelistic ministry of the church.

Doubtless, the best way to enlist workers is through the preaching from the pulpit. Periodically the pastor should preach on the impor-tance of the evangelistic outreach of the church. He should stress very strongly the bus ministry and ask for people who want to dedicate themselves to this ministry to come to the altar. Immediately their names and addresses should be secured and a meeting should be held to organize them into bus workers.

Just recently I was asked to go to a distant state to preach one night on the bus ministry. At the conclusion of the service I gave an invita-tion for those willing to work with the buses. Over forty people vol-unteered to do so. We asked them to meet with us in a departmental assembly room after the service, where we explained the bus ministry thoroughly and organized a new bus ministry. The first Sunday 332 people rode their buses to Sunday school. We should never forget that the inspiration of the pulpit is the important thing about building any phase of a church program.

It should be made clear that any person in the church who desires a bus route may be provided with a bus.

Financing the Work

A bus ministry may or may not become self-supporting. Usually if forty or fifty people ride a bus their offering will amount to at least

$15 or $20, which will finance the bus. We have found that $900 per bus per year is a fair estimate. In fact, we allocate this amount in our budget. Presently we operate forty-five bus routes and soon we plan to have fifty. This means our bus budget for the year is $45,000. This, of course, does not include the purchasing of buses. This is only the expense of maintenance and operation.

This money may be put in the church budget or it may be raised over and above the church budget. Many churches have found it helpful to use the Wednesday offering for the bus ministry. This is an exceptionally good idea. Other churches allocate one Sunday evening offering a month for the bus ministry. This is also a wise suggestion.

Training the Workers

It is a good idea for the director to train the first few workers. A series of classes could be taught and then the director could go with each worker to his area and help him get started. After the first group of workers get the idea and become well trained, it is not difficult for them to reproduce themselves. Then the director may recruit untrained but usable personnel to work with the trained captains and thereby provide a steady flow of trained people. This is simply a revision of the buddy system. After the new worker is adequately trained the team should divide and choose other untrained people to work with each of them.

Upon starting a bus ministry, or anything else in the church for that matter, a weekly meeting of the workers should be held. Our meeting is conducted for about fifteen minutes immediately following the Wednesday evening service. This is a period of training and promotion for the bus ministry.

Promoting the Attendance

1. The pulpit should be promoting the bus ministry constantly. There is no way to have a hot bus ministry and a cold pulpit. Inspiration must come constantly from the pulpit if there is to be a successful bus program.

2. The pastor should share the blessings of the bus ministry with the church family regularly. To be sure, there will be opponents to the bus ministry. Some people will say it is too expensive. Others will not like the class of people brought in. Others will not like the irreverence it causes in the public services. Then there are those who just do not like anything different. The pastor should constantly refute this opposition by sharing the blessings of the bus ministry with the church family.

3. Contests among the buses can be a tremendous thing. Since seventy-five percent of our bus riders are children, we find it very easy to excite them over contests with the other buses. Prizes can be awarded to the top one-third or one-fourth of the bus fleet. In some cases, where fewer buses are operated, the winning bus can receive a prize. At this writing we are in a bus contest. The top ten buses and the workers of these ten buses receive a special prize. Sometimes the prizes may go to the bus workers, and at other times they may go to the entire bus. On one occasion the winning buses were taken to a small airport where each child was taken for a five-minute plane ride. This was not as expensive as it may seem. The children who were waiting on the ground were served refreshments and played games.

4. *Gifts may be given periodically to all who ride buses.* For example, if the Sunday school lesson is on "The Loaves and Fishes" each child may be given a goldfish in a sealed plastic container filled with water. There are any number of little novel ideas that could be applied to God's Word or a specific Sunday school lesson which would delight the average child.

5. *Each captain should also plan his own promotional ideas.* If the director is working to promote the bus attendance, and if the pastor is joining him in such an endeavor, then each captain should also be seeking ways of promoting attendance on his bus. The more people thinking up ideas and working at attendance campaigns, the better it is.

6. *The captains should keep a roll and contact all absentees.* Each captain should consider his bus much like a Sunday school class. Not only should he seek new riders but he should be contacting those who are absent so as to have a minimum turnover on the buses.

Using the Buses for Publicity

The buses should be attractively painted and properly lettered as pictured below:

When the buses are attractive they may be tremendous instruments of publicity for the church. When not in use they can be parked on main thoroughfares. Each bus becomes a signboard or a billboard advertising the church. The bus should be driven around town period- ically. Everywhere the bus goes it is either good publicity or bad publicity for the church. If the driver is courteous and obeys the law, and if the bus is attractive, it becomes a traveling billboard.

A Typical Day on a Bus Route

The driver should start the route in time to pick up the riders and unload them on the church property at least ten minutes before Sunday school begins. The captains then take their riders to their classes directly from the buses. This is very important. The children should not be allowed to go to their classes alone. They should be taken by the captains or an adult appointed by the captain for this specific duty.

After the service is over the captain reclaims his riders at the door of the church or department where the rider is located. The children should never be left to shift for themselves. They should be taken to the door and then, at the door, taken in orderly form back to the bus.

Each child is returned to the front of his home, which is exactly where he was picked up. The captain should then see that the child goes immediately to the door and into the house. He should not leave until the child is safely inside the door.

Starting a Route

After an area is chosen, buses are secured, workers are enlisted and trained, and necessary preparations are made, we come to the actual starting of the route. Many times it has been my privilege to start a bus route. Oftentimes I have gone to the assigned area, found a group of children playing, gathered them around, and asked them how they would like a thirty-mile bus trip with all expenses paid on which Bozo the clown or some other famous character would entertain them. After I got them excited about it, then I went to their home and inquired if their parents would mind the child participating in such an endeavor. The parents are told about the careful planning of the bus ministry. Many of the things already mentioned in this chapter are mentioned in this initial conversation. They should be set at ease con- cerning the safety of the bus, licensing of the driver, choosing of the workers and captains, etc.

Usually the parents will make some excuse like, "We just don't want to get up that early and prepare breakfast for the children." The an- swer to this is a very simple one. Explain to them that in the starting of the route you are providing hot chocolate and doughnuts for the children so they can have breakfast on the bus. Much care should be taken to be friendly, courteous and understanding. Remember, you must sell them on yourself first. The only representative of the church is you and they must be sold on you, the worker. Once two or three families have been enlisted, they can help in enlisting other friends. On the initial bus route a planned activity should be presented. Fun, recreation, breakfast, and other activities are provided to insure a good time for all.

Considering the Liabilities

1. Lack of finances. It should be stressed over and over again that the bus ministry is a missionary project. In many churches it is the largest single evangelistic arm, and in some cases, the bus ministry of the church reaches more people for Christ than all of the missionaries supported by the church. This is not to discredit a foreign mission program but simply to place the bus ministry on a par with other missionary activities of the church, and it should be looked upon as such. If it is a financial liability, the church should accept it as such as she considers the blessings derived and the souls reached through the bus ministry.

2. Delinquent children. This can be a problem but it need not be. In some cases children ride the buses to church, get off the buses, run around the neighborhood until time to reload and never enter into the Sunday school class or the church service. This can be eliminated by the proper use of stamps and stamp pads. Each Sunday school class or department can be equipped with a stamp pad and a stamp with the initials of the church. This stamp should be about the size of a nickel as shown below:

Each teacher or superintendent stamps the back of each child's hand. When the child boards the bus he shows his hand to the driver with the proof that he was in Sunday school. A child who skips Sunday school will not have the stamp on his hand and can be disciplined accordingly.

3. Lost children. As a bus ministry grows it becomes increasingly difficult to avoid children becoming lost. This problem can also be solved with the use of a stamp. Each bus captain stamps the hand of each child with the number of the bus as he boards the bus. For example, the captain of bus #1 places a stamp on the back of each passenger's hand as shown below:

Then each department is provided with a list of buses, bus number, and bus captain. If a child loses his bus, any adult can check the back of his hand for the bus number. The adult can then go to any department and check this list. He then learns the names of the captains and drivers associated with this particular bus number.

BUS NUMBER	BUS CAPTAIN	BUS NUMBER	BUS CAPTAIN
1	Garcia	24	Barker-Zarris
2	Meredith	25	McCarley-Griffith
3	Clark	26	Tunis
4	Faber	27	Bright
5	Phillips	28	Courtright-Bailey
6	McCarroll	29	Belle-Randolph
7	Venander	30	Brown
8	Cunningham	31	Ciesar-Brummitt
9	Barnes	32	Abner
10	Ball-Cantway	33	Litherland
11	Newman	34	Ciesar-Vanderhoof
12	Streeter	35	Grubaugh
13	Moody Bus	36	Lapina-Reeves
14	Waechter-Jonkman	37	VanGorp
15	Wright	38	Morrell
16	Schneider	39	Lord
17	Vezey	40	Nischik
18	Sackville-Pfeiffer	41	Goren
19	Ward-Vaprezsan	42	King
20	Rickey-Sumner	43	Johnson-Mayes
21	Hayes	44	Rodgers
22	Basham	45	Carlin
23	Valandingham	46	Goren-Aldrich

4. Misbehavior in the services. Oftentimes people complain about a bus ministry because of the children's misbehavior in the public services. This problem can be solved in several different ways.

A portion of the church can be reserved for the bus children and volunteer workers can sit with them during the preaching service. One worker for each five to ten children can help discipline them and keep them quiet during the service.

In some churches the bus ministry has grown to such proportions that the church must provide a special preaching service or services for the bus children. In such a case an assistant pastor should preach to them. If the church has no assistant pastor, some God-called preacher or preacher boy could go and preach to these bus children. Of course this would not occupy all of the time during the preaching service. Hence, well-trained workers can be provided to care for them during the church service time. This should not be just a time of coloring and having amusements and entertainment. It should not even be a time limited to a Sunday school type service. There should definitely be preaching. We find it wise to have a choir, special music, offering, sermon, etc. In addition to this church type service, a well-trained worker may have some time of entertainment and inspiration for them. This has proven very helpful in many churches in the reaching of bus children.

5. *Criticism by members*. Probably in every church there are people who will rise in opposition against a bus ministry. These, thank the Lord, are usually in a minority and because they are, they should not be allowed to dictate the policies of the church. They should be dealt with very kindly and yet firmly.

I recall when I first came to the First Baptist Church and started our bus ministry, a well-to-do member came to me and said, "Pastor, what are we going to do with all of these little bus kids?"

I said, "I don't know what you are going to do with them but I am going to love them."

Then the member said, "If they stay, I leave."

Thank the Lord, that is exactly what happened. The bus children stayed and he left. We felt we got the best of the deal. No minority born in the "objective case" and the "kickative mood" should be allowed to stop the progress of God's work and the reaching of hundreds of people for Jesus Christ.

Used properly and organized effectively, a bus ministry can be a tremendous asset to a church, and more important, a church can be a tremendous blessing to thousands of people by the proper use of a bus ministry.

13. The Sick and Shut-ins

"Is any among you afflicted? let him pray. Is any merry? let him sing psalms. Is any sick among you? let him call for the elders of the church; and let them pray over him, anointing him with oil in the name of the Lord: And the prayer of faith shall save the sick, and the Lord shall raise him up; and if he have committed sins, they shall be forgiven him."—Jas. 5:13-15.

One of the most important ministries of the New Testament church was ministering to the sick. Jesus spent much of His life ministering to the sick. The book of Acts is filled with examples of ministering to those who were sick and shut-in. Since this is such a vital part of the church program, let us examine carefully a good ministry to the sick and shut-ins.

1. The people of the church should be trained to call the pastor or the staff when they are ill. It is amazing that people call the doctor and call their friends but simply expect word to get back to the pastor about their illnesses. Constant stress should be upon informing the pastor there is illness. It should also be emphasized that friends of sick people should alert the pastor as to their condition so that no one will be overlooked.

Once a lady came out to the public services and said to her pastor, "Well, I was sick and you didn't come to see me."

The pastor replied, "Did the doctor come?"

"Oh yes, many times," said the lady.

"How did the doctor know you were sick?" the pastor asked.

"Well, I called him, of course."

Then the pastor said, "Maybe I could have seen you many times, too, if you had called me."

It is very important that contact be made with the pastor or the office concerning the sick and shut-ins.

2. A card file should be kept of all visits to the sick and the shut-ins. When a person enters the hospital or becomes sick enough to need prayer, the church office should be called. Immediately, a card should be made in the church office for this person. On the card should be the name of the patient, the hospital, and the room number. Then the pastor or staff member should list each visit made to the patient. This file should be kept as a permanent one for future reference. Oftentimes members may become offended because a certain person was not visited at their request. Proof of this visit can be given if a card file is kept. Below is a card taken from the files of the First Baptist Church, Hammond, Indiana:

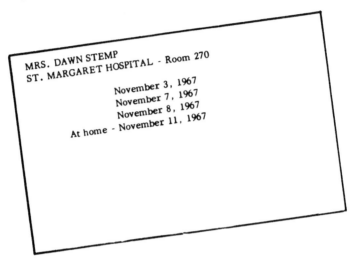

MRS. DAWN STEMP
ST. MARGARET HOSPITAL - Room 270
November 3, 1967
November 7, 1967
November 8, 1967
At home - November 11, 1967

3. *The pastor should send get-well cards to folks who are hospitalized or seriously ill.* Scripture text get-well cards may be purchased from any Bible bookstore and can be a real blessing and help to people when they realize the pastor has thought of them in their illness and has sent them a get-well greeting.

4. *The names of the sick should be included on a weekly prayer list that is mimeographed or printed and given to the people.* When a person calls to say that he is sick or has his name called in as being ill, the entire church family should be notified. The best way to do this is to mimeograph or print a prayer list and give it to the congregation weekly. At First Baptist Church in Hammond we have for years passed out such a prayer sheet in the Wednesday evening service. This prayer sheet is kept by the people for the entire week. Not only are the sick listed but others who request prayer. We have also found it helpful to list the names of the people who are having birthdays during the week, and we encourage our people to pray for each person on his birthday. This enables each member of the church to pray for the entire membership once a year. Below is a sample prayer sheet:

(Illustration on next page)

HAPPY BIRTHDAY TO:

NOVEMBER 23 - Charles Brunson, Ethel Dale, Linda Ham,
Claude Prather, Mrs. Russell Laity, Jr.,
Mrs. Loyce Evans, Michael Stych, Jim
Moffitt, Mrs. Robert Houston, Joann
Gonzales, Sandra Flowers.

24 - Estele Wilson, Jeanette Atkins, Deborah
Ann Darrah, George Laffoon, Dennis
McMinds, Dena McMinds, Mrs. Christopher
Marley, Robert Phillips, Betty Young,
Mrs. Don Hargis, Mrs. Bonnie Karges,
George Vancelette, Dena Zasada.

25 - Richard Seivert, Mrs. Paul McBroom,
Mrs. Ray Pierce, Raymond Sutton, Mrs.
John Vaprezsan, Grace Peters, William
Edwards, Mrs. Jimmy Clayton, Mrs. Jimmy
Ball, Mrs. Alger Waters, Pamela Belcher,
Jane Morgan, Mrs. Helen Anderson, Bobby
Rhodes.

26 - Betsy Auxier, Mrs. Walter Hess, Gary
Zarris, Marvin Oberg, Lori Riechelt.

27 - Roberta Fraker, Emily Hendrick, Phyllis
Moffitt, Rogerlin Charbonneau, Charles
Kenny Patterson, Emily Hendrick, Phyllis
Webb, Dawn Marie Reeves, Cindy Lail.

28 - Jimmy Estes, Pamela Woodcock, Dale Bain,
Marie English, Merle Heath, Sharon Olsen,
Murrell Phillips, Raymond Stewart, Otis
Ritter, Mrs. Thomas Goggin, Oscarlene
Weaver, Sharon Lovings, Glen Gentz,
Warren Dale Austin, Joyce McDonough,
Dan Luchene.

29 - Ray Erickson, Mrs. Donald Forsythe, Mrs.
William Kinney, Maxine Bane, Mrs. Durward
Moles, Judy Spicer, Grover Poole, Anna
Darlene Belcher, Anthony Mayer, Linda
Pence, Carol Pence.

"IT IS A GOOD THING TO GIVE THANKS UNTO THE LORD..."
--Psalm 92:1

FIRST BAPTIST CHURCH
HAMMOND, INDIANA

PRAYER SHEET
November 22, 1967

"But without faith it is impossible
to please Him: for he that cometh
to God must believe that He is, and
that He is a rewarder of them that
diligently seek Him."

--Hebrews 11:6

HOSPITALS

St. Margaret
Mrs. Ida Johnson 278
Mrs. Lula Hinton (Today)
Mrs. Bill Moore and new
baby boy
John Utterback* I.C.
Billy Harris* 4th Flr.
Mrs. Dolly Hobbs 252
Henry Skinner* 101
Cora Purdy* 241
Jane Stevens* 322

St. Catherine
Percival Wilcox* 366
Steve Vargo* 248
Walter Wells* 214
Mrs. Claryce Blair*

Osteopathic - Chicago
Joyce Phillips 307

Porter Memorial - Valpo.
Libby Conn*

The pastor has designated two hours
each week to pray for our people who
have special problems. Please write
your prayer request on paper and
either mail it or give it personally
to the pastor or one of the staff
members and you may be assured that
the pastor will pray for you by
name and for your needs.

ILL AT HOME

George Hiles
Rt. 2, Box 236
Schererville, Indiana

Gladys Fiscus*
561 Forsythe

Faye Kerr
8841 Schneider Dr.
Highland, Indiana

Roger Henson
Route 2, Box 277
Lowell, Indiana

Mrs. Lucy Lopes
6602 Columbia

Baby Scott Hammers
3009 - 100th Street
Highland, Indiana

OUT OF TOWN

Barbara Musgrave, Ill.
Tom Ruiter, Illinois
Mrs. A. L. Douglas, Tenn.
Mrs. Mildred Hinkle, Ill.
Baby Jonathan Abel, S.C.
Mr. & Mrs. J. Whitaker, Ind.

Jake Brown, W. V.
Manuel Gill, W. Va.
Mrs. V. Britton, Tenn.
Mrs. M. Davis, Calif.
Patrick Wallace, Mo.
R. L. Bennett, Ky.

THANK YOU

"I would like very much to thank Brother
Hyles and Brother Colston for their visits
and the many cards from the people at
First Baptist. A special thanks for your
prayers and concern while I was recuperating
from three fractured ribs." --Mrs. Audrey Mickey

"I want to thank the pastors and staff for
their visits while I was in the hospital.
I want to thank the church for their prayers
and cards during my time of illness."
--Mrs. Esther Rice

PASTOR'S HOME PHONE - TE8-8174

REMEMBER IN PRAYER

DEACON FOR THE WEEK----------------Frank Crall
STAFF MEMBER FOR THE WEEK---------Meredith Plopper
SHUT-IN FOR THE WEEK-----------Mrs. Rose Wilkeson,
Colonial Conv. Home, 549 East 162nd Street,
South Holland, Illinois
COLLEGE STUDENT FOR THE WEEK-------George Zarris,
T.T.S. Box T-444, Chattanooga, Tenn. 37404
DEAF STUDENT FOR THE WEEK---------Tommy Holland,
School for the Deaf, Indianapolis, Indiana
MISSIONARY FOR THE WEEK--------Miss Margaret Scipione,
67031 Castel di Sangro (L'Aquila) Italy
SERVICEMAN FOR THE WEEK--------SP4 Raymond Plopper,
US 54809861, 252 Signal Company,
Port Clayton, Canal Zone 09827

CONGRATULATIONS TO:

Mr. and Mrs. Bill Moore on the
arrival of their third son,
William Howard.

GRIEVING--Mr. and Mrs. James Hutton in the loss
of their young son, Brian. Funeral was Friday.

If you know of any member of the church who is
sick enough for a visit by a staff member, please
turn in that member's name and address to the
church office or Maxine Jeffries.

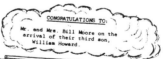

HAPPY THANKSGIVING TO
YOUR FAMILY

5. Regular visits should be made to the hospitals and to the sick. In our church we divide this into four different areas of visitation.

(1.) Local hospitals
(2.) Out-of-town hospitals
(3.) Sick at home
(4.) Shut-ins

Those in local hospitals get a daily visit. Those in out-of-town hospitals, within reasonable driving distance of the church, get a visit once or twice a week. Folks who are sick at home get a weekly visit and those who are shut-in get a lengthy monthly visit. In a large church the staff members may divide these responsibilities. In a smaller church the pastor could care for them all. In some cases, lay people could be chosen for some of these responsibilities.

The Hospital Visit

The hospital visit should be characterized by several things. First, brevity. The patient usually does not feel like having a long visit and is oftentimes made to feel worse by a long visit. The hospital staff will also appreciate the brevity of visits. Second, a visit should be very cheerful. A little appropriate humor, a warm smile, and a cheery greeting is always in order. Bring the patient up to date on the news of the church and the happy events of the outside. Do not tell him of people who have had his illness and died, but be optimistic in the visit. Next, the visit should include words of comfort. These should be brief, encouraging words of interest to the patient and words of assurance of the prayers of the church and friends. Included in the hospital visit should be a witness for Christ if the person is not converted. It might also be wise to speak a cheery word of greeting to each person in the room and take an opportunity to witness to them concerning their spiritual condition.

A few weeks ago I was in a hospital and was witnessing to a dying man. He knew he was dying and had called for a preacher. I found that he had never been saved. Carefully I told him the plan of salvation and led him to the Lord Jesus Christ. Realizing that he would die in a few moments, he was so happy that he had found Christ on his deathbed. I then tried to lead him to assurance and so very soberly and carefully I asked him, "Where are you going when you die?" He looked up at me through tear-filled eyes and said, "Kentucky." We both laughed when we realized that he had misunderstood my question. He was telling me that his body would be shipped back to Kentucky. He laughed as he went to Heaven. It is always important to inquire as to the condition of the soul of one in the hospital.

Then a brief prayer should always be given at the bedside. It should be a prayer of faith, praying for healing, grace, comfort, strength, etc. I have found it helpful simply to hold the hand of the patient as I pray this prayer.

The Shut-in Visit

In a smaller church the pastor could care for the shut-ins. In the church the size of the one I pastor now it requires the help of many to keep up with the sick and shut-ins. We employ a lady to spend one entire day a week working with the shut-ins. Since she has from thirty-five to forty, she is able to visit each shut-in once a month. Here are some observations concerning this vital ministry:

1. *The visit is usually a lengthy one lasting anywhere from twenty minutes to an hour depending upon the condition of the shut-in and the degree of interest the shut-in has in spiritual matters.*

2. *A gift is taken to the shut-in.* Since the visit is made only once a month it is made to be a very impressive one. The pastor may take a gift or his representative may simply say, "The pastor sent this gift to you." Sometimes it is a small box of candy; in other cases, a small bouquet of flowers. A book is a splendid gift for a shut-in. Each shut-in receives a lovely remembrance from the pastor.

3. *A tape recorder is taken by the visitor and a personal taped message is given by the pastor.* The visitor prepares the tape recorder and plays this tape. The pastor speaks to the shut-in something like this:

Message From Pastor to Shut-in

Once again it is a real joy for me to spend some time with my shut-in friends. Many times I have been to the beautiful city of Washington, D. C., and crossed the Potomac River over to the famous cemetery not far from the Washington National Airport. In this great cemetery, where President Kennedy is buried and where the bodies of many of our great statesmen lie, there is a grave called simply "The tomb of the Unknown Soldier." Military guards are posted here, for this man represents the millions of little soldiers who have died for their country. Yes, little as far as man is concerned, but who can say one who dies for his country is little.

When I think of the Unknown Soldier and the unknown soldiers I think of you, our shut-in friends. You write no books that will be read by thousands of people. You preach no sermons that will be a blessing to millions. Your names are never in the headlines of religious periodicals, but I wonder if the Lord has a beautiful monument in Heaven to the unknown soldiers such as you—unknown on earth but well-known in Heaven. I think that among these unknown soldiers would have to be included our shut-in friends.

All of that was said to say this: God knows what you do. He knows your prayers. He knows your sincerity. He knows your heart. What you do for God, the prayers you offer, the kindly deeds you do, the gracious spirit you manifest does not go unnoticed. The great recorder in Heaven records your faithfulness in prayer and the great camera in Heaven records your faithfulness to God. Yes, you are my unknown soldiers, my prayer warriors, and my faithful, loyal friends. May God bless you as you continue to pray for me, other preachers, and other Christian workers. Rest assured that there is a place in our hearts for the "unknown soldiers."

This is always a high hour in the lives of the shut-ins.

4. For those who are able and who desire to hear it, the music and sermon from the previous Sunday are played.

5. The visitor should be a good listener. Realizing that shut-ins talk to few people and want to talk and be heard, it is very vital that the visitor listen carefully to the needs of the patient and be interested in listening.

6. After giving the gift, playing the pastor's personal message, playing the music and sermon from a recent service, and listening and conversing for awhile, the visitor then says, "Could we pray together before I leave?" A prayer is offered which is a little more lengthy than the one at a hospital for there is more time. This prayer should be more personal concerning the needs of the shut-in.

Shut-in Day

The shut-ins are invited to the annual Shut-in Day at the church. On this day the church honors her shut-ins. Wheelchairs, hospital beds, crutches, or any other equipment needed is provided by the church. On occasion an ambulance can be used to transport the shut-ins to the church. This is their day. They come by car, by bus, and by ambulance. They are honored in the service. They are given a special gift from the pastor, and a luncheon is prepared for them after the morning service. This is a high day for them.

Monthly Newspaper

A monthly paper called *Glad Tidings* is mimeographed and mailed to the shut-ins. This little paper informs them of happenings at church and news of other shut-ins. It is just for them. It is their paper and is mailed to their homes each month.

(Illustration on next page)

First Baptist Church ● 523 Sibley Street ● Hammond, Indiana

Jack Hyles, Pastor

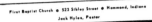

Glad Tidings

Featuring this month . . .

THE PRINCE OF PEACE

To us a Child of hope is born,
To us a Son is given;
Him shall the tribes of earth obey,
Him, all the hosts of Heaven.

His name shall be the Prince of Peace,
Forevermore adored;
The Wonderful, the Counselor,
The great and mighty Lord.

His power, increasing, still shall spread;
His reign no end shall know;
Justice shall guard His throne above,
And peace abound below.

To us a Child of hope is born,
To us a Son is given;
The Wonderful, the Counselor,
The mighty Lord of Heaven.

--Author Unknown
742 Heart-Warming Poems
Compiled by John R. Rice

Especially for you . . .

from Pastor Hyles

This article is being written the day after Thanksgiving. Yesterday, on Thanksgiving Day, I thought of you dear shut-in friends again and again. I thought of how thankful I am for your being faithful to pray for me. The load is especially heavy in these days, and I know I can count on you to pray. My schedule is a busy one, and there are so many, many thousands of things to oversee and to do. I feel a special need of your prayers. I thought of you yesterday and thanked God for you.

And then I thought yesterday of you because you are shut-in. I found myself wishing that you

(cont. page 3)

Something I must tell . . .

By Maxine Jeffries

MERRY CHRISTMAS

AND

A HAPPY NEW YEAR

Well, another year is coming to an end! I was just thinking how wonderful it has been to spend another year with you dear friends. I wish for each of you a very Merry Christmas and a Happy New Year.

The Lord willing, I will be seeing each of you before Christmas time with a small gift from Pastor Hyles for you. So look for me soon.

May God bless each of you in 1968.

"For unto us a child is born..." --Isaiah 9:6

We are praying for . . .

SHUT-IN OF THE MONTH: Mrs. Rose Wilkerson, Colonial Convalescent Home, 549 East 162nd Street, South Holland, Illinois 60473

COLLEGE STUDENT OF THE MONTH: George Zarris, Tennessee Temple Schools, Box T-444, Chattanooga, Tennessee 37404

DEAF STUDENT OF THE MONTH: Tommy Holland, School for the Deaf, 1200 East 42nd Street, Indianapolis, Indiana 46205

MISSIONARY OF THE MONTH: Miss Margaret Scipione, 67031 Castel di Sangro (L'Aquila) Italy

SERVICEMAN OF THE MONTH: SP4 Raymond Plopper, US 54809861, 252 Signal Company, Fort Clayton, Canal Zone 09827

Special prayer requests

for you to remember

St. Margaret's Hospital
Mrs. Jane Stevens*
Mr. Coral Steffey
Radford Smith
Charles Reed*
Betty Quayle*
Dyer Mercy - Dyer, Indiana
Clarence Baldwin
Gary Mercy - Gary, Indiana
Joyce Bozman

SPECIAL PRAYER REQUESTS:
The pastors and staff
Visitation program
Youth program
Deaf work
Retarded work
All our shut-ins
Mission work
The Fall Program (only one week left)
The financial program for 1968
Sunday School classes
Our servicemen
College students as they travel home for Christmas

("Especially for You" cont.)

could be out to the services and other types of activities. This is not possible, of course, but may God give you added grace.

Sometimes someone comes to me and says, "I thought of you yesterday," and it always helps me and encourages me. I just wanted you to know I thought of you yesterday, and I am thankful for you.

Birthdays To Remember

DECEMBER BIRTHDAYS
(No birthdays this month)

JANUARY BIRTHDAYS:

6 - Mrs. L. M. Osborne
4 - 172nd Place
Hammond, Indiana

23 - Mr. Chester Stickler
6821 Huron Street
Hammond, Indiana

HAPPY BIRTHDAY TO YOU!!!

The pastor should never forget that the shut-ins have more time to pray for him than all the rest of the church collectively. Think of the potential power in the prayers of these dear saints. The pastor should constantly be asking for the prayers of the shut-ins and thanking them for remembering him at the Throne of Grace. Here is an untapped source of power in our churches.

For the sake of the church, for the sake of the power of God, and for the sake of the shut-ins, let us not neglect them but make them feel that they are a vital part of the church life.

14. The Youth Program

"Remember now thy Creator in the days of thy youth, while the evil days come not, nor the years draw nigh, when thou shalt say, I have no pleasure in them."—Eccles. 12:1.

Much time, planning, and direction should be given to the youth of the church. The high school student is much like the closing phase of an assembly line. The young person has been through the entire church training program from the nursery cradle into the high school level. We are about to send him off to college, to the service, or to establish his own home. It is very important that these finishing touches be placed wisely and carefully upon the lives of the youth.

God has been good to give us wonderful young people in all of our pastorates. Over eighty young men are now pastoring or serving as evangelists, missionaries, assistant pastors, and music directors who have been saved and trained in our pastorates. It is a great thrill to know as I preach on Sunday morning my own preacher boys are scattered throughout the world preaching the same Gospel that I preach.

There are many ways to conduct a youth program. We will not attempt to give all of them or even many of them but simply to outline the type youth program we have endeavored to carry on in our churches.

1. Every public service is a youth activity in itself. It is a serious mistake to gear the public service only to the adult level. At every service we try to have something that will be both appealing and helpful to the youth. As I go to other churches across America, Canada, and other countries, I find many places where the audience is made up mainly of middle-aged and older people. We simply must gear our services to have an appeal to the young people as well as to the adults. Young people respond to dynamic challenge and dedication. This should be present in our public services.

2. The usual youth activities would include such things as Sunday school, Training Union, and the regular activities of the church. Dedicated, faithful, loyal people should fill these positions. It is just as important that a teacher of young people be an example as it is that he be a speaker. Young people are great hero worshipers. We should place before them the kind of people whom they can emulate and who can be the proper examples for the youth to follow. This same thing is true in the Training Union and other regular activities of the church. There should also be Sunday school parties and Training Union socials as well as spiritual activities sponsored by these groups.

3. The young people should be soul winners. We teach our young people that soul winning is not just for the preacher, not just for the deacon, not just for the adult, but also for the teen-ager. He is periodically taught a course on soul winning. He is trained to be a soul winner just like the adults are. Then a regular night is set aside for youth soul winning. On a recent week, for example, our teen-agers won seventeen people to the Lord Jesus Christ on their designated soul-winning night. Following is a brief outline of this soul-winning activity.

(1.) The prospects are secured from the membership of the church. Periodically we have an announcement made publicly for those knowing of unsaved teen-agers to turn their names into the church office that we might contact them about Christ. Then we also have what is called an inside-church census. This is a survey of all the families of our church. We ask each person to list on this survey the name, address, age, sex, and spiritual condition of each person that lives under his roof or in the same dwelling unit. From this survey we get the names of teen-agers who may be contacted about the Gospel. Prospects also come from visitors to the services, new moves into our area, visitors to the Sunday school departments, and visitors to the youth activities.

(2.) Transportation often poses a real problem as few of the teen-agers are allowed to drive. Hence, transportation is provided by the people of our church who volunteer their own time and the use of their cars to transport the teen-agers from visit to visit. This also provides a chaperon for the young people. They go two by two. This means that there will be a driver and two teen-agers in each car. The driver remains in the car during the visit to enable the teen-agers to do all of the soul winning.

(3.) Boys and girls do not visit together. The boys visit together as teams and they visit male prospects. Men drivers drive the boys. The girls visit together as teams and they visit female prospects. Lady drivers or a man and wife team drive the girls to their assignments.

(4.) Much fanfare is made about the soul-winning visitation. The young people are made to realize just how important it is. Many of these young people have gone out into the world as adults knowing how to win souls, and they continue in the soul-winning business. Many become preachers, missionaries, music directors, etc. The soul-winning program of our young people is a vital part of our church life.

4. The young boys often go soul winning with the pastors. It is not an unusual thing for a pastor to take a teen-ager soul winning with him. It has been my joy to win scores of people to Christ while soul winning with teen-agers in our church. What a thrill this is, both for the pastor and for the youth.

5. *The pastor seeks to counsel with each senior before graduation.* As a young person enters his senior year of high school the pastor seeks a personal conference with him in order that they might discuss the future together. The pastor inquires as to the plans made by the young person. He, in turn, seeks the pastor's counsel concerning decisions that need to be made. Discussed at this conference are such things as vocation, college, the choice of a mate, service, etc. This little get-together lets the young person know that the pastor cares.

6. *The youth choir.* This is discussed in more detail in the chapter on the music program. Each Sunday afternoon at five o'clock the teen-agers of our church meet for a youth choir practice. At this writing approximately one hundred teen-agers attend this practice. Then the youth choir begins the Wednesday evening service by marching into their places in the choir. The boys are required to wear dress shirts and ties and the girls are required to dress appropriately for church. The adult choir is used in the Sunday morning and Sunday evening services leaving the Wednesday evening service for the young people. This is not considered a novelty. The young people are made to feel their importance in this place of service. A title may be given to such a group such as the Teen Choraliers or some other appropriate title.

7. *There are also special activities for college-age young people.* It is wise to provide a special Sunday school class for college-age young people. They have little in common with the high school group and will be much happier in their own Sunday school class. Through this Sunday school class social activity is planned and provided. This is usually a weekly activity. A wide variety of events should be planned.

8. *It is wise to divide the high school from the junior high.* Many of the youth activities include both the junior high and the high school ages, but even on activities that include both groups, the groups could be divided. For example, if two buses are used, the junior high school group could go on one and the high school young people on the other. If one bus is used, one group could sit in the front and the other in the back. It is wise, however, to have activities periodically for the high schoolers only. There is a vast difference between a senior in high school and a student in his first year of junior high. The junior high students do not mind going to activities with the senior high students but the senior high students need to be alone often and such opportunities should be provided for them.

9. *There are many splendid youth camps throughout the nation.* Each Christian young person should have the privilege of attending such a camp. Such an opportunity will provide not only for the spirit-

ual enlightenment but also for the social development of the young person. The cost for such a week is normally less than $25.00. If a church has buses, a camp could be chosen which is some distance away, and the bus trip itself would add to the enjoyment of the week.

10. It is wise that a church secure a youth director. In some cases this could be a full-time employee. In other cases it could be one of many duties of a staff member. In smaller churches, and in some larger ones, it is found necessary to use a volunteer worker from the church membership. Of course, all of the work should be done under the supervision of the pastor and should be church-centered and church-directed.

11. A weekly youth activity should be planned. Young people are on the go. They need to be kept busy. Because of this, it is wise to provide some kind of activity for them each week. We have found it advisable to have this activity either on a Friday evening or some time on Saturday.

12. There are many types of youth activities which can be planned. Some youth directors find it wise to meet with the young people in the junior high and high school departments. At this meeting each person makes suggestions as to the type youth activities he enjoys. From these suggestions a list is made. The youth director then adds his ideas, compiles them with those of the young people and submits the list to the pastor for his approval. These activities should be divided almost equally between spiritual and social. Of course, even the social times should have a time of devotion and spiritual emphasis. For example, as the young people ride to a social event they can sing gospel songs, pass out tracts, give testimonies, and, in general, permeate the atmosphere with Christ-centered activity.

These are planned at least two weeks in advance and usually a month or more in advance. Below you will find a list of youth activities that have been found successful:

1. Christian films
2. Bible quiz
3. All-day outings or trips
4. Banquets and parties
5. Boat rides
6. Sight-seeing tours such as radio and T. V. stations, airports, city, industrial plants, museums, zoo, etc.
7. Camp fire sings
8. Wiener roasts
9. Rescue mission services such as the Pacific Garden Mission, etc.
10. Youth camp—Bill Rice Ranch

13. The list of suggested activities is then submitted to the pastor for his approval. No activity of any kind in the church is planned without the approval of the pastor. This is vitally important concerning the youth program. Any new type of activity should simply be explained to the pastor for his approval. This may be done in writing or through personal conversation.

14. No youth activity, or any other church activity, should be planned during the weeks of revivals, Bible conferences, and other churchwide activities. The young people should attend these meetings regularly.

15. Activities are chosen appropriately to the season of the year. When the weather permits, such things may be conducted as hayrides, wiener roasts, outdoor songfests, etc. When driven to the indoors, attention would have to be turned to parties, quizzes, banquets, films, museum trips, etc.

16. The promotion of these activities is handled in several different ways. First an announcement is printed in our teachers' and officers' paper, the *Echoes*, which is a newsletter for our Wednesday evening teachers' and officers' meeting. The junior high and high school superintendents then make this announcement at their respective Sunday school opening assemblies.

The youth activity is then printed in the church bulletin. This announcement, as all announcements, should involve the meeting place, the date, the time, the activity, and the cost.

The pastor announces and promotes the activity from the pulpit, and then, of course, the next activity is always promoted at the present one.

Then on various occasions the opening assemblies of the departments are visited by the youth director so he may promote the activities personally. Sometimes the young people themselves prepare skits for the promotion of the event.

17. We have found that our adults are very willing to help the young people to grow in grace and to build their lives around the church. Our adults volunteer to help in such matters as bus driving, being camp counselors, cooking for banquets, etc. This is a wonderful way for some adults to serve the Lord Jesus Christ who do not have time or talent to do so in a more spectacular way.

18. Many times bus transportation is used for youth activities. Sometimes this is simply a matter of driving across town. At other times it is driving five hundred miles to a youth camp. Several things are noted when such trips are taken:

(1.) All drivers are properly licensed men from the church.

(2.) The young people are greeted at the door as they board the buses and they are required to fill out a card of registration. (This helps give you prospects for your youth soul-winning visitation.)

(3.) Young people are then reminded that they represent Christ and the church and that they are to act accordingly. They are reminded that there will be no such actions as hand-holding, love-making, etc., and that their behavior must be above reproach.

(4.) They are also reminded as they board the bus that the group goes as a group, stays together as a group, and returns as a group. No one is allowed to drive his own car and meet the bus at its destination. They go on the buses or they are not allowed to go.

(5.) A prayer is then offered asking God for safety and blessing, and off we go for a good time in the Lord.

19. *There are expenditures involved in most youth activities.* We have found that the young people appreciate the youth program more if it costs them something. Add to this the fact that we feel the tithes and offerings should not be used for foolishness. We find it necessary and best to have a small charge for the youth activity. This cost should be kept low and, of course, it should be announced at every activity and at every announcement about the event that those who cannot afford to pay are just as welcome as those who can. The cost would range from as little as 25¢ for a wiener roast up to several dollars for a formal banquet.

It is also wise to have a regular budget set up for the youth activity. There is an item in our church budget for the youth program. This can be used for spiritual activities and for honorariums for guest speakers, singers, etc. First Baptist Church of Hammond allocates only $15.00 a week for the youth fund. This means the youth program must be supplemented by a small charge at most of the activities. It is customary not to plan anything that will cost more than a dollar unless, of course, it is a banquet.

20. *All of the above activities should be adequately supervised by the youth director and adults whom he chooses.* It is wise to have at least one adult for every ten young people. The reasons for this are obvious ones. These adults should be recruited from the congregation, and they should be very faithful, spiritual and separated people who believe in what the church is trying to do.

21. *It is good to have a special time of prayer for the college students.* Each Wednesday evening at our midweek service some time is given to praying for the college students. Each week there is a different "college student of the week." A letter is read from him and prayer is offered on his behalf.

22. *The "College Campus News" is a little paper that relays the news from home to the college students.* It is published monthly and is a link between home and college.

(Illustration on next page)

By no means has this chapter been exhaustive. May God use it, however, to stimulate youth programs in fundamental churches in order that young people may build their lives around the work of Christ and His church.

15. The Church Nursery

There are several reasons why the church should have a well-organized and well-operated church nursery. In the first place, the church nursery can eliminate disturbances in the services. Through the years I have seen many services ruined, or nearly ruined, by crying babies and thoughtless parents. One wonders how many people will miss Heaven because they could not hear of the way to Heaven as expounded by the pastor from the pulpit due to some misbehaving baby who was required to be in the services because adequate nursery facilities were not available or because the parent would not cooperate in the reaching of people for the Saviour.

Not only does a nursery eliminate disturbances in the services and allow visitors to hear the plan of salvation but it also frees parents to work in the Sunday school, sing in the choir, etc. It also provides the ladies of the church an opportunity for service. They will respond to this opportunity if the importance of the task is properly presented by the pastor.

Few things make a better first impression upon visitors as a beautiful, clean, well-organized nursery. Immediately the visitor gets the idea that this church cares and knows what it is doing and does it well.

We will divide this chapter into two main headings: the organization of a nursery and the proper procedure for the nursery.

Organization of the Nursery

1. Choose a competent, spiritual, and hard-working nursery director. This is the key to the entire program. As someone has said, "Everything rises and falls upon leadership." This is certainly true in a nursery. The pastor should bear in mind also that the nursery is one of the few departments of the church in which he is not an expert. If a Sunday school department goes wrong, the pastor knows how to correct it. He is, however, almost at the mercy of the nursery director to see that it operates smoothly. Because of this, much care should be taken in the choosing of a proper director.

2. A census should be taken to find the need. Then a meeting could be conducted with those interested and a list of all of the babies could be made. At this meeting the parents should be invited and they should be set at ease about the future of the nursery. It should be a meeting that is impressive so as to tell the parents that they may feel secure as they place their baby in the nursery that is being organized.

3. *The locating of facilities is very important.* Most churches do not have adequate facilities. However, the best facilities should be given to the nursery. Many churches have lovely adult classrooms and the leftovers are given to the nursery. We have found that the opposite is the wise plan in the drawing of a church. Give your best and most commodious facilities to the babies. The next best should be given to the beginners, then primaries, juniors, and on up. An adult will be more impressed when his children are cared for properly than he will if much care is made for his comfort and little for his children.

When choosing proper facilities, several things should be taken into consideration. The location should be as near the auditorium as possible, yet far enough away so the noise will not interfere with the service. The nursery should be as near the level of the auditorium as possible in order to avoid the danger and discomfort involved when parents are required to carry babies up several flights of stairs.

Tile floor is certainly advisable for a nursery. If this is not available, then some other nonskid material should be used.

If at all possible, there should be a division between the bed babies and the toddlers. It is best to have four rooms for the nursery-age children—one for bed babies, one for toddlers up to their second birthday, one for two-year-olds, and one for three-year-olds. This is, however, often impossible. In such cases, room dividers may be used. At any rate, the children who are on the floor walking should not be allowed to get close enough to touch the bed babies.

It is also wise to have plumbing facilities very near to the nursery or, better still, in the nursery.

4. *The basic equipment for a nursery would include cribs and mattresses.* (These are often donated by members or even by local merchants. At any rate, they could be purchased at discount stores.) Small cribs may be used for babies six months and under and larger cribs for babies approaching their first birthday. Since they take less space, the more small cribs that can be used, the better.

Other equipment needed for the starting of a nursery would be rockers, a cabinet, a blackboard, a coat rack, a clock, a PA system from the auditorium enabling the nursery workers to hear the services and the message, an intercom phone to the ushers' station or a PA room to be used in case of an emergency, bottle warmers, playpens, jumper chairs, and toys. (One-piece washable soft toys are highly preferable.)

Most of the above equipment can be secured through a church shower or a special offering taken for the purchase of such materials. Many people have lovely nursery equipment stored away at home that will probably never be used again. They would love to donate it to the church. In some cases, they can simply let the church borrow the equipment. At any rate, sacrifice somewhere else but provide for the babies and see that they have the best of equipment.

5. *The needed supplies can be brought as donations by the church members.* A baby shower would be very appropriate. These supplies should be secured: sheets, Kleenex, baby powder, Vaseline, plastic bags, washcloths, blankets, and even extra clothing. Oftentimes a baby becomes sick in the nursery and will soil his clothing. It certainly leaves a good impression in the minds of the parents if they can return to find that their baby has been supplied with clean, dry clothing even through the emergency.

Many churches are small and the church nursery budget is limited. As aforementioned, a special shower could be given, a special offering could be taken, or, as many churches have found advisable, the Women's Missionary Circles can provide supplies for the nursery.

6. *The enlistment of workers is a very important phase of any church activity or, for that matter, any thriving institution.* The proper enlistment of workers should include the following:

(1.) All workers should be approved by the pastor. This is true in every phase of the church program.

(2.) A meeting with a group of mothers and faithful ladies of the church can be held where the need for nursery workers is explained and the idea of working in the nursery is sold to them. The pastor could conduct this meeting or, if the nursery director is persuasive, she could conduct the meeting. The need should be presented and the idea should be sold to these ladies. (All the workers in our nursery are mothers.) At this meeting it should be emphasized that working in the nursery is a service for the Lord. It is like teaching, singing, superintending a department, being a deacon, etc. Here is a chance for spiritual service, service that will be rewarded at the Judgment Seat, and service that is pleasing to God. It should be emphasized that this is a means of soul winning. Unsaved people can now hear the message of hope without interruption. How important it is to stress this upon the minds of the group.

(3.) The workers should be well-groomed, clean, pleasant, and faithful.

(4.) Both permanent workers and substitute workers should be used. This should be explained at the aforementioned meeting. Some may have a desire to work regularly on a schedule basis; others, perhaps, would rather be substitute workers to be called in case of emergency. Each job is important and sufficient workers should be enlisted for both permanent and substitute work.

7. *The workers should be assigned.* First, the children should be divided by ages as it is easier to care for children nearer the same

age. As mentioned before, the bed babies should definitely be separated from the toddlers. It is better for the children under two to be separated from the children two and three, if possible. Each worker should have the same assignment each week. In other words, each worker should become an expert in her own particular age level.

It is also advisable to have one worker for each six children. When the attendance is one to six, use one worker; seven to twelve—two workers; thirteen to eighteen—three workers, etc.

It is also advisable to have different workers on Sunday morning, Sunday evening, and Wednesday evening. Now it may be satisfactory for one worker to work two of the three services but because the nursery workers also need spiritual nourishment they should be allowed to be in at least one service a week. It is highly preferable for them to be in two services of the week. Of course, this would fluctuate with the conditions of each individual church.

Proper Procedure for the Nursery

1. The children should be divided by age and no exceptions should be made. Rules are very important in any organization. This one is vital to good nursery procedure.

2. The room should be set up according to the developmental level of the baby. The atmosphere should be conducive to his age level.

3. The nursery should be open at least fifteen minutes before each service. This is a minimum. Thirty minutes is even more desirable. One reason for this is that the Sunday school teachers in the other departments should be in their places at least fifteen minutes before the service. Consequently, the nurseries must be open even earlier for the use of their children.

4. Enroll all babies and keep their cards posted. Below you will see typical enrollment cards:

These cards should be posted on a bulletin board so that the worker may know in detail the needs of each baby. Such things as allergies, special care, etc., are very important to parents and should be important to the worker.

5. *The child's name should be written on a blackboard along with instructions as given by the parents.* Each bed is numbered. When the child is placed in the bed, the number from the bed should be written on the blackboard and beside the number the child's name should be written, and any special instructions for the day should be listed. This is not only a double check but it also gives added temporary instructions that the parent would give the nursery worker that would not be listed on the enrollment card. Also little bins, or cubbyholes, may be made for the purpose of depositing the diaper bag, etc. Each of these little bins should be numbered. The number on the bin, the number on the bed, and the number of the blackboard should correspond. It is very important that the children's equipment such as diaper bags, diapers, bottles, etc., be kept separate. Along with this, bottles, diaper bags, etc., should be marked. Toddlers and babies who play on the floor should be marked with some means of identification. This may be done by writing the name on a bracelet made of bias tape and fastened with a snap or gripper. You may also use a tag that can be pinned to the back of the collar.

6. *The doors should be locked to keep the children in and the parents out.* The nursery is a place for children and not for parents. It is best to have half doors so the baby can be deposited over the half door without the parent entering the nursery. THIS SHOULD BE THE LAW OF THE MEDES AND PERSIANS! When parents come inside, it creates more confusion and causes the children to cry more. It is always best for the children not to see their parents. Especially is this true in the case of the toddlers. When the parents are kept out and the babies are kept in, it helps the organization, sanitation, privacy, and protection of the babies. Babies should be discharged from the nursery only to the parents or to the one who brought the baby, if this is not the parent. When the parents see that the nursery is operated properly, they will be comforted by this kind of arrangement.

7. *Educate the parents and get them interested in the church nursery.* Occasionally send out a mailing to all parents giving the room assignment, marking tag, etc. The proper kind of procedure and the proper kind of communication can sell the parent on the nursery. When the parent is sold, complete confidence is developed and rules are happily followed.

8. *The workers should be in uniform.* White uniforms may be purchased at a nominal cost and will present an efficient appearance. Perhaps few things will do more to settle the minds of the parents than to see a clean, uniformed nursery worker come for the baby. These

uniforms are owned by the church. If possible, a dressing room should be provided so that the ladies can change after they arrive. In some cases uniforms can be secured that simply can be worn over the dresses, then these can be removed and placed in the uniform room or the dressing room.

9. *As implied before, we ask each worker to work one service a week in the same room at the same time.* On Sunday morning this would be both Sunday school and the preaching service. On Sunday evening it would be both Training Union and the preaching service, and on Wednesday evening it would be both Teachers' and Officers' Meeting and the preaching service.

10. *It is always best, if possible, to pay the nursery workers.* Of course, no one will get rich on what they make working in the nursery but if a salary could be paid, for example, a dollar an hour, it would encourage the worker to be on time and be in uniform. It would make him more responsible as an employee rather than a volunteer, and it would give liberty to the nursery superintendent or pastor to call upon the worker for extra service above his regular time. A bulletin board should be secured. The time should be kept on time cards, and the cards should be placed on this bulletin board.

11. *One person should be assigned to get substitutes for the nursery.* This person knows who is to work and is the one to be contacted in case a regular worker must be out. A proper substitute must be chosen. She must be one who meets all of the qualifications of the regular workers.

12. *Appreciation for the workers should be shown.* Periodically at a service, special and public recognition should be given to the nursery workers. Their names could be read, they could stand, and receive a word of commendation from the pastor and a resounding "Amen" or grateful applause should come from the congregation.

It is interesting that oftentimes we overlook the most important things because they seem small. Few things are more important in the building of a church than adequate nurseries. There are many ways to operate a successful nursery. We have offered a skeleton outline of one. May God help it to be used of the Holy Spirit to make our services more conducive to reaching people with the Gospel of Jesus Christ.

16. The Music

Probably nothing affects a preaching service or a congregation any more than music. One might only listen to a well-produced radio broadcast or television program to find the real effect that music has on our emotions. Though we do not realize it, music makes a mystery more mysterious, love more loving, a comedy more humorous, a tragedy more tragic, and subconsciously makes a presentation reach its fullest impact upon the observers. I have often taken a trip only to find myself going slower or faster depending upon the type music being played on the car radio.

A friend of mine once managed a cafeteria. One noon he took me to observe the people as they chose their food. He asked the organist to play a waltz. The speed of the cafeteria line lessened and the people chose their food more slowly and deliberately. He then asked the organist to play a march. Immediately as the tempo accelerated, the customers moved more quickly, though the people never realized the effect music had on them.

Music in a preaching service is either a vitamin or a tranquilizer. It is either an asset or a liability. It is either a stimulant or a sedative. It is needful that our churches know the importance of the right kind and proper use of gospel music. Those involved in the music program of the church need to know how to direct music to the heart and how to prepare both congregation and preacher for the message.

Music plays a big part in the Word of God. When Moses crossed the Red Sea, he sang. Deborah and Barak composed a song at the defeat of Sisera. Hannah sang because of God's promise to give her a son. Mary sang after the annunciation. Others in the Bible such as Joseph, Simon and Hezekiah gave expression of their joy in song. In Revelation 5:9 we find, *"And they sung a new song...."* The psalmist said, *"And he hath put a new song in my mouth."* In Heaven the four living creatures will sing around the throne of God. Singing is one of the enjoyments on earth that can be transferred to Heaven.

In many churches music is a hindrance to the preaching. Probably few things in our churches need to be reevaluated as much as does our music program. The following suggestions are given, not through the eyes of a professional musician but through the eyes of a sincere pastor deeply concerned about music programs in the churches.

Evangelism is an atmosphere. Music can help create this atmosphere. Let us notice, first, music in the service itself.

1. The pastor is pastor of the music program.

It is a dangerous thing for the pastor not to oversee every phase of the church program. It can be a catastrophe for the pastor to take his hands completely off the music. Though the music director certainly should have freedom and liberty to carry out his program, it should all be done with the approval of the pastor. The pastor should constantly retain his right to have veto power. It should be understood that the music director is under the pastor, and that his main concern is to please the pastor and to prepare his heart for the preaching of the Word of God.

It is tragic but true that many preachers would preach better if the sermon preceded the music. In this case the music director is a failure, regardless of the quality of the music or perfection of the presentation. The word "bishop" in the Bible is translated "overseer." The right kind of pastor "oversees." He should oversee the music as well as every other part of the church program.

Many pastors have lamented the day that they turned the music of the church over to a music committee. Often these committees grow in power and authority and make a slave of the music director and a figurehead of the pastor.

We have followed the plan of hiring a qualified music director who is given complete control of the music program *under* the supervision of the pastor. If the music director is not qualified, or if he is not of a disposition suitable for such a plan, he should not have been employed. If he is qualified, he should not be annoyed.

2. A well-planned prelude should set the pace for the service.

If the service is to be evangelistic, the prelude should be evangelistic. It should be started at least ten minutes before the service. It should consist of familiar gospel songs played up to tempo and loudly enough. It should be well planned and well prepared. We allow only sacred music to be played for preludes and offertories.

3. Always start the service on time.

Of course, this will be up to the music director. If one hundred people are present at a service that starts six minutes late, six hundred minutes are wasted. This is ten hours! The Bible says we are to give an account for every idle moment and to redeem the time. I wonder how many hours the preachers and music directors will have to account for at the judgment seat. If the services are to start at 11:00, but then start at 11:03, someone is dishonest.

4. It is often good to start the services with the choir.

An important part of any venture is the beginning. If the choir marches out and immediately presents a well-planned opening song or chorus, it will do several things. First, it will quieten the crowd.

Secondly, it will make friends immediately of the first-time visitors, and then also, it will remind the congregation that this service is well planned and prepared. This opening could be a special choir arrangement, a stanza of a choir arrangement that has been used previously, a chorus of the opening hymn sung well, or a well-prepared chorus. At this part of the service a giddy-type chorus should be avoided. This should be a big-type number, one that will say to the people, "This is going to be a great service. More is to come."

5. *Use gospel songs.*

We feel that the old songs and hymns are the best for congregational singing. We use the same type songs for both morning and evening. Such songs as "Amazing Grace," "How Firm a Foundation," "Rescue the Perishing," "What a Friend We Have in Jesus," "The Old Rugged Cross," etc., are certainly as appropriate for Sunday morning as they are for Sunday evening.

A church that is too formal for such singing is *too* formal. These songs would not necessarily have to be used exclusively, but to exclude them completely because it is Sunday morning will eventually act as a sedative on evangelism.

6. *The pastor chooses the appropriate songs.*

It has been my policy for many years to go through the songbooks and approve songs we use for congregational singing. I do not choose the particular ones to be sung on a given Sunday, but simply decide what songs may be used in our services. There are some songs in the book that are not good for congregational singing and some that the pastor might feel would not help the desired end for the services. The use of these can be avoided by simply going through the songbook and checking the songs the pastor approves for congregational singing.

7. *Introductions should also be planned ahead.*

After the pastor has approved the songs to be used for congregational singing, the music director or the organist should decide on a good, short introduction for each hymn and mark it in the hymnals used by the organist and pianist. In this way the accompanists will never be unprepared for the playing of a good, lively introduction regardless of the song named by the song leader. Many services have been harmed because the organist played introductions which were much too long and musically incorrect.

8. *The choir should practice congregational songs.*

The choir should practice the next Sunday's congregational songs in the choir practice. This will serve a twofold purpose. First, it can serve as a warm-up for choir practice. This also prevents "hallelujah breakdowns" during the song service on the Lord's Day. If the choir members know the songs to be sung, it can often save embarrassment to the song leader at the public service.

9. The pianist and organist should have the list of numbers.

The pianist and organist should have the list of page numbers prior to the service so they can have their books open to the proper page *before* the song is announced. They should start playing immediately upon the announcement of the numbers. Because we have found it best to have the numbers announced twice, at the conclusion of the second announcement the organist and pianist immediately start playing the "marked" introduction.

10. Announce the page numbers distinctly.

We announce each number twice. These numbers are easily misunderstood: 270 could be 217; 350 could be 315; 118 could be 180. It might even be wise to announce such numbers first as "number one hundred eighteen," and then announce as "1-1-8."

11. Song leader selects and records hymns used in public services.

It is wise for the song leader to keep a record of the hymns used in the public services. In this way he guards against overusing a few gospel songs and excluding other good songs approved by the pastor.

In selecting the songs for a particular service the song leader should choose a peppy one for the first number. Too many services begin with a slower hymn, such as "Saviour, Like a Shepherd Lead Us," and this is not conducive to establishing an atmosphere of evangelism. "Love Lifted Me" or "He Keeps Me Singing" would be better at the beginning of a service. The slower songs could be used later.

12. The congregational song leader should leave the preaching to the preacher.

Occasionally one comes across some song leader who likes to tell his favorite story between stanzas and will pause and preach awhile during the song service. The song leader should remember that his job is to lead the singing, not to philosophize or exegete the song before, during, or after it is sung.

13. Have a familiar gospel offertory.

The pianist or organist should never be used just as a "filler." The offertory is a definite part of the service. It should be carefully and prayerfully planned and well presented. Though I have a great love for classical music, I feel that the church is definitely not the place for it, and we do not allow its use in our services. Our offertories are taken from well-known hymns and songs so that the people can be blessed while the music is played. In fact, no instrumental selection is ever played unless it is a familiar one so that the people can be blessed by the message. If a trombonist, organist, pianist, or harpist were to play an unfamiliar number, people should be given the page number so they could open to the song and follow its words.

14. We should remember that music is a means to an end.

Music is not an end itself. It should never take the place of preaching. Let us prepare the people's hearts for the preaching of the Word.

In nearly a quarter of a century of preaching we have yet to take a Sunday morning or Sunday evening strictly for a musical program. It is always preaching. If a cantata is presented, it is presented on a weeknight, Sunday afternoon, or right before a service. People know that they can always find preaching at our church. Our music is not an end but it is an important means to an end.

15. The choir should set the pace for the service.

In other words, the choir should be an example for the congregation. The choir should not whisper or misbehave in any way. They should be obviously responsive to the preaching so as to set a pattern for the congregation to follow. The first thing the visitor sees is the choir, and since the first impression is often a lasting one, it should be a positive one.

16. The invitation number should not be announced secretly to the choir during the sermon.

It is not uncommon for a pastor's message to be hindered by the music director whispering the number to someone in the choir and then the chain reaction starts. It is certainly disconcerting for choir members to be opening their songbooks at the most crucial part of the message.

17. The organist should not take liberties during the invitation.

The pastor is in complete charge of the invitation. The organist should never decide to play softly at the close of the message or at any time during the invitation. The organist should play only at the pastor's request.

18. Start each invitation with the same song.

This is so the choir will know what the number of the invitation will be, avoiding the error in the aforementioned part. For years we have started our invitation with "Just As I Am." People know what it is going to be. The choir knows what it is going to be. Hence, much confusion is avoided.

19. We use only the choir on the invitation.

We do not want the people reaching for their books. Even this much movement will take the sinner's mind off the Gospel. We simply stand for the invitation, and the choir starts to sing. For this reason our choir never goes down to sit in the congregation during the sermon. They are always behind the preacher, ready to sing the invitation hymn.

20. The choir rehearses the invitation numbers at choir practice.

The invitation song is always sung up to tempo, never slowly. It is led by the music director as a special number is led. It has been rehearsed at choir practice and sung in full voice as a special number would be sung.

It is a shame the way an average invitation is sung so slowly. It is no wonder that people do not respond quickly to the invitation.

21. Use the same invitation song as long as people are responding.

It can be detrimental to the service for one song to be stopped and another started while folks are walking the aisle and others are in the "valley of decision." For this cause we continue to sing the same song as long as people will respond. We simply repeat the verses over and over. When folks stop coming forward, then we consider changing the number.

22. Only the pastor changes the invitation song.

It is the pastor who feels the heartbeat of the invitation. It is the pastor who knows when another song is needed. The invitation can be changed with the following statement of the pastor: "Now as the choir sings, 'Softly and Tenderly Jesus Is Calling,' would you come forward and receive Christ as your Saviour." Note that the page number is not announced. The choir knows it and the congregation does not need it. Hence, all of the invitation numbers are changed only by the pastor if he feels led to make the change.

23. The choir should sing after the closing prayer.

In our service we do not use a benediction, nor do we use a choral response, or a sevenfold amen. Hence, the service is closed with a prayer followed by the choir singing such songs as "He Lives," "A New Name Written Down in Glory," etc. This sends the people home on a joyful note.

24. The organist and pianist play a joyful postlude.

The service should be closed on a high plane, and the people should leave with a spirit of joyful thanksgiving. The right kind of postlude helps to stimulate this mood. This should also consist of familiar hymns. "Praise Him! Praise Him!" and "Ring the Bells of Heaven" would be the appropriate kind of hymn to play for a postlude.

25. The piano and organ should be tuned regularly.

Few things can hurt a service any more than having the musical instruments out of tune. Little things should be cared for in a public service. The tuning of the piano, proper lighting, proper heat and ventilation, proper adjustment of the public address system and other things are of vital importance for the success of the service.

26. Special groups, as duets, trios, quartets, should be well prepared and well planned.

No such number should be sung unless it has been rehearsed properly. Those who sing should be sitting in the choir or right in the front together. We have found it wise to have a special number after a prayer. As soon as the prayer is closed, they should be behind the pulpit and the instruments should play the introduction immediately. There should be no lulls in the service.

Normally, our singing groups are not introduced. They should be dressed properly and taught to stand properly. They should avoid of-

fensive gestures, smiles and facial gestures at the people in the audience, and improper posture.

Why should the Lord's work be done less efficiently than a television program? Why should a nightclub be better prepared than a
church? God's business is the biggest business in the world. Let's
act like it. The slipshod way the average church operates its music
program is a pity! It is evident that time is not given to planning and
preparing the special numbers. Special numbers are oftentimes given
by people who are not prepared and who dress sloppily, slouch up to
the pulpit, clap their hands, chew their gum, smile at the boyfriend,
and go through the motion of trying to be a blessing. The local bur-
lesque plans better than we do. God pity us.

27. Special groups should be organized.

(1.) Each singing group should consist of people approved by the
pastor *before* they are approached about singing in a special group.

(2.) There should be a weekly practice for each singing group. It
might be wise for all ladies' groups to practice at the same time,
having the nursery open or a baby sitter available for all of the children. A good time to have these ladies practice would be during the
graded choir rehearsals. This provides a place for the children while
the mothers practice.

(3.) Each group should consider the possibility of dressing alike.
Certainly each group should carefully plan their attire when singing in
the service.

(4.) A singing group should be named. This name should be something more than "Ladies' Trio," "Men's Quartet," etc.

(5.) The pastor or music director should keep a card file on each
group. On this card should be listed every song this group knows well
enough to sing and when and if they have sung it. From this file the
pastor and music director will know at any moment what group and
numbers are ready for presentation.

(6.) Each group should have a captain who can be contacted by the
pastor or music director. The captain is responsible to inform other
members of the singing group.

(7.) The music director should either practice with each group or
have a competent person in charge of each group to insure the best
preparation and presentation.

28. Have an active graded-choir program.

Remember that the efficiency and effectiveness of such a program
will not only give the challenge to learn music better but gives the
lasting impression as to the way God's work should be carried on.

(1.) The choirs should be graded by departments. There should be
a beginner choir, a primary choir, a junior choir, and a teen-age
choir.

(2.) There should be a weekly rehearsal. This may be any time suitable to your situation. Many churches find it convenient to have it after school. At one pastorate we found after school on Monday to be a splendid time. We could announce it heartily on the Lord's Day and then it would be fresh in the minds of the boys and girls for Monday.

(3.) There should be some definite rules about dress at the rehearsals. Boys should be required to wear ties and girls should be required to dress neatly. At one church we even provided white shirts and ties for the boys and matching skirts and blouses for the girls. Of course, there were those who complained, but they felt a sense of pride, and it also taught the boys and girls to dress properly. This is greatly needed in these days.

(4.) There should be a weekly workers' meeting for the discussion of curriculum, etc. This meeting could be held immediately before the choirs meet or at any other convenient time during the week. We have found it helpful to keep a definite order of curriculum in our choir programs. Such things as scales, rules of music, song leading, etc., may be taught to a smallest boy or girl. A meeting of directors may help with the planning of such a program.

(5.) Children line up at the door and march in. This is a time much like the Daily Vacation Bible School. This will help the children to learn obedience and will also help the order and discipline for the entire session. They will line up at different doors of the auditorium and march in quickly and quietly for an opening assembly of all choirs. Then each choir is sitting together during this assembly.

(6.) Have a fifteen-minute fun time or assembly time with all of the choirs present. This can be a get-acquainted session, a time of action, or a time of devotion-type assembly. This creates a school spirit. This is much like a Sunday school departmental opening assembly followed by individual classes.

(7.) Choirs then march in line to the individual practice rooms. Notice before the child is ever taught music, he is taught how to dress properly, he is taught discipline, and he is taught to follow orders. These are vitally important to any organization.

(8.) Use choruses first in the choir rehearsal. Boys and girls should get the idea that choir practice is fun. Start off with choruses that they like to sing and gradually work into the curriculum of the day. This curriculum should always contain the learning of some musical knowledge as well as the rehearsal of some song the choir plans to sing. It should include such things as constant practice on how to stand and sit together, how to hold the songbook, how to stand during performance, etc. The same methods of standing, sitting, holding books, etc., we use in the adult choir should be taught to the entire program. By the time the children become members of the adult choir, this habit will have become part of them subconsciously.

(9.) Have a surprise once a month. This surprise will be in the form of refreshments or a guest, such as a ventriloquist or magician, etc. The actual day of the surprise should not be announced. It should be about once a month on a different day of each month and should come as a complete surprise to the boys and girls. This should help them to come regularly.

(10.) A different choir should sing in the church service once a month. This should keep the boys and girls interested and keep the parents happy. It will also help the attendance at the public service.

(11.) A roll should be kept of choir members and a letter sent to absentees. We have found it beneficial to have three types of letters and cards sent. One for the first absence, one for the second absence and one for the third. These are sent to each absentee each week. It simply lets them know we care.

29. The adult choir should be properly organized and well trained.

Members should be enlisted properly. The enlistment of choir members should be done the same way that Sunday school teachers are enlisted and a challenge should be presented to a potential member personally. To ask folks in the congregation to come to the choir shows the sign of both the lack of concern and the lack of preparation. How a choir member is enlisted will determine to a great extent his interest and faithfulness to the program.

30. Choir practice should always start on time.

Nothing encourages tardiness like the leader being tardy in starting. If only two people are there, he should start the moment it is scheduled to start. Nobody wants to miss anything. Then, too, we aid our people in developing slipshod habits if we are delinquent in starting on time.

31. Choirs should be organized properly.

The choir should have a president and he should be given time to preside briefly at each choir practice. He could welcome new ones in the choir, say a word about any social activity the choir is planning, and briefly make necessary announcements. Then it is often wise to have group captains and maybe even a secretary, social chairman, etc. The practice always should be well planned and conducive to conducting God's business with dignity.

32. Each group captain should keep an attendance record.

Absentee letters and postcards should be sent and even visits made to insure a good choir practice attendance.

33. Each choir member should have his own seat.

He should be required to see that it is filled at all times. Some churches even find it wise to have the person's name on the seat.

34. The choir practice should last approximately one hour.

It should include the rehearsing of congregational songs for the next Sunday. It should be spiritual as well as informal and gay.

35. It is wise to practice a special at least three weeks before it is presented.

This will insure each choir member having enough practice to guarantee a good presentation.

36. It is good to present some new numbers to the choir each week.

Nothing will hurt choir practice attendance any more than a lack of a challenge. Few things present less challenge than an excessive number of "repeats." People respond to something new, and the choir is challenged to faithfulness by knowing that something new is waiting for them at every practice.

37. The choir director should choose choir music carefully.

In our church services we use no anthems. We use arrangements of gospel songs. The choir director should select these carefully so that the performance of these arrangements will add to the atmosphere of evangelism.

The choir arrangements should be suited to the overall ability of the choir. The use of extremely simplified arrangements fails to challenge the members. Interesting selections will keep up their interest if care is taken to avoid overly difficult numbers which would discourage and embarrass the choir.

38. The choir arrangements should be studied by the director before the rehearsal.

Because the director is the "leader," he should be prepared to *lead* the music. It is disconcerting for choir members to give their time to the rehearsing of selections with which the director is not thoroughly familiar.

When a choir director is personally prepared, he can more efficiently and confidently lead the choirs in their rehearsing of the specials for the Lord's Day.

39. The choir should have some social life together.

About four times a year the choir should have some planned social activity. This would help develop a choir spirit. This is necessary for the success of any organization.

40. Some general music suggestions.

(1.) A piano class. Many churches are plagued by a lack of qualified pianists. The church pianist could have a piano class one hour each week. In a year's time these people would be qualified enough to play the simple gospel songs and could be used as accompanists as needed.

(2.) A song leaders' class. Most churches need departmental song leaders. Adult men could be trained for this by the church music director. This should also be a weekly matter. In a few months the Sunday school could be staffed with qualified departmental and class song leaders.

As the reader has probably surmised, music is very important to this preacher. It is important enough that we should be giving it our best. This is the greatest business in all the world and is worthy of nothing less than our best!

17. The Women's Missionary Society

Many Women's Missionary Societies have deteriorated into nothing more than Ladies' Aid Societies, civic clubs, etc. Several years ago at the First Baptist Church in Hammond we completely reorganized the women's work, and it has been a joy and a blessing ever since. We have received many letters and inquiries from pastors concerning this work. Upon the receipt of one such letter I asked Mrs. Erma McKinney, who was serving at that time as W.M.S. president, to answer the letter. Following is the letter from Mrs. McKinney to the inquiring pastor and the outline she enclosed:

JACK HYLES, *Pastor*
June 24, 1966

Pastor E. Wayne Wall
2520 Sunset Blvd.
W. Columbia, South Carolina 29169

Dear Brother Wall:

Pastor Hyles has passed on to me the copy of his reply to you, dated June 21, I am happy to send to you an outline of the "ingredients" included in the organization and the program of our Women's Mission Society. I hope that I have thought to include all that should be given.

By way of introduction, we are happy to say that <u>we work very closely with our pastor</u> in planning, in choosing workers, etc. He has written me letters offering his services in counseling for planning programs, for choosing speakers, and for approving ladies whom I would have in mind to fill positions of responsibility. The nominating committees each year meet with him to get approval of those whom they have in mind to fill the slate of officers. In other words, this work of the church, we are very happy to say, is as much pastored as any other work. We find that this prevents serious mistakes from being made; this also aids us in maintaining among the ladies the sweet spirit that ought to prevail in every avenue of the local church's work. <u>We have no constitution</u> -- we used to have one years ago. It was laid aside and then in one meeting we just made the announcement that we can happily say that this work is directed by the Holy Spirit; we are operating without a constitution. <u>The missionaries for whom we do service</u> are those that are written into our church budget. <u>Any other work is done</u> to help our own church local program. With this positive aim, whenever the Red Cross, the Community Chest, or anyone's personal-interest missionary or relative calls for help, we can answer them that we cannot step into these phases of work because our services include our missionaries and our local work; this is really all that we can take care of.

I am trusting that the enclosed will be of help to you.

Sincerely yours,

Erma McKinney
(Mrs. Tom McKinney)

Enclosure   INDIANA'S LARGEST SUNDAY SCHOOL

WOMEN'S MISSION SOCIETY WORK
of
First Baptist Church
Hammond, Indiana
June 24, 1966

I. PURPOSES
1. To provide Christian fellowship for the ladies of our church.
2. To inform the ladies of missionaries of history and of the present time.
3. To provide a means for the ladies to assist the missionaries whom we support, and to suggest missionary projects for our Girls' Lamplighter Society.
4. To provide assistance in our local work.

II. ORGANIZATIONAL STRUCTURE
1. Elected Officers: President, Vice-President, Program Chairman, Secretary, Assistant Secretary, Treasurer, Assistant Treasurer, Song Leader, Pianist.
2. Appointed Officers: Spiritual Life Chairman, Used Clothing Chairman, Membership Chairman, Circle Leaders, Registration Chairman.
3. Duties of each officer:
  (1) President: To oversee the entire work of WMS, to appoint officers, to preside at all the general meetings, to call meetings of circle leaders and general officers as needed, to visit each circle during the course of the year in order to learn the pulse of each group and to get acquainted with the ladies of these groups, and to perform any other duties that would involve arranging for general meetings and aiding the circle leaders to organize their meetings and groups.
  (2) Vice-President: To preside over the general meetings in the absence of the president, to take care of newspaper publicity, to type announcements for the pastor to make from the pulpit and to be printed in the Sunday bulletin, to work very closely with the president as the president's "sounding board" before bringing ideas or recommendations to the other officers and circle leaders.
  (3) Program Chairman: To arrange for the main speaker and program for the general meetings.
  (4) Secretary: To keep minutes of all the general meetings and all the officers' and circle leaders' meetings.
  (5) Assistant Secretary: To read and take minutes in the absence of the secretary.
  (6) Treasurer: To take the offerings at the general meetings; to care for paying the bills; to have the checks for nursery

workers, speakers, any who have spent money for general meeting expenses; to send checks to those organizations that are written into our budget; to keep the books; and to read the report at the general meeting. (The books are audited by two ladies at the close of each WMS year—these ladies are appointed by the president. A checking account is maintained at the local bank so that everything is done "decently and in order.")

(7) Assistant Treasurer: To read the treasurer's report in the absence of the treasurer at the general meeting and to assist in taking the offering at the general meeting.

(8) Song Leader: To choose the music to be used at the general meetings and to arrange for special music at the general meetings.

(9) Pianist: To play the piano at the general meetings.

(10) Spiritual Life Chairman: To meet with the president during the summer to choose a spiritual theme for the WMS year that begins in September; to choose Scripture verses to fit this theme for each month of the year; to compile the monthly prayer sheet that is used in the general meeting; and to arrange in advance for a lady to lead in prayer during the prayer time of the general meeting. (The prayer sheets are mimeographed in the church office, but the subject matter is provided by the Spiritual Life Chairman. She compiles the news from letters received from our missionaries and adds the verse for the month and a poem on devotional thought. Occasionally all the missionaries, the college students, or the servicemen are listed in addition to the missionaries' prayer requests. Enough copies of the prayer sheet are made so each lady can take one home to use in her daily devotional time.)

(11) Used Clothing Chairman: To assist the superintendent of the mission in keeping the church's used clothing room organized. (We maintain a used clothing room, with racks and shelves for clothing, shoes, scarves, etc., brought by members of the church from time to time.)

(12) Membership Chairman: To send each new lady member of the church a form letter which welcomes her to the membership of our church and also invites her to attend the WMS general meetings and circle meetings. (Periodically a list of the names, addresses and approximate ages of ladies who have recently joined the church is obtained from the church office. The membership chairman utilizes this list as do the leaders of the circles in personally inviting the new ladies to attend the meetings.)

(13) Registration Chairman: To take registrations after the Sunday services for the general meeting that is to follow the next Tuesday, to take registrations over the phone at her home until noon the Monday before the meeting, to arrange the names of the registered ladies into alphabetical order so that she can receive their payment for the luncheon as they arrive for the general meeting. (We never sell anything or serve any meal with the purpose of "making" money. All the work of our church is carried on by offerings. The luncheon cost cares for the expenses of the general meeting.)

(14) Circle Leaders: To act as president of her own circle, organizing her group with volunteer and/or appointed officers.

(15) Nursery Chairman: To call nursery workers for each general meeting, giving their names to the treasurer so that they can be paid the $2.00 for the afternoon that we pay in addition to furnishing their luncheon meal.

4. Members: Every lady member of the First Baptist Church of Hammond is automatically a member of the WMS. She is therefore welcome and invited simply to attend in order to become active. No dues are paid and there is no required number of meetings to attend in order to join. Every announcement concerning a general meeting of WMS is for every lady and her guests. Every circle announcement is made with her in mind if she cares to come.

5. Groupings

(1) The general meeting: The entire group meets together once a month in what we call the general meeting.

(2) The circles: The entire group is divided into circles, each circle meeting separately once a month at a time other than the time of the general meeting.

III. PROGRAM

1. General Meetings

(1) The Luncheon: We meet at 12:30 the first Tuesday of each month in the church fellowship hall. A different circle each month takes care of the meal, and another circle cares for the decorations. We charge 75¢ for adults and 25¢ for children. The money collected for the luncheon is allocated in the following manner:

a. The serving circle is allowed $35.00 for purchasing food in addition to the dishes they prepare individually. (Those serving are not required to pay the 75¢ charge.)

b. The decorating circle is allowed $4.00 for supplies.

c. The two nursery workers each receive $2.00.

d. In order that the serving ladies need not miss the meeting,

our rescue mission men clean up the kitchen and are paid
$3.00 for this task.

 e. Any remaining funds are applied to the cost of decorations
for the annual Mother-Daughter Banquet, which is held in
May.

 f. Payments to outside speakers are made from the offerings
taken at the general meetings.

(2) Agenda

 a. *Group singing* is led by the song leader while tables are
quickly cleared.

 b. *Business* includes the following:

  (a) Reading of the minutes of the previous general meeting
and the officers' meeting as well.

  (b) The treasurer's report.

  (c) Announcements of future WMS meetings.

  (d) Announcements of any plans for the work of WMS.

  (e) Recommendations. (Any recommendations brought to the
ladies have been discussed thoroughly by the officers or
officers and circle leaders so that a minimum amount of
time is spent on voting or any items of business.)

 c. *Special music* is presented.

 d. *A prayer time* for our missionaries is conducted.

 e. *The program* is presented.

(3) Types of Programs

 a. *Speakers:*

  (a) The director of the Pacific Garden Mission in Chicago.

  (b) The lady in charge of the women's work at the Pacific Garden Mission.

  (c) Any of our missionaries who are in the area.

  (d) Our own staff members.

  (e) Devotional speakers from within our own group of ladies.

 b. *Films* of the mission fields where our missionaries are
serving.

 c. *College meetings* conducted by our own college students
singing, testifying, and speaking. Also, films of colleges
we would recommend are shown so that the parents can be
informed.

 d. *Skits* portraying the work of our staff.

 e. *Christmas musical programs* presented by our own singing
groups.

 f. *Tape recordings* from our missionaries. (These are provided by us, but made by the missionary so we may "get
acquainted.")

 g. *Tours* of our parsonages, our rescue mission, and the Pacific Garden Mission.

h. *Installation service* for the new officers.

2. Organization

   (1) *Division of the ladies* is based upon various things — young married ladies' circle, deaf ladies' circle, single ladies' circle, others with mixed ages contain ladies convenient to a central location. The ladies are free to choose any convenient circle.

   (2) *Names of the circles* are chosen from the names of countries where our missionaries serve. (If more countries' names are available than needed, one circle could bear two countries' names until there is need for another circle to be formed; for instance, Japan-Mexico Circle.) If the church should at any time decide not to extend support to a certain missionary for some reason such as retirement, etc., the change is more gracefully made if the circle is not named for individual missionaries but rather for the field in which they serve.

   (3) *Meeting time* — once a month. Some meet in the afternoon, some in the evening, some the second Tuesday of the month, some the third Tuesday — the meetings vary. Sometimes a potluck is chosen by a circle to be served at lunch or supper time; sometimes the circle chooses to work at the church during the day on some project that can better be done there; or they meet at their regular meeting time in the home of one of the circle members.

   (4) *Officers of the circles* — leader, co-leader, secretary-treasurer, corresponding secretary, devotional chairman, project chairman.

   (5) *Program followed in a circle meeting:*

     a. A time of *devotions and prayer* is led by a member of the circle arranged for by the devotional chairman. The devotions are given either from a book selected by the WMS officers, who have purchased a copy for each circle, or from the thoughts compiled by the person presenting the devotions.

     b. A *report* on a missionary's work is presented. This is in the form of a book report about some past missionary or a compilation of letters and materials obtained from missionaries whom we now support. Two methods have been used for these reports. Some years a list of books is given to each circle, and a schedule is drawn up for ladies of the circle to present the reports to their own circle. Other years "roving speakers" are selected. Each speaker (a lady from our church) presents her book report to a different circle each month according to a schedule drawn up by the WMS president. Both methods work well if careful check is kept on them — books selected and "roving speakers."

   c. *Correspondence* is read from the circle's missionary, shut-in, college student, and/or serviceman.

   d. Time is spent on a *project* which requires sewing, etc.

   e. *Refreshments and fellowship* usually conclude the meeting.

IV. PROJECTS

  1. For our missionaries: The types of projects which we undertake for our missionaries are, of course, dependent upon their needs and the feasibility of shipping because of weight, duty involved, etc. If we can determine duty ahead of time, we'll send to the mission board of the particular missionary a check designated for that missionary in the amount of the duty which he will have to pay on the package. We write and ask the missionaries what their needs are, asking them to state specifically their personal needs and the needs of their mission field. Of course we can guess their personal needs many times. We know, if they have a family, items of clothing and reading material, such as subscriptions to *Reader's Digest, Sword of the Lord,* etc., might be enjoyed by them. Food items that they cannot buy would be a real treat to them: cake mixes, soft drink mixes, certain canned goods, etc. On some fields used clothing is badly needed and boxes of it can be sent. Bibles can be purchased through Bible societies and sent in our name to the mission field. Quilts are a needed item on many fields, both for the use of the missionary and also the people on their field. We make and buy baby clothes each year, for these are needed items in many places.

  2. Local:

    (1) The used clothing room on the church property is well stocked. We keep not only donated clothing but also newly-made quilts and baby clothes to be distributed among our own needy.

    (2) Baptismal robes constantly need replacing and repairing.

    (3) We help bereaved church families. It is determined how much food is needed for the meal after the funeral (and perhaps for longer periods of time than this) and decided what kinds of dishes and how many should be brought. Circles take turns providing dishes and help. The church budget allows for buying a large ham for any bereaved family.

    (4) Our ladies do things around the church that are not included in the custodian's duties: wash the artificial greenery in the auditorium, mend songbooks, clean the church kitchen (cabinet, refrigerators, etc.).

    (5) Our church maintains a rescue mission. The ladies make personal effects bags and fill them with shaving cream, toothbrush, toothpaste, etc. They also bring handkerchiefs, socks,

etc. We have had schedules for the different circles to bring dessert dishes to the mission.

(6) Each circle is provided with names of shut-ins, servicemen, and college students from our church family. On their birthdays and at other special oocasions cards are sent with the assurance that the ladies are praying for them. To the shut-ins visits are made periodically, taking baskets of fruit and other gifts at Christmas, Thanksgiving and perhaps at birthdays.

V. FINANCIAL STRUCTURE

1. Budget—General Meetings: The budget is set up at the beginning of each WMS year (the fall) designating sums to different organizations, such as Child Evangelism, World Home Bible League, Pacific Garden Mission, etc. We try each year to review the merits of each designation, and if we feel that there is some reason for not using the Lord's money in support of a group, we do not recommend to the ladies that we support them again.

2. Extra Needs—General Meetings: When we hear of special needs throughout the year, we consider them and vote upon whether we can send money.

3. Circles' Finances: The offerings taken in the circle meetings are disbursed according to the wishes of the ladies attending that circle. Many times recommendation is made by the general group that all the circles help in one certain project.

VI. THE YEAR'S WORK

1. How decided:

(1) By officers and circle leaders during the summer.

(2) With a twelve-month period in mind, plans are made for September through August. (New officers are installed in the June meeting and actually take office in July, carrying out plans for the July and August general meetings that were made by the outgoing officers.)

(3) By individual circles. (Some choose to meet during the summer; some do not.)

2. Yearbooks:

(1) Made up by officers.

(2) Contents to be of aid to all ladies attending.

(3) About 4" x 6" in size, mimeographed and bound in book form. Listed are the names of all the officers with their phone numbers; names of our missionaries and their addresses; a separate page for each month of the year showing the verse for that month, the names of the serving and decorating circles for that month; circle names, times of meeting and their leaders' names and phone numbers; and other helpful information to which the group can refer throughout the year.

18. The Baptismal Service

"Who baptized Jesus?" asked a beginner department Sunday school teacher. After a few moments of deliberation little Johnny raised his hand and answered, "John the Baptist did."

"That's right," replied the teacher. "Now another question: Who baptized John the Baptist?" This was a real stumper. Finally, after much deliberation, little Johnny's hand went up again. "All right, Johnny, who did baptize John the Baptist?"

"Brother Hyles did," replied the boy.

This took place in a little country church in east Texas in 1949. I was the pastor of the little country church. The teacher was one of our fine teachers, and Johnny was one of our beginner boys. Johnny said a great deal about his pastor in that little statement. He was saying, "My pastor must have baptized almost everybody because he baptizes so much." He was also saying, "My pastor puts a great stress on baptism and even John the Baptist would have been pleased to have Brother Hyles baptize him."

Johnny was right in one respect. Brother Hyles does place a big emphasis on baptism. To be sure, baptism is not necessary to salvation, but it is necessary to obedience. There are several reasons why it is important. The first is, baptism pictures the death, burial and resurrection of Jesus Christ. We should tell the world immediately upon salvation that we believe in these basic truths.

Then, baptism also pictures what has happened to us at salvation. It is somewhat like an X-ray. An X-ray reveals internal conditions to the human eye; baptism reveals salvation to the human eye. One says to the world, "Look, let me show you outwardly what happened to me inwardly. As I go down into the water, I am showing you that I have buried the old life; and as I rise from the water, I am showing you that I have risen to walk in the newness of life. I am a new creature and I want you to see it."

Then, baptism also identifies us with Jesus Christ in His death, burial and resurrection.

Baptism is one of the few things that we can do exactly as Jesus did. Oh, yes, we are to strive to be like Him. We are to follow His example. The first and best way for a Christian to do this is by obeying His command of baptism. Jesus places a great deal of emphasis on baptism. This is shown so vividly by His inclusion of this ordinance in the Great Commission. Had it not been important to Him, He would not have included it in what we commonly call "The Great Commission."

In March of 1965 I went on a tour of Bible lands. It was my privilege to baptize four people in the Jordan River. We walked out into the Jordan River just where the Sea of Galilee flows into the Jordan. With the Sea of Galilee in the background and the Promised Land framing the scene, I, like John the Baptist, baptized in the Jordan. As the five of us walked into the river, a group of nineteen believers sang:

> On Jordan's stormy banks I stand,
> And cast a wishful eye
> To Canaan's fair and happy land,
> Where my possessions lie.
>
> I am bound for the promised land,
> I am bound for the promised land;
> O who will come and go with me?
> I am bound for the promised land.

What a thrill it was to baptize in the Jordan River!

It is, however, my privilege to enjoy that same thrill Sunday after Sunday, as newborn babes in Christ follow the command of the Saviour in believers' baptism. It is my desire in the next few pages to help pastors and churches around the world increase their number of converts and the number of baptisms. May God use these remarks to fulfill that purpose.

1. Baptize both Sunday morning and Sunday evening, and baptize the converts immediately upon salvation. We should make it easy for people to be baptized. It is a step of obedience. It is the *first* step of obedience after salvation. Many churches could double their baptisms simply by baptizing on Sunday morning as well as Sunday evening, by having the baptistry filled at all times, and by having necessary preparation for such services.

This is not foreign to New Testament practice. In fact, in the New Testament, baptism immediately followed salvation. Acts 2:41 says, "Then they that gladly received his word were baptized: and the same day there were added unto them about three thousand souls." Notice the words "the same day." Hence, on Pentecost the converts were baptized immediately.

Now turn to Acts 2:47. "Praising God, and having favour with all the people. And the Lord added to the church daily such as should be saved." Notice that the converts were being added to the church daily. Since the converts were being baptized before being added to the church, this would lead us to believe that they continued baptizing converts immediately upon salvation.

In Acts 8:37 and 38 we read, "And Philip said, If thou believest with all thine heart; thou mayest. And he answered and said, I believe that Jesus Christ is the Son of God. And he commanded the chariot to stand still: and they went down both into the water, both Philip and the eunuch; and he baptized him." Now here was a man whom Philip had never seen. He was of another race and another country. He was just traveling through, yet he was baptized immediately.

Now turn to Acts 9:17 and 18. "And Ananias went his way, and entered into the house; and putting his hands on him said, Brother Saul, the Lord, even Jesus, that appeared unto thee in the way as thou camest, hath sent me, that thou mightest receive thy sight, and be filled with the Holy Ghost. And immediately there fell from his eyes as it had been scales: and he received sight forthwith, and arose, and was baptized." The Apostle Paul likewise was baptized soon after his salvation.

We also found the same thing in Acts 10:47 and 48. "Can any man forbid water, that these should not be baptized, which have received the Holy Ghost as well as we? And he commanded them to be baptized in the name of the Lord. Then prayed they him to tarry certain days." In the house of Cornelius Peter had preached. Many had been saved. Then they were ready for a baptismal service.

In Acts 16:14 and 15 we read, "And a certain woman named Lydia, a seller of purple, of the city of Thyatira, which worshipped God, heard us: whose heart the Lord opened, that she attended unto the things which were spoken of Paul. And when she was baptized, and her household, she besought us, saying, If ye have judged me to be faithful to the Lord, come into my house, and abide there. And she constrained us." Here again we have a convert. Here is a lady that perhaps Paul had never seen before, yet she was saved and immediately baptized. In this same chapter we have a similar story. Look at Acts 16:33. "And he took them the same hour of the night, and washed their stripes; and was baptized, he and all his, straightway." Note the words "the same hour."

Believing that our church should follow the New Testament pattern, the First Baptist Church of Hammond has practiced this for a number of years.

2. *Have a baptistry.* It is absolutely amazing how many churches have no baptistries. It is even more amazing to find Baptist churches without baptistries. Because the word Baptist means baptizers, it is unbelievable to find that many churches will have pews, chairs, choirs, pulpits, etc., but no baptistry. It seems to me that the first thing a Baptist church would want to have would be a baptistry. Not only should a church have a baptistry, but it should be filled at every service for immediate use.

3. *Clothing.* In many cases people are asked to bring an exchange

of clothing with them to the baptismal services. This, of course, means that the convert cannot be baptized in the same service when he is saved. It is far more convenient for the church to provide baptismal robes or smocks for the new converts to wear. This is a worthy project for the ladies' group in the church such as the W. M. S. We have found it wise to have all sizes and keep a generous supply available. We also keep an ample supply of underclothing for the converts.

4. *Scores of towels are kept available for the converts to use.* This means that the convert has to bring nothing with him for baptism. He may be baptized on the "same day," as was the case in the book of Acts.

5. *We have found it wise to keep a generous supply of hair dryers available (especially for the ladies).* These are especially useful for preventing the converts from catching colds, etc., in the wintertime and in colder climates.

6. *We provide plastic caps for the ladies with which to cover their hair if they prefer not to get their hair wet.*

7. *Both men's and women's dressing rooms must be provided for the preparation for baptism.* In these rooms are kept the aforementioned supplies such as hair dryers, smocks, towels, etc. It is also wise to have restroom facilities adjacent to these dressing rooms. Inside the dressing rooms there are little stalls about the size of a telephone booth where people dress for baptism. It is best to have the dressing rooms on either side of the baptistry with a door leading from each into the water. These rooms should be attractive, well lighted and clean.

8. *Helpers are needed.* There are many people involved in making an immediate baptismal service possible. First, there are the folks who work at the altar talking to the new converts and explaining to them that they can be baptized immediately. These workers also point them to the door leading to the stairs and to the baptismal room. Just inside the door there is another worker who is waiting for converts pointing to the stairs leading to the baptistry. Then at the top of the stairs there is another worker to show which is the ladies' room and which is the men's. Then there are three to five ladies who work in the ladies' dressing room and three to five men who work in the men's dressing room passing out towels, smocks, etc. In general, they simply help the converts in their preparation for baptism. Then there is another worker at the top of the steps leading down into the baptistry who explains to the convert how to be baptized before he enters the water.

There are two other men helping me in the water. While I am baptizing a man, one of my helpers in the water is getting a lady down into the water. While the male convert is leaving the baptistry, the lady convert is entering. While she is being baptized, my other helper is preparing another convert and helping him down into the water. After the lady leaves, a man comes, then a lady, then a man, etc. This enables us to baptize four or five converts a minute without any appearance of rushing and without taking less time with each person in the actual experience of baptism. We will baptize an average of twenty-five to thirty each Sunday morning, and the entire baptismal service takes only about ten minutes.

9. *The baptismal service should be an impressive one.* It should be done smoothly and gracefully. People should get the idea that it is not a hard thing to get baptized. Often people do not want to get baptized because they are afraid of the water. Many times this fear is created, or at least enhanced, by a pastor not taking the proper care in the actual administering of the ordinance. If it is done in a crude, jerky way, it may strike fear into the hearts of people, especially little ones who will not want to get baptized because they are afraid of the ordeal.

The pastor stands facing the people and points the convert facing to his left in front of him. He then moves a little to the right of the convert so the congregation can see him. It has been my policy for years to raise my right hand in the air and put my left hand on the elbow of the person being baptized. Then I say,

"In obedience to the command of our Lord and Master, and upon a public profession of your faith in Him, I baptize you, my brother (or sister), in the name of the Father, the Son, and the Holy Spirit. Amen."

Keeping my left hand on his elbow (the arms of the convert are now folded) and putting my right hand on the back of his neck, I lower him carefully into the water until everything is under the water but his face. I then pause very briefly to let him know that I am about to put his face under the water. Then I take a handkerchief, which has been in my left hand, and move my left hand from his elbow, place the handkerchief over his nose, quickly lower his face in the water and back up. At this time I am holding my right hand behind his neck and my left hand with the handkerchief over his face. When he comes up out of the water I immediately place my left hand on his elbow again and raise him to the upright position.

Often I am asked why I do not allow the convert to hold on to my arm or wrist as I lower him under the water in order to give the convert more assurance. This is because I believe baptism is a picture of salvation. Salvation is by grace through faith and not by holding on, hence, I do not like for the convert to hold on to the preacher. It is a small point, to be sure, but I feel that salvation is not perfectly pictured if the convert is holding on to the pastor. I would certainly not make an issue of this point, however.

10. Include the subject of baptism in a sermon almost every Sunday. Just one sentence could be said about baptism each Lord's Day. In other words, the general atmosphere of the church should be that for a Christian not to be baptized is a sin and that to be obedient a new convert must be baptized. The people should get the idea that baptism has nothing to do with salvation. However, they *should* be made to feel that it is a very important step, and that when they get saved, God wants them to be baptized. This certainly does not deviate from the scriptural practice and the example as set forth in the Book of Acts.

Now look at Matthew 28:19 and 20. "Go ye therefore, and teach all nations, baptizing them in the name of the Father, and of the Son, and of the Holy Ghost: Teaching them to observe all things whatsoever I have commanded you: and, lo, I am with you alway, even unto the end of the world. Amen." Notice, if you would please, the imperatives in these verses: Go, teach, baptize and teach. You will notice the simple command of Christ is that we go and tell people how to be saved, baptize them after they are saved, and teach them to do what God commanded us to do. Since God's command to us was go, get people saved and get them baptized, then we are to teach others to go, get people saved and get them baptized. Notice the divine order: Go, teach all nations, baptize and then train them to be soul winners. This is God's plan.

It is sad that many churches make it difficult to get baptized. Take this same logic and use it about other things that a new Christian should do. Should we let a new Christian wait awhile before he tithes? Should we make it hard for him to tithe? Should we make it hard for a new Christian to quit drinking and smoking? Should we advise him to go back to the bar for awhile until he is sure he is saved? Or should we make it easy for him to quit his sins and start tithing? The sad thing is that many of us do not look upon baptism as being an act of obedience on the part of the believer. So in many cases we actually hinder him from being obedient in baptism.

Let us carry out the Great Commission to its fullest, remembering that people are lost without Christ and need to be saved, and they, too, need to be baptized and trained to go back and bring others to the Saviour.

Let's increase our converts and our baptisms.

19. A Soul-Winning Experience

Doug Hiles was won to Christ in his home in the fall of 1960 by Pastor Hyles. The experience was relived so that others could "hear" how to win a soul.

His growth in grace is evidenced by the fact that Brother Doug has become a deacon in the First Baptist Church of Hammond.

MRS. HILES: Hello.

PASTOR: Hello. Mrs. Hiles?

MRS. HILES: Yes.

PASTOR: I am Brother Jack Hyles, pastor of the First Baptist Church in Hammond.

MRS. HILES: How do you do.

PASTOR: Your name is spelled H-I-L-E-S, is it not?

MRS. HILES: That is right.

PASTOR: And mine is spelled H-Y-L-E-S. I wonder if maybe our great, great, great, great, great, great, great, great grandfathers didn't come over on the Mayflower together. Perhaps the spelling has been changed through the years, but I have never seen anyone in all my life outside my own family named Hyles. It is very interesting to me that we have the same name.

MRS. HILES: It is not too common a name.

PASTOR: It is not too common. Mrs. Hiles, I understand that you were in our service recently. Is this right? Let's see—Sunday morning or evening?

MRS. HILES: Both services.

PASTOR: Oh, both services? Well, wonderful, and you were back again on Sunday evening and Wednesday evening also. Was your husband with you?

MRS. HILES: Not on Wednesday. Would you like to come in and meet him?

PASTOR: Well, thank you, thank you, I will. My, it is nice to be inside. It is a little cool outside. Who plays the guitar, Kathy?

MRS. HILES: Doug.

PASTOR: Oh, is that right?

MRS. HILES: This is Doug.

PASTOR: Hello, Doug. How are you?

MR. HILES: How do you do.

PASTOR: I am glad to know you. I am pastor of the First Baptist Church. We are so glad that you came to see us last Sunday. Kathy tells me that you are a guitar player. Is that right?

MR. HILES: Yes, I play a little bit.

PASTOR: Is that a fact? Where do you play, Doug?

MR. HILES: Well, I'm not playing anywhere right now. Before we moved here I did a little work in Nevada in some of the clubs.

PASTOR: Oh, did you?

MR. HILES: Yes, when I was in service, I played.

PASTOR: Well, how interesting. I admire a fellow who plays the guitar. What kind of guitar is this, Doug?

MR. HILES: It is a Gretsch.

PASTOR: A Gretsch? Is it a steel, standard or what?

MR. HILES: Well, it is a regular Spanish guitar.

PASTOR: Oh, a regular Spanish guitar. Wonderful. Are you folks new in town?

MR. HILES: Yes, we are.

PASTOR: Well, fine. From where did you come?

MR. HILES: We came from Wisconsin. I was attending school up there.

PASTOR: Where did you go to school, Doug?

MR. HILES: I went to Milwaukee Civil Engineering for awhile and then I switched over and went to the Automation Institute—IBM school.

PASTOR: You have a varied background—Wisconsin, Nevada, guitar playing, engineering training, etc. Well, this is tremendous. Where do you work here, Doug? Are you employed here in our area?

MR. HILES: Yes, I am with Lever Brothers Company.

PASTOR: What do you do there?

MR. HILES: I am an IBM operator.

PASTOR: Did you learn this in Wisconsin at school?

MR. HILES: Yes, in the Automation Institute.

PASTOR: I see. How do you like it there?

MR. HILES: I like it real well.

PASTOR: I hope you will like it. We want to welcome you to our area. We are glad that you are here and do trust that you will enjoy living in the Calumet region. I also want to say on behalf of our church that we are so glad that you came to see us last Sunday. It is always a joy to have visitors. We are glad that you came.

MRS. HILES: It is a large church.

PASTOR: Yes, it is a very large church.

MR. HILES: We enjoyed the choir very much.

PASTOR: Wonderful. That is good. You know, I like good music. I guess you do because you play the guitar.
I think that you will find, Kathy, that we do have a lot of people, but

I think you will find our church to have a little-type spirit, maybe. We don't play big. We don't act big. Actually, we are just a lot of little people and we love the Lord. I think that you will find after you have been here awhile that we are like the country church back home, and we hope you will come back to see us again. What church did you belong to, Kathy? Do you have a church membership?

MRS. HILES: Yes, in Nevada, I was a Southern Baptist.

PASTOR: Oh, is that a fact? Then you have been saved, have you?

MRS. HILES: Yes, I have.

PASTOR: Do you know, Kathy, that if you died today that you would go to Heaven?

MRS. HILES: I certainly do.

PASTOR: Well, wonderful. When were you saved?

MRS. HILES: When I was about thirteen.

PASTOR: Well, that is good. I am so glad. Doug, are you a Baptist too?

MR. HILES: No, I was raised Methodist. We have been looking around in the area for a church. We have been investigating the Catholic religion.

PASTOR: Oh, I see. Then you were reared a Methodist, were you?

MR. HILES: Yes.

PASTOR: My mother was reared a Methodist. She became a Baptist after I started going to a Baptist church. You are not attending the Catholic church, are you?

MR. HILES: Well, we attended some in Wisconsin. We just have gone to a few around here. We are looking for a church.

PASTOR: Oh, I see. You are interested in the Catholic religion?

MR. HILES: Yes, we have been looking into it.

PASTOR: Well, that is very interesting. We have almost an ecumenical movement right here, don't we? I am a Baptist and Kathy is a Southern Baptist. You are a Methodist and you are thinking of attending the Catholic church. You know the wonderful thing about it, Doug and Kathy, is that you don't have to belong to a church to go to Heaven. It does not matter what church you belong to. If you do know Jesus Christ as your own personal Saviour, you can go to Heaven regardless of the church.

I always say that the church is like a bus station. It doesn't take you to your destination; it is simply a good place to meet the bus that will. So the transportation to Heaven is Jesus Christ. A lot of people meet Him at the church, but you can flag the bus down on the highway too and catch it. So you can be saved in your home as well as you could at church.

Let's forget for a few moments, Doug, that I am a Baptist and that you are considering Catholicism, and let's just think about one thing. I know in our Baptist churches oftentimes people come to me and say, "Pastor, though I have been a Baptist for many years, I really do not know that I am going to Heaven." I am sure that in the Catholic church, or even the Methodist church, there may be numbers of people that may belong to the church but, as some Baptists, they do not really know that if they died they would go to Heaven.

Let me ask you, Doug, do you know that if you died tonight that you would go to Heaven?

MR. HILES: I don't think anyone can really know until they die.

PASTOR: I see. Then you feel that a person cannot know he is saved until he dies. Is that true?

MRS. HILES: I am sure that Doug is a Christian. He reads his Bible a lot.

PASTOR: I see. Well, that is admirable. I am sure that the fact that you have been in the Baptist church, the Methodist church and are now looking into the Catholic religion, means that you are sincere and that you do want to know the truth. I am sure of that. You strike me, Doug, that you are a very sincere man. Let me ask you this, Doug. Suppose that I could show you in the Bible how you could know that if you died, you would go to Heaven, and you could see that a person could know. If you could see it and see what to do, would you do it?

MR. HILES: Yes, I believe that I would if I could agree with you on that point.

PASTOR: In other words, if you could agree that the Bible does teach that you can know, you would do it?

MR. HILES: Yes.

PASTOR: Of course, I John 5:13 says, "These things have I written unto you that believe on the name of the Son of God; that ye may know that ye have eternal life...." I want to go a little further into it. Then if you could see what to do, and if you could agree with me on what the Bible teaches, you would do it?

MR. HILES: Yes, if I knew what to do.

PASTOR: There are only four things that you have to know to go to Heaven. The Bible says that faith cometh by hearing and hearing by the Word of God. You are right. A person should investigate the Word of God to learn what he should do in order to be a Christian.

The first thing that you have to know is that you are a sinner. Let me show you here in the Bible, Doug. In Romans, chapter 3 and verse 10, I want you to notice the first thing I mention is that we must know that we are sinners if we go to Heaven. Do you see right there? Romans 3:10, "As it is written, there is none...."

MR. HILES: "...righteous...."

PASTOR: "...righteous...." That is right. "...no, not one." Do you see that?

MR. HILES: Yes.

PASTOR: Now, this entire third chapter of Romans tells us the condition of the heart of man. Look at the last part of verse 12. We find "...there is none that doeth...."

MR. HILES: "...good...."

PASTOR: "...good...." Right. "...none that doeth good, no, not one." In verse 23, it sums up the entire chapter by saying that we all what?"

MR. HILES: "All have sinned...."

PASTOR: "All have sinned and come short...." Of what?

MR. HILES: "...glory of God."

PASTOR: "...glory of God." Now what this teaches is that all of us are, by nature, sinners. If there is none righteous, that means that I am not righteous, doesn't it?"

MR. HILES: Yes.

PASTOR: And if there is none righteous, that means Kathy is not righteous. Of course, you know that she is not righteous already. But that means that she is not righteous. That means there is none righteous. That means that Jack Hyles has sinned. That means that Kathy Hiles has sinned, and Doug Hiles has sinned, for all of us have sinned. Do you understand that?

MR. HILES: Yes.

PASTOR: So the first thing we know is that every person is by nature a sinner and there is none righteous.

The second thing you have to know, Doug, to become a Christian is that God has placed a price on sin. All of us are sinners and there is a price that must be paid. That price is found in chapter 5 and verse 12, where it says, notice, "Wherefore, as by one man sin entered into the world..." and what by sin, Doug?

MR. HILES: "...death..."

PASTOR: "...death by sin...." And so what?

MR. HILES: "...death...."

PASTOR: "...death passed upon all men, for that all have sinned." About the same thing is said in chapter 6 and verse 23. "For the wages of sin is...."

MR. HILES: "...death...."

PASTOR: "...death...." Right. All right, we find then that all of us are sinners, and we find that God has placed a price on this sin. This price is death. Here is what it means: God made a man and a woman. He put them in the Garden of Eden and said, "You can eat of every tree in this garden but one and that is the tree of the knowledge of good and evil. Adam and Eve, you cannot eat of this tree. If you do, you are going to die." They did eat of the tree. You remember that. The Catholics believe that, the Methodists believe that, and the Baptists believe that. So they did eat of this tree. When they did, they died. They did not drop dead physically. It was first a spiritual death, though the curse of physical death did come upon man. Immediately he ran from God and was separated from God which means that he died spiritually. If man lives without God, he has to die without God. If a person dies without God, he has to live in eternity without God— this is called Hell. It means, Doug, in the final analysis, sin takes us to Hell.

The first thing we notice is a person is a sinner. The second thing is there is a price on sin and that price is death, which ultimately will take the person to Hell. Do you understand that? That is the second thing.

MR. HILES: Yes.

PASTOR: Now, so far in our story, I am a sinner and you are a sinner. Is that true?

MR. HILES: Yes.

PASTOR: And so far in our story, I am going to Hell and you are going to Hell. Is this not true?

MR. HILES: Yes.

PASTOR: The third thing, Doug, that you have to know is found in Romans, chapter 5 and verse 8, and that is that God has paid the price for us already. Look at chapter 5 and verse 8: "But God commendeth his love toward us, in that, while we were yet sinners, Christ...." What?

MR. HILES: "...died for us."

PASTOR: "...died for us." Now what are the wages of sin?

MR. HILES: Death.

PASTOR: Death. What did Christ do for us?

MR. HILES: Died for us.

PASTOR: Right. That means that whatever sin cost, Jesus paid. Does it not?

MR. HILES: Yes.

PASTOR: All right. Then we are sinners, and the wages of sin is death and separation from God. Jesus died for us, which means that Jesus has paid the price for our sins. God sent His only begotten Son into the world. He was God in the flesh. He was born of a virgin. He lived a perfect life. He Himself never sinned. So He Himself did not have to go to Hell, did He? But when He had been here for thirty-three years, He went to the cross. On that cross He said, "My God, my God, why hast thou forsaken me?" This means that He was paying the price for your sins. He was your substitute, your sacrifice, paying your price for sin. So do you understand that now?

MR. HILES: Yes.

PASTOR: Now, Doug, the fourth thing you have to know is that if we would put our faith in Jesus Christ as our Saviour, God will see that faith, and count it for righteousness, transferring all of our sins to Jesus and imputing His righteousness to us. This means the moment that you put your faith in Jesus Christ, God sees Jesus with your sins and sees you with His goodness. Wouldn't it be a wonderful thing to-day to know that every sin was forgiven?

MR. HILES: Yes, it would. But faith is a big word. I mean it takes in quite a scope. You have to live according to the Old Testament and the Ten Commandments and things like this and live a good life, too.

PASTOR: Well, I think that it is admirable that you ought to live a good life. But the thing that happens when you are saved is that God gives you His Holy Spirit, and the Holy Spirit comes in you to live. He lives through you in your Christian life. He is the "Baby Sitter" who takes care of you.

Now, we cannot keep the commandments or even live a good life unless we have God's help. A person must be first born again, receiving Christ by faith and when our faith is placed in Christ, the Holy Spirit comes in us to live. Then He lives through us, works through us, and lets us live the kind of life we ought to live. But it is the faith that makes us God's children.

Now, Doug, let me ask you this: Romans 10:9 and 10 says, "That if thou shalt confess with thy mouth the Lord Jesus, and shalt believe in thine heart that God hath raised him from the dead, thou shalt be saved. For with the heart man believeth unto righteousness [that is the way you do righteous-believing]; and with the mouth confession is made unto salvation." Did you see that?

MR. HILES: Yes.

PASTOR: Doug, let me ask you a question. Do you realize today that you are a sinner?

MR. HILES: Yes, I do.

PASTOR: Do you realize that because we are sinners there is a price on sin which means that if you died tonight, you would go to Hell? Do you realize this?

MR. HILES: Yes, I do.

PASTOR: Doug, that is a very serious matter. Kathy is a Christian, and you are not a Christian. If your apartment were to burn tonight and both of you would go out into eternity, Kathy would go to Heaven and you would go to Hell. You would never see her again. That scares me, Doug. Do you believe, Doug, that Jesus Christ took your sins and died for you on the cross that you might have eternal life?

MR. HILES: Yes, I do.

PASTOR: Do you believe that if you would be willing tonight to bow your head and say, "God, the best I know how, I am trusting Christ in faith as my Saviour and this moment I receive Him," do you believe that God would take you to Heaven if you would mean that?

MR. HILES: Well, I think He would.

PASTOR: He surely would. Doug, let's bow our heads and have a prayer and let me pray that you would do it tonight. Let us just bow our heads and close our eyes. Our Heavenly Father, I am so grateful that Doug has heard the Gospel. Here is a young couple starting out together. They have all of their lives ahead of them, but more than that, all of eternity stretches out before them. Here is Kathy. She is a Christian. She is going to Heaven. Here is Doug. He needs to be a Christian. I pray tonight that he will say yes to Jesus Christ.

Doug, while our heads are bowed and our eyes are closed, I am going to ask you to do something that God would have you to do. I am going to ask you to talk to God in your own words and ask God to forgive you and tell Him tonight you are receiving Jesus Christ as your Saviour. Go ahead and do it, Doug. God will help you. Go ahead, out loud. I hope you will.

Well, Doug, maybe it is a little hard for you to pray. Maybe you can't think of the words. I am going to ask you then to repeat after me this prayer. If you mean it with all of your heart and you do tonight want to receive the Saviour, I am going to ask you to say to God from your heart now, "Dear Lord, forgive my sins."

MR. HILES: Dear Lord, forgive my sins.

PASTOR: And save my soul...

MR. HILES: And save my soul...

PASTOR: Be merciful to me a sinner.

MR. HILES: Be merciful to me a sinner.

PASTOR: I do now receive Jesus Christ as my Saviour...

MR. HILES: I do now receive Jesus Christ as my Saviour...

PASTOR: And I trust Him to take me to Heaven when I die.

MR. HILES: And I trust Him to take me to Heaven when I die.

PASTOR: Doug, while our heads are bowed, if you meant that prayer and you did receive Christ as your Saviour, making this the hour of hours of your life, I am going to ask you, as a token of it, to take my hand. Amen. God bless you.
Our Heavenly Father, I am so glad that Doug has received Christ tonight. I am glad that he by faith has turned to the Saviour. I pray now that you will help him to realize that if he is sincere that his faith has been counted for righteousness and he is your child. In Jesus' name. Amen.
God bless you, Doug.
Now let me ask you a question, Doug. Over here in the Gospel of John, in the third chapter (one of the greatest chapters in all of the Bible) I want you to see this verse: "He that believeth on the Son hath everlasting life." Doug, are you believing on the Son of God tonight?

MR. HILES: Yes, I am.

PASTOR: According to that verse, where would you go if you were to die tonight?

MR. HILES: Well, I would go to Heaven.

PASTOR: Right. Because the Bible says it, that is your hope for Heaven. Doug, turn to Kathy and say, "Kathy, I have just become a Christian."

MR. HILES: I just became a Christian.

PASTOR: Isn't that wonderful? That's wonderful. God bless you, Doug.

Doug, now that you have received Christ as your Saviour, the next thing you ought to do is come to the services and let me tell the people that you received Him. This doesn't mean, necessarily, that you are joining the church but simply means that you are telling the whole world that you are a Christian. Would you be willing to come Sunday to the services and when the invitation is given at the closing of the service, would you be willing to come forward and let me tell the people what has happened in your home today?

MR. HILES: I believe we could do that.

PASTOR: Well, would you promise God that?

MR. HILES: Well, yes, yes, I will.

PASTOR: Let us bow our heads and would you just say this prayer: Dear Lord...

MR. HILES: Dear Lord...

PASTOR: I do promise...

MR. HILES: I do promise...

PASTOR: That I will come forward...

MR. HILES: That I will come forward...

PASTOR: At the First Baptist Church in Hammond...

MR. HILES: At the First Baptist Church in Hammond...

PASTOR: Next Sunday morning.

MR. HILES: Next Sunday morning.

PASTOR: Amen.

MR. HILES: Amen.

PASTOR: God bless you, Doug. I will be going. I have a deacons' meeting. I am a little late. I hope that they don't vote to fire me before I get there. So nice to have met you. Kathy, it was such a joy to meet you. God bless you and I will see you Sunday morning. Goodbye.

III. The Pastor

20. The Wedding

"Marriage is honourable in all, and the bed undefiled: but whore-mongers and adulterers God will judge."—Heb. 13:4.

One of the most wonderful things about pastoring is the privilege of sharing with the people their joys and their sorrows. After a man of God has been with people for many years and shared with them such experiences as praying for their babies, marrying their youth and burying their dead, a tie akin to Heaven should develop.

Few events link a pastor and his people like a beautiful and impressive wedding ceremony. In this chapter we will take into consideration the church wedding with a few comments about a simple private wedding ceremony. As has been said in previous chapters concerning other subjects, an event of such magnitude as a wedding ceremony must of necessity be governed largely by the customs of the area, the church, etc. Then, too, there are many different ways of conducting a beautiful ceremony. In this chapter we simply present one of them. Following is a discussion of the plans and preparation for an impressive wedding ceremony that has provided many blessed experiences and wonderful memories for young couples.

The First Contact

1. The couple should contact the pastor concerning the setting of a date for the marriage and gaining his consent for performing the ceremony. At this first contact the pastor should question the couple very carefully so as to make his decision immediately whether or not he can perform the ceremony. Some pastors do not marry divorced people. Other pastors marry divorced people only under certain circumstances. Some pastors do not marry saved people to unsaved people. Still others do not marry unsaved people at all. The pastor should have his convictions about these matters, and his decision should be governed by them without exception.

If the pastor finds that his convictions will allow him to perform the ceremony, the church calendar should then be examined and the date for the marriage should be set. It is also wise to decide on the rehearsal date at this meeting. It should be stressed to the couple that all members of the wedding party must be present at this rehearsal.

2. *Either at this initial contact; or at a later date; the pastor should talk with the couple concerning their marriage plans.* He should discuss with them the size of the wedding party, expected attendance, etc. At the First Baptist Church in Hammond we give to the couple at this meeting a mimeographed sheet on which are listed some of the rules of our church concerning marriage.

INSTRUCTIONS FOR WEDDING CEREMONIES

Experience has taught us that proper planning and preparation makes for a successful marriage ceremony. Since we want yours to be successful and beautiful, we have found it necessary to make the following suggestions and observations concerning your coming marriage:

1. The following people should be at the rehearsal: Bride, groom, all ushers and attendants, the bride's mother, organist, and soloist. If one or more of these cannot be in attendance, the following are absolutely necessary: Bride, groom, best man, maid of honor, at least one male attendant and lady attendant, and at least two ushers. These would be the bare minimum. In other words, we could not have a successful rehearsal without these present.

2. The bride and groom are responsible for securing their own organist and soloist. The Pastor will be happy to make suggestions and recommendations concerning satisfactory ones, but the responsibility of contact will rest with the bride and groom.

3. There are no set fees for wedding ceremonies or for the use of the fellowship hall or auditorium when the people marrying are members of the First Baptist Church. It has become a tradition, however, for even church members to give a little donation to the custodians because of the many extra hours they work. Oftentimes remuneration is given to the organist and soloist as well. None of these is compulsory, however.

4. For people who are not members of our church, there is a fee for the use of our buildings. There is a $50.00 fee for the use of the auditorium and a $50.00 fee for the use of the fellowship hall, making a total of $100.00 if both wedding and reception are conducted here.

5. Very soon after the setting of the date, the bride and groom should contact the custodians concerning preparations for the wedding and reception. The purpose of this is to discuss the lighting, arrangement of equipment, etc. in the auditorium and fellowship hall. The custodian in charge of the auditorium is Mr. Clarence Goren, 532 Sibley Street, Hammond (931-8602). The custodian for the fellowship hall is Mr. Harold Sullivan, 5508 Calumet Avenue, Hammond (932-5085).

6. No smoking is allowed on the church property during rehearsal, marriage, reception, or any other time. We would appreciate compliance with this rule.

7. No one will be allowed to participate in any rehearsal or wedding who is under the influence of intoxicating beverages. Several times such cases happened at a rehearsal, and the wedding was marred because the person did not properly learn his part at rehearsal time.

8. We ask that no shorts or slacks be worn in any church building at any time.

9. No wedding will be conducted in our auditorium when intoxicating beverages are served at the reception, even if the reception is held away from the church property.

We want yours to be the sweetest and most impressive wedding possible. The above suggestions and rules have been made to make yours exactly that. May God bless you in these days of preparation for one of the most important steps in your life.

These rules should be understood clearly by the couple and should be strictly followed.

It is also a good idea for the pastor to present a good book on marriage to the couple. This book may be a gift or it may be loaned, but they should both agree to read it before the marriage ceremony. The pastor should suggest other books that they could read and make a few general suggestions about marriage itself.

The Rehearsal

1. The rehearsal should be conducted a night or two before the wedding. Without exception, the pastor should be in charge of the rehearsal. In rare instances people are employed by the bride's family to prepare the entire ceremony, etc. In such cases, the pastor should still be in charge of the rehearsal. The marriage ceremony is his, and though he may seek help and advice from others, he should be the director of the rehearsal.

2. All must be present for the rehearsal. This is very important. A typical wedding party would include the bride, the groom, the pastor, the best man, the maid of honor, the ring bearer, the flower girl, two groomsmen, two bridesmaids, and two ushers. (In some cases the groomsmen also act as ushers.) Also at the rehearsal should be the bride's father and mother, the groom's father and mother and any others who might be having a part in the ceremony. It is best for all to be present. In some cases, a few may be unable to attend but no wedding rehearsal should be conducted without the following present: the pastor, the bride, the groom, the best man, the maid of honor, the ring bearer, the flower girl, and the majority of the attendants. It is not uncommon for an usher to fail to attend the rehearsal because he feels that his job is not important. The truth is that the usher's job is the most important in the wedding as far as detail planning is concerned. To have a beautiful wedding there must be a good rehearsal. Mistakes at weddings are oftentimes the result of an improper rehearsal. Hence, all should be present.

3. The rehearsal should start with prayer. This prayer should be offered by the pastor. It should be a simple, sincere and direct request for God to give wisdom so that the ceremony will be spiritual, beautiful, and impressive.

4. The pastor leads the party in going through the wedding three times. First, he talks them through it. The wedding party sits in front of him as he describes the ceremony to them. In some cases he may want to demonstrate, but usually it is sufficient simply to explain to the party the wedding procedure. Then, the wedding is rehearsed quickly. The party simply goes through the motions briskly. Everything except the songs is rehearsed, but it is done at a rapid pace at this particular time. After this quick rehearsal the pastor then asks if there are any questions. When the questions are all answered, it is rehearsed for the final time exactly as it will be carried out on the wedding day. During this final practice the songs may or may not be sung, but everything else is rehearsed in detail. After this final rehearsal, the party is again brought together and the pastor answers any final questions.

5. *The pastor then makes general suggestions concerning the wedding ceremony.* He should remind the party concerning mistakes. If an obvious mistake is made that everyone sees as a mistake it may be retracted. However, most mistakes that are made at wedding ceremonies are made without the knowledge of the audience. If the audience does not know a mistake is being made, it may be carried through to its completion and will appear to be planned.

For example, suppose someone comes in before his or her time. In such a case, he may simply proceed with his mistake, take his place at the altar, and the audience will feel it was a part of the plan. Mistakes should certainly not be given away with grinning, giggling or amateurish behaviour.

It is also a good idea for the pastor to remind the party not to keep their knees locked or their bodies stiffened while standing at the altar. Such a position encourages fainting. Though a person should not be slouchy at the altar, neither should he be stiff.

The male members of the wedding party are reminded as they stand at the altar to keep their hands in front of them with the left hand over the right. If this is not the procedure, they should at least be instructed to act uniformly.

6. *The plan of salvation should be presented and a brief invitation given.* This is only, of course, when the pastor does not know concerning the salvation of the entire wedding party. In most cases, this will be unnecessary but we have had some wonderful experiences by simply closing a ceremony with a very brief explanation of what it means to be a Christian. It is explained to the party that since marriage is a Christian rite and the home is a Christian institution, it would be wonderful if all parties participating were Christians. Within five minutes these few words and the plan of salvation can be given.

The pastor may then simply say, "May we bow our heads for prayer. While our heads are bowed perhaps there is one here tonight who has never received Jesus Christ as his personal Saviour. This would be a wonderful time to make such a decision. If there is one in this gathering who would like to make that decision tonight, would you please signify it by lifting your hand." Then the pastor may lead in the closing prayer. If there are those whose hands have been raised, they should be sought out privately after the rehearsal and not embarrassed in front of the people.

7. To close the rehearsal, a public word of affection and gratitude should be given to the couple. Perhaps words like these would be appropriate: "Now in closing, may I say to the couple how much we appreciate your choosing us to be a part of this wedding. It is a delight and privilege for us to have been chosen to share with you in this happy occasion. Those of us who will participate with you in your ceremony pray that God will help us to do our best to make the ceremony beautiful and one that will provide lasting and precious memories for you. Then, too, we wish for you a long and happy life together. Good night and God bless you."

The Church Wedding

1. The groom and his attendants should meet the pastor in his study fifteen to thirty minutes before the wedding. There the pastor may care for such things as preparing the marriage license, the pinning on of boutonnieres, etc.

2. The bride should arrive at the church at least an hour and a half before the ceremony. This is only if the bride dresses at the church. If possible, the church should provide a dressing area. Our church has a bride's room where the bride and her party may dress. At any rate, the bride should arrive in ample time so as to avoid rushing on her wedding day.

3. The ushers should start seating people as they arrive. One usher should seat the groom's guests and the other, the bride's guests. Care should be taken not to use the center aisle for the seating of guests. The usher should extend his arm to each lady as he escorts her and her husband to their seats. In the case of several ladies being in one party he should extend his arm to the one he thinks is the eldest. He should remain on the outside of the section where his party is to be seated. In other words, the lady is to be nearer the section of seats. He proceeds to the row where he plans to seat the party. He then turns and faces the rear of the building, showing with his hand the seat to the guests. This procedure is continued until the beginning of the wedding.

4. The wedding begins with the seating of the groom's parents. The usher extends his arm to the groom's mother and escorts her to her seat. The father follows. This is the first use of the center aisle thus far. After seating the groom's parents the usher returns to the back of the auditorium.

5. Next is the seating of the bride's mother. When the groom's parents are seated, the usher who has been seating the bride's friends extends his arm to the bride's mother and escorts her to her seat. The bride's mother should be seated at the front on the first or second seat, just to the left of the center aisle. She should leave enough room for her husband to join her after he gives the bride away. The groom's parents are seated just across the aisle from the bride's mother on the corresponding pew. The usher then returns to the back and joins the other usher immediately for the lighting of the candles. It is best for each usher to come down a side aisle. Each lights one of the two candelabras from the outside candle in. Care should be made to stay together. After the lighting of the last candle each usher extinguishes his lighter (usually a candle or a specially prepared candle lighter), walk to the center where the ushers meet and prepare to walk up the center aisle to the back of the auditorium.

6. *Rolling out of the carpet is done next if one is being used.* In many weddings, the ushers roll out a white carpet in preparation for the coming of the wedding party. This carpet is usually in a roll at the altar. A handle is provided on each side of the roll. The ushers reach down, take the handle, and roll the carpet up the center aisle. After this is finished, the ushers may stand at the back doors for the seating of late comers. If the ushers are also acting as groomsmen, they must hurriedly go to their places behind the platform where they join the pastor, the groom, and the best man in preparation for their entrance.

7. *The first wedding song is then sung.* This song should be a typical wedding song such as "Because," "I Love You Truly," "Always," etc. The organist, who has been playing appropriate music since the seating of the first guest, now plays a brief introduction and accompanies the soloist in the first song.

8. *The pastor enters.* He normally enters from a door to the right (facing the platform) of the altar. He proceeds to the altar taking his place at the center facing the people.

9. *The groom, best man, and groomsmen enter.* Approximately fifteen seconds after the pastor enters, the groom enters followed at a comfortable distance by the best man and the groomsmen. He takes his place at the altar in front of the pastor, facing toward the rear of the auditorium so he can see the bride as she enters. The other men in the ceremony take their places in order beside the groom. They also face the rear of the auditorium.

10. *The bridesmaids enter.* As soon as the men are in their places the first bridesmaid starts down the center aisle. When she reaches the altar she takes her place opposite the groomsman on the extreme end. When she is in place, the second bridesmaid comes to her place. If there are more than two bridesmaids participating, they continue coming one at a time until all are in place.

11. *The maid of honor enters.* Once the bridesmaids are in place, the maid of honor comes down the center aisle taking her place at the altar opposite the best man.

12. *The ring bearer and flower girl enter.* In some cases there is
no ring bearer, in other cases there is no flower girl, and in rare instances there are neither. If the wedding includes both the ring bearer
and a flower girl, the ring bearer follows the maid of honor. He starts
down the aisle as soon as the maid of honor is in place. When he is in
place (which is at the side of the best man), the flower girl enters
spreading flowers as she walks the aisle until she comes to the altar
where she takes her place at the side of the maid of honor. The entire
party is looking toward the rear waiting for the entrance of the bride.

13. *The bride enters.* The organist begins playing the wedding
march more loudly as the bride enters on the arm of her father.
(Customarily, the bride is on the right arm of her father. In some
areas, however, custom dictates that the bride be on the left arm of
the father. This enables the father to give the bride's right arm to the
groom at the altar.) The bride and the father proceed slowly down the
aisle until arriving at the front pew. (In some cases, the second or
third pew may be preferable.) The bride and her father stop, the organist plays more softly, and the pastor says, "Who gives the bride
away?" or "Who giveth this woman in marriage?" The father replies,
"I do," or "Her mother and I do" and in turn gives the bride to the
groom. The groom offers the bride his left arm and the two of them
approach the pastor. As they take their final step toward the pastor
the wedding party turns to face the pastor forming a semicircle
around him.

14. *As the party is at the altar, the soloist sings another appropriate wedding song.* It is good for those at the altar, if at all possible, to look at the soloist. Of course, this is impossible for the pastor whose back is to the musicians.

15. *Following the second song, the pastor then enters into the ceremony proper.* This includes a few fitting words, the saying of the
vows, the exchanging of the rings, the pronouncing of the couple as
husband and wife, and the closing prayer. Oftentimes, the closing
prayer is preceded by a prayer song such as "The Lord's Prayer" or
"The Wedding Prayer." This is followed by the pastor's closing
prayer.

16. *The kiss follows the prayer.* As the pastor finishes his prayer
the bride and groom turn toward each other. The groom lifts the
bride's veil and places a brief, but impressive, kiss upon her lips.
The pastor quotes, *"What therefore God hath joined together, let not
man put asunder."* This is to be the length of the kiss. When the kiss
is over, the bride and groom turn facing the people. The pastor steps
to the side of the bride, places his left hand on her right elbow and
gestures with his right hand to the people as he says, "I now present
to you Mr. and Mrs. John Doe." He then steps back to his original
place as the organist plays the recessional. The bride and groom

march together to the rear of the building followed by the ring bearer and flower girl, the best man and the maid of honor, and each grooms-man with his corresponding bridesmaid. They then march to the rear of the auditorium or to the reception hall where they form the receiving line. Following is the order of the receiving line: Mother of the bride, father of the groom, mother of the groom, father of the bride, the bride, the groom, the lady attendants in order of honor, the ring bearer and flower girl. The best man, groomsmen, and ushers are not to stand in the receiving line.

The Reception

If the reception is being held on the church property, it is wise for the pastor and the bride and groom to proceed to the fellowship hall or the place of the reception where the bride and groom may participate in the cake-cutting ceremonies. Then the pastor gives instructions as to the refreshments and leads in prayer. While the people are being served the wedding party may return to the auditorium to reenact the ceremony for pictures.

The Pictures

The pastor should always recommend that a photographer be secured and that pictures be taken. This is vitally important. It is not fitting for pictures to be taken during the actual ceremony. The photographer should arrive several minutes before the ceremony. He should get some good casual shots of the groom as he waits in the pastor's study, of the pastor or best man as he pins the flower on the groom's coat, or perhaps even of the groom signing the marriage license. The photographer may then proceed to the bride's dressing room where he may photograph the bride's helpers preparing her veil, etc. A splendid picture may be taken of the male members of the wedding party as they wait outside the door of the auditorium. Then pictures may be taken of the bridesmaids as they enter as well as of the flower girl, ring bearer, maid of honor, and bride. Once the wedding party is at the altar, however, the photographer should be seated in order to add to the impressiveness of the ceremony.

After the ceremony, pictures should be taken of the cake-cutting ceremonies and much of the ceremony should be reenacted at the altar. A picture of the entire party should be taken in their places just as they were during the ceremony itself. Pictures should be taken of the exchanging of the rings, the kiss, the pastor giving the marriage license to the bride and groom, the parents with the bride and groom, and single shots of the bride. Other pictures as the bride and groom request should be taken at this time.

Other Suggestions

1. The atmosphere. The pastor and all who participate in the wedding ceremony should work to make it a sweet and appropriate occasion. It should not be stiff or starchy but the atmosphere should lend to make it exactly what it is—two young people who love each other are sweetly becoming one.

2. A recording could be made. One of the most treasured things that a young couple could receive as a wedding gift would be a tape recording of the ceremony. This may easily be prepared by the thoughtful pastor and the wise church.

The Private Wedding

The marriage can take place in the study or the parsonage. The pastor should always encourage young people to have public weddings. However, there are times when this is impossible or unwise. In such cases, the wedding may be conducted in the pastor's study or even in the parsonage. On some very rare occasions the pastor may even be asked to go to someone's home to conduct a wedding ceremony. In any of the aforementioned cases, the pastor should see to it that the wedding is a very impressive one. He should insist that someone take pictures and he should spend much time talking to the couple about the seriousness of the occasion.

Even if the pastor refuses to marry a couple, he should have a personal conference with them. It is unwise to say "no" to a couple over the telephone even if you know that you cannot perform the marriage. Many times I have talked to a couple by phone to find that one, or both, were unsaved. Since I do not marry unsaved people I could have given an immediate "no" answer but rather than that, I told them I would like to talk with them in my study. I have won many to the Lord Jesus Christ thereby enabling them to meet the qualifications so I could marry them. This is an excellent chance for a soul-winning opportunity.

21. A Wedding Ceremony

(Following is an actual wedding ceremony recorded and transcribed as conducted at the First Baptist Church of Hammond on Saturday, September 30, 1967.)

(The organ is played approximately twenty minutes as the guests are seated and the ushers light the candles and roll out the bridal carpet.)

Solo by Mrs. Jack Hyles:

> Because you come to me with naught save love,
> And hold my hand and lift mine eyes above,
> A wider world of hope and joy I see,
> Because you come to me.
>
> Because you speak to me in accent sweet,
> I find the roses waking 'round my feet,
> And I am lead thru tears and joy to thee
> Because you speak to me.
>
> Because God made thee mine I'll cherish thee
> Thru light and darkness, thru all time to be,
> And pray His love may make our love divine,
> Because God made thee mine.

(The organ is played as the bridal party enters, followed by the entrance of the bride and her father, who stop at the front seat.)

PASTOR: Who gives the bride away?

FATHER: Her mother and I do.

(The bride takes her place at the altar by the groom.)

Solo by Mrs. Jack Hyles:

I'll be loving you, always
With a love that's true, always,
When the things you've planned
Need a helping hand,
I will understand, always, always.

Days may not be fair, always
That's when I'll be there, always,
Not for just an hour,
Not for just a day,
Not for just a year, but always.

Pastor's Prayer

PASTOR: Let us pray together. We thank Thee, our Heavenly Father, that for a Christian man and a Christian woman who love Thee and marry in Thy will, marriage is not for just a day, or even a year, or even 'til death parts them, but we thank Thee it is for always. Even death itself cannot part the people of God, for we have a home eternal in Heaven prepared by Thee. We thank Thee for these two young friends who have found Thy will for their lives and Thy partner for life. Now we invoke Thee to be with us at this altar. We pray that Thou wouldst solemnize the vows and make sacred the words that we say. Bless the home that is to be established. In Jesus' name. Amen.

Pastor's Comments

Ronald Hilliard and Mary Ann Sallade have come to me expressing their desire and their conviction that it is God's will that they become husband and wife. It must be a wonderful, wonderful thing for a mother and father to invest their lives in an only child such as Ron, and then to come to the occasion such as this where they see the fruit of their labors in a fine Christian lad such as Ron. Then it must be equally gratifying to know that he is marrying the kind of young lady that is pleasing to God and that will make for him a dedicated, Christian wife. Then it must be a wonderful thing for a couple to invest their lives in an only daughter and have her become a sweet, charming, dedicated Christian as is Mary Ann. It must be equally gratifying for them to realize that God has given to her a fine Christian young man for a husband. We rejoice because of this hour.

It is certainly fitting, Ron, for you and Mary Ann to be married here at this altar. At this altar so many wonderful, wonderful things have happened to you. At this church so many fine things have happened. Ron was saying to me awhile ago that everything he has asked God for since he's been right with the Lord, God has given it to him. Certainly, this event this evening is an answer to one of those prayers. They met here at First Baptist Church. In fact, I believe, Mary Ann and Ron, it was back at the back door near where you came forward a minute ago, that you first met. I think it was on the way to the Pioneer Sunday School class, if I am not mistaken.

Ron walked this aisle, knelt at this altar, and gave his life to God. Mary Ann was reared in this church, and we have no finer people than Mary Ann and her family. It was at this church where they did their courting. We rejoiced as we saw them fall in love with each other. It is very significant, I think, that it was on the way to prayer meeting on Wednesday night when Ron gave the engagement ring to Mary Ann. In these days of what we call juvenile delinquency and in these days of divorce, and homes breaking up, it is refreshing—yea, wonderful, for us to come to an occasion such as this.

Ron, this is your wedding day. You are about to become a husband with all the privileges, and, yea, responsibilities involved. You said to me before we walked in a minute ago, that you hoped God would help you become the kind of husband you ought to be. You take upon yourself a great responsibility today. This is one of the greatest responsibilities of life. May God give you leadership as you say to Mary Ann, "Mary Ann, follow me as I follow Christ."

Mary Ann, this is the day of all days for a young lady. This is your wedding day. You are about to become a wife, the queen of a home, a helpmate of a godly young man. Today you fulfill the purpose for which God made you. For God looked one day and saw that man could not make it alone. That man needed a helpmeet and He took from his wounded side a rib and from that rib He made a woman. He brought the woman to the man that she might be a helpmeet. This is the purpose for woman and you fulfill that purpose this evening. As your pastor, as your families, and as your friends, we wish for you the best of God's blessings both here at this altar and in the days to come.

Vows

If you, Ronald Hilliard, and you, Mary Ann Sallade, have freely and deliberately chosen each other as partners for life, would you please join your right hands.

Ron Hilliard, will you have this woman to be your wedded wife; will you love her, honor and keep her in sickness as in health, in poverty as in wealth, and forsaking all others, keep thee only unto her so long as you both shall live—do you so promise?

RON HILLIARD: I do.

PASTOR: Mary Ann Sallade, will you have this man to be your wedded husband? Will you love him, honor and keep him in sickness as in health, in poverty as in wealth, and forsaking all others, keep thee only unto him so long as you both shall live—do you so promise?

MARY ANN SALLADE: I do.

PASTOR: Ron, would you repeat after me the following words, please: I, Ronald Hilliard...

RON HILLIARD: I, Ronald Hilliard...

PASTOR: Take thee, Mary Ann Sallade...

RON HILLIARD: Take thee, Mary Ann Sallade...

PASTOR: To be my wedded wife.

RON HILLIARD: To be my wedded wife.

PASTOR: To have and to hold...

RON HILLIARD: To have and to hold...

PASTOR: From this day forward...

RON HILLIARD: From this day forward...

PASTOR: For better, for worse...

RON HILLIARD: For better, for worse...

PASTOR: For richer, for poorer...

RON HILLIARD: For richer, for poorer...

PASTOR: In sickness and in health...

RON HILLIARD: In sickness and in health...

PASTOR: To love and cherish...

RON HILLIARD: To love and cherish...

PASTOR: 'Til death do us part...

RON HILLIARD: 'Til death do us part...

PASTOR: Mary Ann, would you repeat after me the following words, please: I, Mary Ann Sallade...

MARY ANN SALLADE: I, Mary Ann Sallade...

PASTOR: Take thee, Ronald Hilliard...

MARY ANN SALLADE: Take thee, Ronald Hilliard...

PASTOR: To be my wedded husband...

MARY ANN SALLADE: To be my wedded husband...

PASTOR: To have and to hold...

MARY ANN SALLADE: To have and to hold...

PASTOR: From this day forward...

MARY ANN SALLADE: From this day forward...

PASTOR: For better, for worse...

MARY ANN SALLADE: For better, for worse...

PASTOR: For richer, for poorer...

MARY ANN SALLADE: For richer, for poorer...

PASTOR: In sickness and in health...

MARY ANN SALLADE: In sickness and in health...

PASTOR: To love, cherish, and obey...

MARY ANN SALLADE: To love, cherish, and obey...

PASTOR: 'Til death do us part.

MARY ANN SALLADE: 'Til death do us part.

Exchanging of Rings

PASTOR: May I have the rings, please. I suspect no way has been found to show one's love for another any more typically of true love than the exchanging of a ring. A ring is beautiful as is love. A ring never ends, and your love will never end. You join millions of people who through the generations of mankind have said to each other, "I love you and I express that love by giving you a ring."

Ron, as you give this ring to Mary Ann you are saying, "Mary Ann, I love you with a love as beautiful and as never-ending as this ring." To show that love for her would you take this beautiful ring and place it upon the third finger of her left hand. As you do, you will give it to her because you love her, and she will wear it to show the world her love for you.

Now, Mary Ann, you are saying, "Ron, I too want to show you my love, and I show you that love by placing this ring upon your finger. I give you my life, my love, and my heart." In so doing would you please place the ring upon the third finger of his left hand. You will give it to him because you love him, and Ron, you will wear it because you love her.

Pronouncing of Husband and Wife

For as much then as you, Ronald Hilliard, and you, Mary Ann Sallade, have offered yourselves each to the other, believing it God's will that you become one flesh, and believing that God has led you to this place, as your pastor, an officer of the laws of the State of Indiana, and a minister of the Gospel of Jesus Christ, in the presence of your family, these friends, and our Heavenly Father, I take great pleasure in pronouncing you as husband and wife. Let us pray.

Solo by Mrs. Jack Hyles:

> Our Father, which art in Heaven,
> Hallowed be Thy name.
> Thy kingdom come.
> Thy will be done in earth,
> As it is in Heaven.
> Give us this day our daily bread.
> And forgive us our debts,
> As we forgive our debtors.
> And lead us not into temptation;
> But deliver us from evil:
> For Thine is the kingdom, and the power,
> And the glory forever. Amen.

Closing Prayer

PASTOR: Our Heavenly Father, it was at this altar that we first met Ron. It was here on this corner where we first met Mary Ann. It was here where they each met the other, and now we come to the same place to observe them as they become one flesh. We thank Thee that this shall be the place where they shall grow in grace and where they shall continue to know Thee better and love Thee more. Bless their home. Bless their life together. May peace, love, joy, and all the blessings and goodness of God be given to each of them. In Jesus' name. Amen.

(The bride and groom kiss, then turn and face the audience.)

PASTOR: What...God hath joined together, let not man put asunder." It is a real joy to introduce to you Mr. and Mrs. Ronald Hilliard.

(Organ music is played as bridal party exits.)

22. The Funeral

Few things should endear the pastor to the hearts of the people more than a dignified, appropriate and comforting funeral service. We are admonished by the Scriptures to "weep with them that weep." We should mourn with those who mourn. May we learn to do it more like the Master did.

1. The pastor should prepare himself for the service. This, of course, would include preparation for the message and preparation of his own heart. It has been my policy for years to spend a few moments before entering the service to picture myself sitting in the seat of the bereaved family and then to wander back to that day when I did sit there. By placing himself in the position of the bereaved, the pastor will be prepared to speak words of comfort.

2. The beginning of the service will vary with the customs of an area. Customs and practices at funeral services often vary even within an area. For example, sometimes the pastor begins the service by leading the family down the center aisle. The pastor enters the auditorium by the rear of the building. He proceeds down the center aisle, walking slowly, and is followed by the family. He then enters the pulpit and when all the family is in place, the pastor and family are seated.

In other cases, the pastor enters the pulpit from a side door just before the family enters. He then asks the people in the audience to stand as the family enters. The audience stands as the family comes down the center aisle to their appointed place.

In other areas, the pastor simply waits until all are seated and then he quietly enters through a side door. His entrance marks the beginning of the service. In my ministry, this is the plan I have followed through the years.

3. The order of service will also vary with the customs of the area but it has been our practice to have this very simple order of service:

1. Song
2. Obituary, Scripture, and prayer by pastor
3. Song
4. Message by pastor

4. Use appropriate songs. Oftentimes, the family requests the use of certain songs. By all means, these requests should be granted. If, however, the choosing of the songs is left to the pastor or to the singer, appropriate songs should be chosen. I personally prefer songs of comfort to the family rather than songs about Heaven, etc. Of course, either type is appropriate but what could be more helpful at a funeral service than songs like "Does Jesus Care?" and "What a Friend We Have in Jesus."

5. The reading of the obituary is standard procedure in some areas. It seems wise for the pastor to give the name of the deceased at least. The minimum would be something like this: "These lovely flowers, this beautiful music, and our attendance in this place today are in memory of the long and beautiful life of Mr. John Doe, who served his Lord, his church, his family, and his community well. May God bless and strengthen those who mourn his passing." From this simple statement to a complete obituary listing the survivors, etc., is appropriate.

6. Read an appropriate Scripture. Once again, I think it best that this Scripture be directed to the grieving. I like passages on comfort, strength, and God's promise to help. The Twenty-third Psalm is always appropriate. The Ninety-first Psalm is a wonderful funeral passage. The pastor also may decide to choose to read the Scripture from whence he will speak. The Scripture may, or may not, be connected with the funeral message. It should not be too lengthy a Scripture.

7. A brief prayer should then be offered. This prayer, as are the aforementioned, is basically for the grieving. It is too late to pray for the deceased but the grieving need strength and help.

8. The prayer is followed by another appropriate song of comfort and help.

9. The message should definitely be appropriate. On some rare occasion, perhaps it could be a eulogy. More often, however, it should be directed to those who mourn. In any case, the deceased should be mentioned and, if appropriate, a few words of eulogy given. The pastor should avoid unwise and unkind remarks. If the deceased was an unsaved person, the pastor may direct his entire remarks to the living.

It is usually best to make the funeral message brief. From fifteen to twenty minutes is usually adequate, and if the message is prepared and sincerely delivered, much comfort can be given. Much good can be done in this brief period.

10. An invitation should be given. Now by this I do not mean that the same type of invitation should be given as would be given in a revival meeting. I have made it a policy for many years simply to ask the people to bow their heads at the close of the message. I will say something like this:

"Now with our heads bowed, I'm wondering if in this small gathering today there is someone who has never received the Lord Jesus Christ as Saviour. If such is the case, may I lovingly and tenderly tell you what a wonderful thing it is to be a Christian, and may I recommend the Saviour to you. If there is someone in the service today who has never received the Saviour but would like to at this moment, would you please signify by quietly lifting your hand while every head is bowed and every eye is closed. Thank you and God bless you."

Then immediately the pastor prays again. This is the closing prayer of the service. Be very careful here not to offend and to be very gentle and gracious.

11. The pastor then proceeds to the head of the casket. He remains there as the people walk by and view the body. As the immediate family comes to the casket the pastor should step beside them and speak words of comfort. A simple reminder that this is not the deceased but simply his body, sometimes helps. Oftentimes, simply a pat on the back or a touch of the elbow helps. The pastor, once again, should be very appropriate in this trying time.

12. The pastor then precedes the casket as the pallbearers carry it to the hearse. Very slowly the pastor walks in front of the casket, Bible in hand. When he arrives at the door of the hearse he stands to the side as the casket is loaded. Then he proceeds to his own car, or to the funeral director's car, as he chooses, for the ride to the cemetery.

13. The pastor leads the casket to the grave. When the family and friends arrive at the grave, the pastor stands at the door of the hearse as the casket is unloaded. He then precedes the pallbearers as they carry the casket from the hearse to the grave. He stands at the head of the casket for the graveside service.

14. Have a brief and appropriate graveside service. In some cases the reading of a passage of Scripture and a prayer is all that is necessary. In other cases, just a brief word would be appropriate. This depends upon the situation and the area. It is best here to read some Scripture about the resurrection or the coming of the Lord Jesus Christ, reminding the people that the body shall rise again. Passages from I Thessalonians 4 and I Corinthians 15 are very helpful here.

15. The pastor then speaks a word to nearest of kin. This may be done by a handshake and a word of comfort before the service is dismissed after the closing prayer, or it may be done after the service is dismissed on the way to the cars. Just a brief word assuring the bereaved of the pastor's concern and prayers is all that is necessary.

16. The people of the church should be trained to have funeral services in the church building. Now, of course, it is not a sin to have a funeral service in a funeral chapel but there are many of us who still believe the church building is the best place to have a funeral. I stress this to my people and have through the years. Funeral directors oftentimes do not prefer this. In fact, most funeral directors would prefer having the services in the chapel. This is certainly understandable, but it is also understandable that a person who serves God in his church through the years would want to have his service in the church building.

17. The pastor should always remember to be appropriate in his dress, words, and manners. A funeral service is no time to spring your most recent novel idea and it is no time to spring a surprise. Always be appropriate.

18. Before the funeral service the church should be very helpful to the bereaved. Someone in the church should be given the responsibility of contacting the family and arranging for food to be brought from the church members. The pastor should go by for a brief visit discussing the service and offering the services of the church in any need that might arise.

23. A Funeral Service

(Saturday, February 18, 1967 — 11:00 a.m.)

Mr. Fay Ault, Deacon Emeritus of the First Baptist Church, went "Home" on Wednesday, February 15, 1967. The funeral service was conducted the following Saturday morning by Pastor Hyles. Assistant Pastor William J. Bednar of the Calvary Baptist Church of Binghamton, New York, son-in-law of Brother Ault, read the Scripture and prayed.

(The organ is played as the people are seated.)

Duet by Mr. and Mrs. Lindsay Terry (the music director and his wife):

In the Sweet By and By

There's a land that is fairer than day,
And by faith we can see it afar;
For the Father waits over the way,
To prepare us a dwelling-place there.

Chorus:

In the sweet by and by,
We shall meet on that beautiful shore;
In the sweet by and by,
We shall meet on that beautiful shore.

We shall sing on that beautiful shore
The melodious songs of the blest,
And our spirits shall sorrow no more,
Not a sigh for the blessing of rest.

To our bountiful Father above,
We will offer our tribute of praise,
For the glorious gift of His love,
And the blessings that hallow our days.

PASTOR: This tremendous crowd and these beautiful flowers are here in honor of the long and wonderful life of our brother and friend, Fay Ault. It is our desire as pastor and musicians that God will help us to help you and help lighten the load a bit. We trust that His grace shall be sufficient and that He will use us today as we celebrate the

Home-going and hold the Commencement Exercises for the graduation of our brother, who truly graduated with honors.

In a pastorate of nearly eight years (and many of you have shared almost all of these eight years with me) a pastor and people share many unusual, wonderful, and yes, sorrowful experiences. In just two hours and forty-five minutes from now, this pulpit will be removed, and, instead of tears and heartache, there will be joy, the throwing of rice, the opening of gifts, and the sharing of wonderful expressions of congratulations. These are typical of the joys and sorrows that we share as pastor and people. In a church the size of ours, and in a church, I think, with the greatness of ours, it is wonderful that God can let us, seemingly, rejoice and sorrow at the same time.

We come together this afternoon as friends, pastor and people because a member of the body of Christ has been taken, which means that we other members of the same body are suffering. When my hand suffers, I suffer all over. When a member of our body here at First Baptist suffers, each of us suffers. We would have you know, Mrs. Ault and family, that we suffer with you. We do not quite understand the extent of your suffering, but we want you to know that we too suffer. Our hearts weep, not as much as yours, but as really as yours.

READING OF THE SCRIPTURE AND PRAYER

MR. WILLIAM J. BEDNAR (Assistant pastor of the Calvary Baptist Church, Binghamton, New York, son-in-law of Mr. Fay Ault): I have selected three portions from God's Word familiar to many of us, just reassuring us of that blessed hope that we have in Christ. I would like to have you think just a moment upon that passage in I Corinthians 15:12-26:

"Now if Christ be preached that he rose from the dead, how say some among you that there is no resurrection of the dead? But if there be no resurrection of the dead, then is Christ not risen: And if Christ be not risen, then is our preaching vain, and your faith is also vain. Yea, and we are found false witnesses of God; because we have testified of God that he raised up Christ: Whom he raised not up, if so be that the dead rise not. For if the dead rise not, then is not Christ raised: And if Christ be not raised, your faith is vain; ye are yet in your sins. Then they also which are fallen asleep in Christ are perished. If in this life only we have hope in Christ, we are of all men most miserable. But now is Christ risen from the dead, and become the firstfruits of them that slept. For since by man came death, by man came also the resurrection of the dead. For as in Adam all die, even so in Christ shall all be made alive. But every man in his own order: Christ the firstfruits; afterward they that are Christ's at his

coming. Then cometh the end, when he shall have delivered up the kingdom to God, even the Father; when he shall have put down all rule and all authority and power. For he must reign, till he hath put all enemies under his feet. The last enemy that shall be destroyed is death."

Then Paul in his Thessalonian letter has this to say in I Thessalonians 4:13-18:

"But I would not have you to be ignorant, brethren, concerning them which are asleep, that ye sorrow not, even as others which have no hope. For if we believe that Jesus died and rose again, even so them also which sleep in Jesus will God bring with him. For this we say unto you by the word of the Lord, that we which are alive and remain unto the coming of the Lord shall not prevent them which are asleep. For the Lord himself shall descend from heaven with a shout, with the voice of the archangel, and with the trump of God: and the dead in Christ shall rise first: Then we which are alive and remain shall be caught up together with them in the clouds, to meet the Lord in the air: and so shall we ever be with the Lord. Wherefore comfort one another with these words."

Then Peter has a few words for us in I Peter 1:3-8:

"Blessed be the God and Father of our Lord Jesus Christ, which according to his abundant mercy hath begotten us again unto a lively hope by the resurrection of Jesus Christ from the dead, To an inheritance incorruptible, and undefiled, and that fadeth not away, reserved in heaven for you, Who are kept by the power of God through faith unto salvation ready to be revealed in the last time. Wherein ye greatly rejoice, though now for a season, if need be, ye are in heaviness through manifold temptations: That the trial of your faith, being much more precious than of gold that perisheth, though it be tried with fire, might be found unto praise and honour and glory at the appearing of Jesus Christ: Whom having not seen, ye love; in whom, though now ye see him not, yet believing, ye rejoice with joy unspeakable and full of glory."

May God add His blessings to this reading of His infallible Word.

Shall we unite our hearts together in prayer.

Our Father, we thank Thee for the glorious hope that is ours in Christ Jesus. We thank Thee, our Father, for His faithfulness in the light of these promises. And we thank Thee, Father, that He is coming again to receive unto Himself those who have left our presence and also those, our Father, who remain. We thank Thee for that place that we have in Christ now—those from among us who have passed on into Thy presence. We thank Thee for the testimony of our beloved one. We thank Thee for his influence upon this immediate family and upon others outside the family. We thank Thee, our Father, that Thou hast seen fit to usher him into Thy presence because his work was finished here. We thank Thee, Father, that he is now seated in the heavenlies in Christ Jesus today. We thank Thee that he is rejoicing, no doubt, with the other saints of old who have long since entered into Thy presence.

We would remember, our Father, those who possibly know not Christ as our beloved one knew Him. There might be some, our Father, who have yet to receive Christ as their Saviour. We pray that through this experience they may come to realize their need of Jesus Christ and receive Him as their Saviour. And then should Thou come to receive them, we know that they will be ready to be ushered into Thy glorious presence.

Father, we pray for loved ones. Be with Mrs. Ault. Strengthen, uphold and encourage her. Our Father, we pray that because of this experience she may have a new light shed upon the glory that Thou hast for each and every one who professes to know Thy name. We pray for strength for the other members of the family. We pray that Thou wilt comfort their hearts. Console them by Thy presence.

We thank Thee, Father, that Thou art the Answer to every need in our lives. Whenever there are seasons of refreshing, we can thank Thee. When there are seasons of depression and distress, we still can thank Thee. We thank Thee, our Father, "that all things work together for good to them that love God, to them who are the called according to [Thy] purpose." Bless the ministry of this hour to the furtherance of the gospel testimony here and far. We pray in Jesus' name. Amen.

Solo by Mrs. Jack Hyles:

A Child of the King

My Father is rich in houses and lands,
He holdeth the wealth of the world in His hand!
Of rubies and diamonds, of silver and gold,
His coffers are full, He has riches untold.

Chorus:

I'm a child of the King,
A child of the King:
With Jesus my Saviour
I'm a child of the King.

My Father's own Son, the Saviour of men,
Once wandered on earth as the poorest of them;
But now He is pleading our pardon on high,
That we may be His when He comes by and by.

A tent or a cottage, why should I care?
They're building a palace for me over there:
Tho' exiled from home, yet, still I may sing:
All glory to God, I'm a child of the King!

Message:

The Will of Mr. Fay Ault

PASTOR: We come this morning to execute the will and to distribute the inheritance of Mr. Fay Ault. From the time I heard, walking through this door the other day, that he had passed away, until today, one Scripture has been on my mind. It is strange how this happens. You don't think about the Scripture until someone is gone and then upon their Home-going it seems that one Scripture (I have never preached at a funeral on this Scripture before) comes to mind. This Scripture came to my mind as I thought about Mr. Ault, and, of course, as I pictured him in his usual place here in the church: "To an inheritance incorruptible, and undefiled, and that fadeth not away..." (I Pet. 1:4).

I think for a few moments that we will leave the usual type of funeral message and execute the will, for he did leave a will. He left in his will something for each person in this room today. If you will, allow me to be the executor and distribute the inheritance. I will list for you a few of the things that I find in the will of Mr. Fay Ault.

He Left Something for the Grandchildren

We first find something in the will for the grandchildren. Oh, I doubt if you will be rich the rest of your lives because you are the grandchildren of Fay Ault. I doubt if your bank account will swell a great deal because you had the privilege of being in his family.

Far more valuable are the contents of this will for you than if he had left you a million dollars. Our Lord says, "A good name is rather to be chosen than great riches, and loving favour rather than silver and gold." So, grandchildren, Mr. Ault left you the memory of a grandfather who walked with God and loved God and yet also a grandfather who was your pal.

I have been reminded since his death that he was a real buddy to his grandson Keith, and I am sure to others. Just a few days ago, as they were fiddling with the tools in the basement, I understand he made this statement: "In a few days, Keith, these tools will be yours." Exactly what he meant by that statement none of us, I guess, really understands. There is one thing that we do know, and that is that he left you the inheritance, grandchildren, of having a grandfather who was not only a great man, a great Christian, but also a great pal.

He leaves for you two bits of advice. He said to his granddaughter Gail, just before he died, "Are you well prepared?"

He was doing the thing that he did so often and that was bringing somebody to church or taking somebody home from church. Many an afternoon at 4:45 or 5:00 I would be leaving the office and I would find him waiting for Erma (one of Mr. Ault's daughters and a secretary on our staff). I used to love to kid him. I would say to Erma, "Is this man still bothering you?"

She would say something like this, "Yes, and I enjoy it." We would kid awhile and chat awhile. It seems like most of the times that I saw him he was bringing someone to the church building or coming to get someone. It is significant, I think, that he was bringing Gail to have a part in the nationwide Pastors' School, and he asked her the question just before he graduated, "Are you well prepared?" Never forget that, grandchildren. That is tremendous advice. He left you this advice in his will: Always be prepared.

After Gail said (as she always, of course, can say), "Yes, I am well prepared," he replied something like this, "Do your best." As far as we know, these were the last words that he said.

What a tremendous inheritance is yours! I believe that I had rather have those two bits of advice than all of the silver and gold. To me, I think, I had rather have a grandfather say to me as he died, "Be prepared and do your best," than for him to leave me stock in Eastern Airlines, or the Hilton Hotel chain.

This will be one, by the way, that is not taxable, and one that, as you spend it, will keep replenishing itself. You will never spend the contents of this will. It will grow larger and larger with the passing of days.

He Left Something for the Children

As we execute the will of Mr. Ault, we come to what he left the children. I find that he not only cared for the grandchildren in his will but he also cared for the children. The song, "I'm a Child of the King," that Mrs. Hyles sang awhile ago was the one that the children heard him sing, I understand, as he prepared for Sunday school every Sunday morning. Perhaps you wondered why this type of song would be sung at a funeral service.

I find in the will for the children a good name. You mention the name "Ault" in the city of Hammond and that is as good as gold. You mention the name "Ault" in the First Baptist Church and everyone thinks well. He left you a good name. The wisest man that ever lived apart from our Saviour said, "A good name is rather to be chosen than great riches."

If we gathered around today to open the will and found, to your surprise, that he was rich, you still would not have riches as valuable as the name that he left. He left you integrity, honesty, character, decency, virtue, cleanliness, Christian love, and all of the things that we so greatly need in America today. Truly, as I said to our brother awhile ago, he was a man of the old school, and God increase his tribe! What an inheritance!

My mother's sister died a few years ago, and we went to the funeral service. My mother's sister was very wealthy, and each of her children was left a great deal of money. We were driving home from the cemetery and mother began to pout a little bit, as mothers sometimes do who cannot give to their children all that they feel like they would like to. She said, "I wish I could leave a lot of money for you and Earlyne (my sister) when I die." I hugged her and I said, "The money that she left for her children couldn't pay the down payment on what you will leave when we open your will." We may have to pay for the funeral expenses and borrow money to do so, but there are some things more valuable than gold, and the things that I find in this will for the children are among them.

He Left Something for the Wife

I also find something in the will, as I execute it, for the wife. Mrs. Ault, he left you something. He left you a storehouse of tremendous memories. The truth is, you are entering into that part of life when the sweetest part is memories. The Bible says that old people (though I am not saying you are an old person) dream dreams and visions and think of the experiences of life. That is what it means in Ecclesiastes 12:1, where it says, "Remember now thy Creator in the days of thy youth." Then when you get old you can remember sweet memories of youth. That is exactly what you can do. You lived a beautiful life in youth, and now you can have beautiful memories in old age.

He left you something more than that, Mrs. Ault. He left you two wonderful girls, two fine boys, and some wonderful grandchildren—someone for whom you can live! If I could seclude you and me off for a few minutes and just talk with you, I would like to say that you have a lot to live for, and you have a lot of people who need you to live for them. As you continue to live for your children, grandchildren, church, Christ, and friends, may I congratulate you for the tremendous inheritance that your husband left you.

He Left Something for His Church

I find the family is not all he included in his will. He left something for his church. Oh, I do not think that we will receive any big check from his will, but we have received and will receive, as long as there is a First Baptist Church, dividends from the life of Fay Ault. He left us his family. In his will he left us a wonderful church secretary, a tremendous Beginner Department superintendent—and I say—simply the best in the world. He left us his wife, his daughter, his grand-children, and then he left us a life of dedication and service to our church. He was once a deacon. He was once the chairman of our deacon board.

He Left Something for His Pastor

Could I be a little bit personal for a few minutes and say as I look at the will, I find that he included something for me. He left much for his grandchildren, his children, his wife, and his church, but he also left something for his pastor in his will. He left to me and to all of those who lead in the First Baptist Church a tremendous demonstra-tion of loyalty to his pastor. I do not believe that we talked together an hour total, but his eyes spoke volumes as I preached, and his smiles of encouragement spoke volumes when I needed encouragement. He always sat right over here. He had one of those faces at which a preacher looks. (I must reveal a secret we preachers have. We have a few faces that encourage us, and we look at them very often.) He had one of those faces. If I were preaching on something a little con-troversial, I would always look over this way because he would be shaking his head and grinning. So he left for me memories of a loyal member who never doubted his pastor and never criticized his pas-tor's leadership.

When I first came to this church, I was told that Mr. Ault had once been chairman of the deacon board. With a new administration and new type pastor (each man has his own particular characteristics and traits) I wondered how the ex-deacon chairman was going to treat the new preacher. I didn't wonder for long because of a warm handshake, a squeeze of the hand, a pat on the back, a shake of the head, and a smile. He was always encouraging the pastor in the times when the pastor was in desperate need of encouragement. So I am grateful that he included me in the will.

He Left Something for Each of Us

As we continue to execute the will, I find not only that there is something in the will for his children, grandchildren, wife, church, and pastor, but there is something for each of us. You, too, are in-cluded in the will. He left for you, his friends, an example of the way a life ought to be lived. He left for each of us a pattern to follow.

We have executed the will of Mr. Ault and with gratitude, let us use the inheritance wisely.

Let us pray.

24. The Pastoral Counseling

One of the delights of my ministry is to look out in the congregation on a Sunday and see families sitting together with whom I have counseled, and realize that their homes have been salvaged because of our counseling. We live in a confused world—a world of nervous breakdowns, a world of divorce, a world of juvenile frustrations, a world of dope addiction, a world of alcoholic beverages, and many other things that lead to frustration, unhappiness, and discontentment. This means that the average pastor who loves his people must spend hours in counseling with them. This also means that there are too many people needing help for the pastor to care for them all. Deacons and other spiritual Christians should be interested in counseling. Following are some suggestions to help in this vital ministry:

1. *All counselors need plain wisdom.* James said in his epistle, chapter 1, verse 5, "If any of you lack wisdom, let him ask of God, that giveth to all men liberally, and upbraideth not; and it shall be given him." Wisdom is a gift from God. How we need it if we are going to help people become happily adjusted in this maladjusted world.

2. *The pastor should counsel in his office.* If he uses his own home, it will infringe upon the privacy of his family and this is not wise, proper, or fair. If he counsels with women in their homes he would have to take another person with him, and this oftentimes would prevent the troubled persons from being open and frank in their discussion. Hence, it is wise for the counseling to be done, if at all possible, in the privacy of the pastor's study. This prevents children interfering, the telephone ringing, the doorbell ringing, etc. If the children must be brought to such a session, a nursery worker could be provided for them and the church nursery could be open.

3. *For matters of less than major importance, a good time to counsel is after the public services.* This will prevent the pastor from having to make an extra trip to the church. It will enable him to have more time with his family and it, also, will require some people to attend the public services that otherwise would not. It is wise to remember, here, that we should not set a certain time for this conference. It should be simply after the services. If, for example, the time is set for twelve o'clock, the person may miss the service and come for the private conference. If the time is set for after the serv-

ice, he would almost have to be in the service or take a chance on missing his appointment.

4. *Unless it is an emergency, set the appointment up for at least one day in advance.* Many problems have a way of solving themselves and many problems can be solved by giving the parties involved twenty-four hours to cool off and discuss the differences involved.

5. *In the case of a marital problem it is far better to have both husband and wife present.* It is extremely difficult to solve a marriage problem without both parties cooperating. I have found it wise to insist strongly that both husband and wife come at the same time for the appointment. Rarely have I seen a marriage saved when both parties were not present.

6. *Talk with each party privately.* In our church we have a little waiting room outside the pastor's office. Some reading material is provided. The pastor asks one party to wait outside while he talks to the other. He then asks for the party in his study to tell the story as he, or she, sees it. As they talk, the pastor makes notes. On one sheet of paper he writes questions that he would like to ask. On another sheet of paper he writes suggestions that he would like to make. As soon as the conference is finished, the parties exchange places and the same procedure is followed with the one who has been waiting outside.

7. *Let each party tell his entire story while you listen.* Do not interrupt unless something is not clear. Do not give your advice until you have listened carefully, and at length, to each side of the story.

8. *Have a comfortable atmosphere.* In my study I have a sofa and two comfortable chairs in a little living-room-type atmosphere. I have found that people are more free to talk if they feel comfortable. I also have a small refrigerator where I keep refreshments. Often it sets a person at ease if he can hold a glass of juice in his hand and sip on it while presenting his problem.

9. *Always set the couple or person at ease.* Do not act like a strange, mysterious person from outer space. Be friendly, personable, and happy. Let them know that at one time or another we all have troubles and need help. With this kind of treatment a person will not feel that you are acting as a "holier than thou" or that your piety is showing excessively. Chat awhile with them. Talk about general things: their work, their hobbies, etc. Become friendly so the conversation can be free before entering into the problem at hand.

10. *As you counsel, enter into their lives.* Feel that you are a member of their family and that your home depends upon theirs. The solving of their problem is the greatest thing in the world. Feel for them and with them as you listen and as you talk. Be sure that your compassion and concern is transferred to them and that they know you care.

11. After they finish, the counselor should ask questions. No questions should be asked while they are talking unless something is not clear. When they have finished with their story, if it is a marriage problem, ask questions about their relationship with their in-laws. Ask questions about their financial condition. Ask questions about their spiritual activity, their church attendance, and such things as having a family altar, saying grace at the table, reading the Bible, etc. Also ask questions about their physical love life in case of sexual maladjustment. These areas cause much trouble in a home and in a marriage. Be sure that you know all that you can find out about each of these areas. Let us list them again: in-laws, money, church, and physical relationship.

12. There are four things that husbands and wives ought to be. These things should be stressed:

(1.) Lovers
(2.) Pals
(3.) Christians
(4.) Partners

13. It is usually best not to counsel alone with a lady in her home. The pastor may take his wife with him or, in some rare cases, (very rare, indeed) he may simply send his wife.

14. During all of the aforementioned conversation the counselor should be listing suggestions that he feels would be helpful to the home or to the problem.

15. After you feel you know the case properly and have the suggestions listed, ask them to listen as you give suggestions. This is one of the main reasons why they should not be interrupted as they talk. Now it is your time to talk. You can expect to proceed without interruptions. Remind them not to interrupt as you talk, for you are going to give suggestions to them that will help in the solving of their problem.

16. Be kind and understanding as you advise. Do not make them feel that you are being critical or looking down upon them. You are a kind brother trying to help. They should feel that this is true.

17. Show scriptural reasons for your advice, if at all possible.

18. Show the possible alternatives and the one that you would advise they follow.

19. The information should be held in strict confidence. This is very important. It does not take long for word to get around that the pastor or counselor does not keep things told in secrecy in strict confidence. Your opportunity to help will be seriously hindered.

MISCELLANEOUS SUGGESTIONS TO THOSE HAVING MARITAL PROBLEMS

Volumes have been written and could be written about marriage counseling. Neither time nor space will permit such elaboration here. However, following is a list of general suggestions that we have given to folks having marital difficulties through the years. They are time tested and have been used of God.

Four Great Causes for Divorce

1. Financial problems: (Not having a proper understanding concerning the handling of money, excessive installment buying, and extravagant spending.)

2. Improper relationship with in-laws: (Criticism of in-laws and living too close to them.)

3. Lack of emphasis on spiritual life: (Failure to say grace at the table, have family devotions, and attend the public services of the church.)

4. Failure in love life: (Including failing in common courtesies, in open expressions of love, and in sexual adjustment.)

Four Things That Married Couples Ought to Be

1. Christians
2. Lovers
3. Pals
4. Partners

General Things to Remember

1. Marriage is life's biggest relationship. It is also the longest and the closest.

2. Get help from an outsider when marital problems arise. This help should be from a spiritual person and should be sought immediately.

3. Become an expert on marriage. A young lady who plans to be a nurse will spend years in preparation. One preparing to be a schoolteacher will spend even more years. One who plans to spend her life as a wife oftentimes doesn't even make one hour of preparation for life's greatest work for a woman.

4. Talk over your marital problems with your husband or wife, and do it as Christians and as adults.

The Divine Order of the Home

1. God (What He says is what we are to do.)

2. Man (Man is the leader of the home in purity, in spiritual life, and in love. —I Cor. 14:34, 35; Josh. 24:15; Acts 16:31.)

3. Woman (The woman is to be in subjection to the husband. —Gen. 3:16; Eph: 5:22-24,33; I Tim. 2:11-14; I Pet. 3:1,2. Note the words "submit," "subjection," "obey," "reverence," etc.)

4. Children (The children are to obey their parents. They are to be disciplined by their parents. —Prov. 29:15; 19:18; 23:13,14; 29:17; 13:24. Also, the parents are not to refuse to have children. —Gen. 1: 28).

Some Things for the Wife to Remember

1. To be a failure as a wife is to be a failure in life.
2. The purpose for woman's creation was to be a wife.
3. Give your husband first place in your life.
4. Do not brag on other men in your husband's presence.
5. If your husband is unsaved and the least bit antagonistic toward the church, do not discuss the church with him or tell how much you enjoy it in front of him.
6. Be sure that you boost your husband. Do not tear him down. Remember, you are a helpmeet.
7. Make your husband feel important. The only way for you to be a queen is to make him a king.
8. Keep the home atmosphere as pleasant as possible.
9. Do not argue with the children or attempt to correct them in the presence of the husband.
10. If you are more efficient than he is, appear to be less efficient. Show your need of him.
11. Put your husband before the children.
12. Love your husband and let him know it.
13. Spend time with him regularly.
14. Be interested in his activities.
15. Always submit yourself to your husband.
16. Be beautiful and appealing.
17. Dress as he wants you to dress. Think of him in choosing your wardrobe.
18. Talk to him very frankly about his needs.
19. Be a good conversationalist and a good listener.
20. Don't forget to be more romantic and more appealing with the passing of the years.
21. Be very frugal financially.
22. Never criticize his parents.
23. Encourage him to take the lead of the family spiritually.
24. If your husband refuses to be the spiritual leader of the family and you have to have the family altar, have it alone with the children and not in his presence, unless he so desires.

25. Arrange to eat privately with your husband often. (This can be done in a restaurant, in a drive-in hamburger place, or even at a picnic table in the park. A husband and wife should be together for a meal alone once a week.)

26. Learn to have fun together. Maybe a hobby could be started.

27. Do not boss your husband. Do not tell him what to do around the house. Courteously, lovingly and kindly you may ask him; but keep clear of any strong suggestions or orders.

28. Do not take the children's side when your husband disciplines them. Stay together on discipline.

29. Do not spank a child when you are angry. Simply send him to his room. Spank him privately, carefully and prayerfully, explaining to him why.

30. Be sure that the degree of discipline given to a child is proportionate to the degree of guilt. In other words, when a child tells an untruth, he should be spanked harder for this than when he accidentally breaks a vase.

31. If your husband is guilty of fornication, you then have scriptural grounds for divorce. This does not mean that you are commanded to divorce, but it does mean that you are permitted to divorce. If the home is saved and forgiveness is offered, do not bring up the past.

32. Be very careful with your relationship with the opposite sex. Do not place yourself in positions where temptations will arise or criticism could be given.

33. Read a good book on the home by some Christian author. Read a sensible book on marriage by some good doctor. Certainly, read what the Bible has to say about marriage.

34. Plan to be home when your husband is at home.

35. Do not be preoccupied with duties or thoughts of duties when you are with your husband unless, of course, the duties are being performed together.

Suggestions for Husbands

1. Love your wife and let her know it.

2. Be thoughtful and expressive to your wife. Bring her flowers, perfume, etc.

3. Be gentle in all of your dealings with your wife. Never be harsh or physically abusive.

4. Assume your place of leadership in the home.

5. Never brag excessively about another lady in the presence of your wife.

6. Always keep appointments with your wife.

7. Always come home from work at the time expected. If this is not possible, call as soon as you can.

8. Hold your relationship with your wife very sacred. Do not reveal it to others. Let her know it is a very precious thing to you.

9. Eat out with your wife at least once a week.

10. Have fun with your wife. Somebody has said, "Couples that pray together, stay together." Perhaps it should be added, "Couples that pray together and play together, stay together."

11. Lead in spiritual activities. Say grace at the table. Lead in the family devotions. Come to church with your family.

12. Be as pleasant as possible at home.

13. Go shopping together. Enjoy the commonplace things of life with each other.

14. Never criticize her parents.

15. Be sure that your wife is happy with your love life.

16. Help her in some of the household duties.

17. Be interested in what your wife's activities were for the day.

18. Do not take the children's side when your wife disciplines them. Stay together on discipline.

19. Do not spank a child when you are angry. Simply send him to his room. Spank him privately, carefully, and prayerfully, explaining to him why.

20. Be sure that the degree of discipline given to a child is proportionate to the degree of guilt. In other words, when a child tells an untruth, he should be spanked harder for this than when he accidentally breaks a vase.

21. If your wife is guilty of fornication, you then have scriptural grounds for divorce. This does not mean that you are commanded to divorce, but it does mean that you are permitted to divorce. If the home is saved and forgiveness is offered, do not bring up the past.

22. Be very careful with your relationship with the opposite sex. Do not place yourself in positions where temptations will arise or criticism could be given.

23. Usually it is best for the husband to handle the finances, giving his wife an allowance for groceries and incidentals. A little extra should be included in this allowance so that the wife will have a little spending money.

24. Read a good book on the home by some Christian author. Read a sensible book on marriage by some good doctor. Certainly, read what the Bible has to say about marriage.

25. Do not be preoccupied with duties or thoughts of duties when you are with your wife unless, of course, the duties are being performed together.

25. The Relationship of Pastor and His People

Few ties and few relationships should be as close as the relationship that exists between a Bible-preaching pastor and his people. To be sure, a Bible preacher should be fearless, free, and uncompromising, but this should not take away the love and devotion that he should have for his people. To preach against sin is necessary. To do it with love and a broken heart is equally necessary. May God use this chapter to encourage and instruct the pastor to have the right spirit, attitude and relationship toward his flock, and to encourage the flock to understand, love and follow the undershepherd that God has given them.

1. *The pastor and people should share glory and defeat.* It is tempting for the pastor to accept the glory for a victory and evade the blame for defeat. When the church enjoys a victory, the pastor and people should share equally; and when the church suffers defeat, the pastor and people should each assume a portion of the responsibility.

When I was a young preacher I used to scold the people when the attendance was down. Suddenly I realized that those who were there were not absent and did not need the scolding. Let us be very careful to realize that there are not self-made men, and there are no victories won without a successful leader and loyal followers.

It was said of Saul, when he was anointed king, "And Saul also went home to Gibeah; and there went with him a band of men, whose hearts God had touched." When Aaron and Hur lifted up the hands of Moses, the battle was won. When his hands were lowered, the battle was lost. When one reads very carefully the letters of Paul, he is reminded over and over of Paul's awareness of his helpers.

Read the last chapter of the book of Romans and notice how Paul gives credit and recognition to lesser lights.

2. *The pastor and people should compliment success and performance of duty.* The pastor should always be aware of the work that his helpers do and should give them due praise and credit. On the other hand, the people should be very careful that they take time to encourage the pastor for his labor of love.

Each Sunday evening we read a list of names of people in our church who fill jobs and do them well. We ask the people to stand as their names are read and remain standing until all of the names are read.

One Sunday evening we will honor the nursery workers; the next Sunday evening, the ushers; then the PA men, the choir, the deacons, the Sunday school workers, those who do odd jobs around the church, etc. As the people are standing the pastor will say something like this: "On behalf of our entire church family may I thank you dear people for the job that you are doing. You are making a contribution to our church and the work of the Lord, and you are doing it faithfully and lovingly. Our entire church appreciates your sacrificial service and your dedicated lives. May God bless you for doing your job and doing it well." The pastor will then give the people an opportunity to respond by either a chorus of "Amens" or an occasional applause.

Letters of appreciation should be written often. Phone calls and personal conversation can be used as an expression of appreciation.

3. *The pastor and people should express their love openly to each other.* Recently, Mrs. Hyles and I were driving down the street. We happened to see a family crossing the street. "Those people are faithful members of our church," I said to my wife. "Those are wonderful people." However, they could not hear me. They did not know that I said it, so I made a note to drop them a line and express my love and gratitude to them. Often I receive love letters from my people. These are simply letters of affection and gratitude that are always an encouragement and a boost. Let's express our love openly.

4. *Pastor and people should seek counsel from each other.* Now to be sure, a church member should lean heavily upon the counsel of his pastor. Most of this counsel can be gleaned from the public services and his messages. However, there will come times when the member will need individual attention. A phone call may be all that is necessary. A letter may suffice or it may even be needful to plan a private conference. On the other hand, the pastor also needs counsel. He should seek it from time to time from people in the church. Maybe a godly deacon, or maybe the deacon board, or maybe someone who is an expert on the subject at hand could be of inestimable value to the preacher.

There is probably no one in the church more lonely than the preacher (unless it is his wife). He needs prayer, encouragement and counsel. I have found it very helpful to seek counsel from my wife. I also ask for counsel from my staff almost daily. From time to time I ask my deacons for advice. This is a very important part of the pastor-people relationship.

5. *The pastor should be quick to accept suggestions from his people.* Now this does not mean that the pastor should always follow the suggestion. It simply means he should accept suggestions as favors rather than criticisms, that is, if they are given in the spirit of love and kindness. It does not mean that a pastor is losing his freedom if he listens to a suggestion. In some cases he might be losing his free-

dom if he followed the suggestion, but to say the least, he should be very gracious to accept the suggestions and prayerfully consider them. Let it be understood, however, that he should not obey or follow unless he feels led of the Lord to so do.

6. *The pastor should learn to be careful of intimate friendships.* As aforementioned, the pastor is a lonely man. He must be very careful not to show partiality or favoritism. This means that normally he cannot invite members into his house and he cannot enjoy the luxury of intimate friendships with his people as he would want to do. Close friends may be developed from preacher friends, staff members, and family, and though the tie with the people is close and the love should exceed many other relationships, the manifestations of that tie must be limited so as not to show partiality.

This is one reason why the pastor's family should be a very close unit. The pastor should find in his family relationships the satisfying of his hunger for intimacy. The pastor's wife should be closer to him than most wives are to their husbands. Likewise, the pastor's children should feel closer to Dad than most children.

Pastor, love your people with all your heart. Weep when they weep. Laugh when they laugh. Rejoice when they rejoice. Mourn when they mourn, but be careful of developing pets and favorites in the congregation.

7. *The pastor should learn to take a joke on himself.* Few things will endear a person to his followers as the learning to be the object of jokes and kidding gracefully.

For example, I cannot sing. To me this is a real sorrow and heartache. I love good music and would give much to be able to have a good voice. My wife has a lovely voice and sings solos in church. My daughters all sing and my son David has a good voice. I am the black sheep of the family. When the family gathers around the piano to sing, what a time they have; that is, until I join in. I will slip up behind them and try to carry the bass part and someone will invariably say, "Somebody is off." Someone will suggest maybe that I should not sing the next stanza. Sure enough, the problem is solved.

Now, I always laugh about it though on the inside I am sad. I want to sing. I would love to sing. Music is in my bones. I would love to be able to sing duets with my wife but that is impossible. Now I have learned to joke about it. My people kid me about it often and I kid myself in front of them. This is a very important part in leading people.

Like most men, I am losing my hair and, like most men, I am doing it with weeping and wailing and gnashing of teeth. I am not enjoying it, but I find myself being joked a great deal about it. To take this gracefully is very important. In fact, I oftentimes make myself the object of such a joke. People appreciate a pastor who is not sensitive and, by the way, a pastor appreciates people who are not sensitive.

8. *The pastor should keep everything "above the table."* As a pastor leads his people he should be careful not to have secrets concerning the church business or church affairs. It is very important that the people are kept abreast with the church affairs and church business. (See chapter on Church Business Meetings.)

9. *The pastor should pray with and for his people.* I have found it helpful to set aside two hours a week when I pray by name for the people in my church who need my prayers. Then I also pray briefly each day for those who are in special need of prayer. When the pastor makes contact with the people he should remember to pray. A hospital visit should be ended with a brief prayer for the patient. A house call should be ended with a prayer for the home. A visit to the office should be ended with prayer. This is perhaps more to the people than the pastor will ever realize. To some it is a never-to-be-forgotten experience to hear their pastor pray for them by name.

10. *The pastor and people should not be retaliatory.* A servant of God is going to be criticized. Sometimes it will be a Shimei who will follow us and haunt us with criticism. At other times it will be a surly Joab who will remind us through the years of our faults and weaknesses. At other times it will be a jealous Saul who will seek to kill our ministries. Let us follow the example of David in each of the above cases when he left retaliation and vengeance to the Lord. A church member will never realize the criticism that is directed toward a pastor. The temptation to retaliate publicly is a tremendous one but it should be avoided.

Those of us who have played in athletic contests are aware that it is the man who hits the second blow who usually gets penalized. Perhaps an opposing player will be dirty and underhanded throughout the entire contest. The referee never sees it. Then our patience is worn thin and we retaliate one time. Invariably, the referee will see our retaliation and the penalty will come to our team.

Along this line it is wise for the members not to burden the pastor with little criticisms. Now, if a serious matter arises he should be alerted, but a little insignificant word of criticism should not be relayed to the pastor.

I suppose every pastor has had that member who meets him at the door just before he enters the service on Sunday morning and says, "Pastor, I'm with you no matter what they say." All throughout the message the pastor is saying to himself, "What did they say? What did they say? What did they say?" The message is ruined either by the pastor's lack of concentration or by the pastor's public retaliation to the criticism. Most criticism is less serious than we think and oftentimes we use an atomic bomb when a BB gun would do. Many churches have had serious trouble develop because of a misevaluation on the part of the pastor of the size of the problem. In most cases ninety-five percent of the people do not even know of the problem and it is often made known to them by the retaliation of the pastor.

11. The pastor should not burden his wife with unnecessary and needless problems. The pastor's wife can be a much more congenial and enjoyable person if the pastor does not relay to her every little problem that arises in the church. Remember it is her job to encourage and boost the pastor. A discouraged wife can hardly encourage a discouraged preacher. Now to be sure the pastor should share his burdens with his wife but they should be of big enough magnitude to warrant a serious discussion before the wife is brought into the problem. Many pastors have built for themselves discouraging wives while, on the other hand, many pastors who are wise and prudent have built the kind of wife who is a constant source of encouragement because she is not burdened down with every wind change in the church.

12. The pastor should never turn down a love gift from a member. Dr. George W. Truett used to say, "Never turn down even a drink of water when offered in Jesus' name." Shortly before this writing I observed my forty-first birthday. I received many remembrances and gifts. My Sunday school class gave me a new suit. A fine family gave me money for a new sport coat. But perhaps the greatest gift was that of a little boy who gave me a homemade birthday card with two quarters Scotch taped on the inside. I suspect I treasure that gift more than them all. One poor lady gave me a ballpoint pen worth 19¢ (God bless her!). I felt guilty accepting it except to her it was probably the best 19¢ she had ever spent.

Along with the acceptance of these gifts let every pastor develop a sense of sincere gratitude to his people. Professionalism can develop easily since the pastor is usually the recipient of many wonderful gestures of love and kindness. Let us never become adjusted to that little piece of candy given by a child, to that pie or cake baked by the loving hands of a Martha, or to that shirt carefully and thoughtfully made by some faithful Dorcas.

13. The pastor and people should always be friendly. A warm smile, a friendly handshake, and an affectionate pat on the back are always in order between God's people. The pastor should be very friendly both publicly and privately.

Not too many years ago a lady in our area gave our church two buses (valued at approximately $14,000.00) simply because one day the pastor was friendly to her when he was out visiting. This should not be the purpose for our friendliness. Nevertheless, we should be always friendly to each other.

14. The pastor should be willing to make enemies because of his position but not because of his disposition.

15. The pastor should never use his people to build the work but should use his work to build the people. It is so easy to use patients to build a hospital or to use students to build a school or to use people to build a church. Never forget the purpose of a hospital is to make people well, and the most important thing about a school is the student. The object of the work of a pastor is to build people, not buildings and not churches. Our people should sense that they are the most important thing of our work and should feel that the pastor's great work is in building great Christians.

Oftentimes a pastor will come by on a weekday wanting to see my work. Of course, I know what he means but I always tell him that my work is at school, at home, at the office, and at the shop. The buildings are but a tool used to help the people. We must always keep this in proper perspective.

It is a tragedy to see people critical of their pastor and to see a pastor who does not properly love his people. Let it be said of each pastor as was said of Saul, "There went with him a band of men, whose hearts God had touched."

26. The Relationship of Pastor and His Staff

As a church grows, the work soon becomes too big for one man. The pastor then finds that he must have help. There are few days in a pastor's life more crucial than the day when he seeks and chooses this help. He must realize that what is happening is that the pastor is growing. The staff is the pastor. The staff is an enlargement of the pastor. The staff's heart should beat with the pastor's heart and its mind should be in tune with the pastor's mind. Careful planning and prayerful choosing must be done at this critical time in the life of a pastor and a church.

The Enlistment of Staff Members

It is my feeling that the first staff member that a pastor needs is an efficient secretary. There are many things that a pastor does which could be done by a faithful secretary. If a church does not need a full-time secretary, a fine soul-winning lady could be chosen who could be a secretary in the mornings and a soul-winning visitor in the afternoons. I have found it very helpful to choose secretaries from the church roll. Now, if a secretary is chosen from outside the church, much care should be given. I am constantly amazed that churches will choose a pastor and a pastor will choose staff members with less care than a Five and Ten Cent Store chooses a clerk.

When staff members are chosen from the church roll there is always one advantage—they chose the church before the church chose them. There will be only the adjustment to the new job and not the adjustment to a new church. This is of great advantage.

There are several things that should be considered when choosing a staff member. First is loyalty. This is the outstanding characteristic that should be possessed by every staff member—one hundred percent unquestioned loyalty. Never a reflection or a doubt should be expressed by a staff member concerning the pastor and his work.

When employing our present music director, I watched him very carefully for two years though he did not realize he was being considered for employment. I would give him opportunity after opportunity to express just a little criticism of his pastor. Had he done so, his name would have been erased from consideration. It was only after months and months of careful observation of his loyalty to his pastor that he was employed by our church. No amount of talent, conviction or devotion can substitute for loyalty to the pastor.

Secondly, a staff member should be chosen because of hard work. For example, if a secretary is being employed, go to her home and see what type of housekeeper she is. Check very carefully with former employers. Diligence and hard work are essentials!

Presently we have thirteen members on our staff. My music director, as aforementioned, was employed from outside the church. My other three assistant pastors were called to preach and ordained under my ministry. Each has college training but is a home-grown product. My private secretary was a junior high schoolteacher before she came to work for us. One of our ladies was employed with the Sword of the Lord for thirteen years before coming to us, though she was already a member of our church before we employed her. Our records secretary was a social science teacher in the local high school. Our director of literature grew up in our church. Our music secretary was a first-grade schoolteacher in the Hammond, Indiana, school system. Our publications secretary is my sister whose loyalty is beyond question. Our financial secretary was a faithful member of our church and employed from the church roll. She, too, was reared in the church. Our receptionist was saved and baptized in our church; in fact, her entire family was saved during the few years before this writing. I consider all of us together as pastor of the church. We form one team. The pastoral work became too big for one man, and then it became too big for two, and then it outgrew three, etc. In the Lord's work we are as one.

Rules for Handling the Staff

1. Duties should be kept separate. It is always wise to outline very carefully a staff member's duties and responsibilities. The staff member should be kept within his own field and not allowed to have his duties overlap with those of another. If he is to be responsible for his work, he must be the only one who does the work. This is a cardinal rule of our staff. We keep each staff member's duties separate.

2. Show appreciation publicly for the staff. It is not easy to be a second man or play "second fiddle." It is important that the first fiddler give due public respect and appreciation to the second fiddler. The people should realize and recognize the pastor's appreciation for his staff and the fact that the pastor shares the credit for success with those who labor with him.

3. A staff spirit should be developed. It is good that a staff have esprit de corps. There should be a patriotism, a loyalty and a spirit on a church staff. This could be encouraged by weekly staff devotions periodic staff parties, etc. Our staff has an annual Christmas party. We then observe birthdays with staff get-togethers and parties. We have a devotional period each Monday morning and, in general, take real pride in the staff. It is a team, a unit, and each member is proud and happy to be a part of the team.

4. *The pastor should be very discreet in his conduct with the lady staff members.* When the proper spirit exists on the church staff the pastor becomes the object of much affection. The staff members respect him and often nearly revere him. The pastor should never mistake this for anything more than affection for a godly man. For that matter, the lady staff members should always interpret their affection for the pastor in this light. The sad thing is that if the relationship is misinterpreted, the beauty of the proper relationship must be forfeited. Once a relationship goes beyond its bounds, it then, sad to say, eliminates the beautiful relationship that existed beforehand.

It is wise for a pastor not to be in a car alone with a lady staff member. It is wise for the pastor to choose ladies who have devotion and love for their husbands. The pastor should be careful to use restraint in his conversation and behavior with the ladies both on the staff and off the staff as well.

5. *The staff members should have responsibilities.* Bearing in mind that the pastor is the overseer of all the church program and should approve every step made, nevertheless, the staff member should have an area in which he or she can work at a responsibility that he can carry. Do not look over the staff member's shoulder as he works. Place confidence in him. Give him work to do. Expect him to do it and believe that he can do it.

6. *The pastor and staff should manifest unselfishness to each other.* As mentioned beforehand, it is always a critical time when the pastor chooses a staff. Up until now the pastor has been the recipient of all of the cherry pies, peach cobblers, green beans, etc. Now suddenly, he finds competition. How he accepts this competition for the courtesies of his people will largely determine the kind of staff he will have and the contribution they will make to his ministry.

I well recall when I hired my first assistant pastor. He came to the church one evening licking his lips and saying that he had certainly enjoyed the fresh green beans. I knew that he did not have a garden so I asked, "Where did you get those green beans?"

He then replied, "Mrs. So-and-so brought them by the house."

A green-eyed monster named jealousy ran through my mind as I said, "She didn't bring me any." It was then and there that I was convicted that if I would have the advantages of an assistant, I must be willing to share him with the people and share the people with him.

I recall one day when I had just burned up a transmission trying to get unstuck from the snow, my assistant pastor came by and asked me why I didn't have snow tires. I told him I couldn't afford snow tires and then he said, "Mr. Blank gave me some." I had just burned up my transmission, and it cost me nearly $300.00 to have it repaired. My first thought was, "Why didn't Mr. Blank give them to me?" Again I was reminded that the right kind of relationship between the pastor, staff and people must be one of unselfishness. Your people will not love you any less because they also love a new person. In fact, the loving of a new person oftentimes increases their ability to love and they will love you even more. To be sure, your manifestation of unselfishness will increase their love for you.

7. *The pastor should be very careful to compliment the staff before other people.* The pastor is always in the public eye. He is the spokesman for the staff. He will always get his share of the compliments if the staff gets its share. The pastor will have to give out the bouquets. How important this is.

8. *The staff members must have a feeling of equality.* There is no place for a caste system on a staff. The pastor should realize that the staff members should be as high socially as is he. He should treat them as his equals. This does not mean that he loses his authority over them. It simply means that it is his position that gives him authority and not his superiority. The staff members should never feel that they are beneath the pastor. They should feel that the pastor needs them and that each is making a contribution to the pastoral work of the church.

9. *The pastor should see to it that the staff is paid proportionally to his own salary.* Most churches barely get along financially, and so it is often the case that the salary level of a church secretary is beneath the level of a secretary in the business field. Bear in mind that the people will feel the importance of the staff members only as the pastor feels and expresses their importance. When the staff is exalted or elevated in the minds of the people, it is easier for the pastor to lead the people to pay adequate and proper salaries. I have found that if the pastor is more concerned about the staff members' salaries than his own, they will be more concerned about his needs than their own.

10. *A growing church is usually in need of space; however, it is very important that a staff member have adequate office space.* Privacy is important. Room to have a filing cabinet and a nice desk is very important. Much care should be taken in preparing for each staff member adequate office space.

11. *The staff member should not have to sacrifice his right to have a pastor.* One of the first things that I say to a new staff member is that he remember to consider me as his pastor. I remind him of his right to come to me any time as a church member to seek my counsel and advice. This is one reason why a pastor will oftentimes have to

exercise restraint with his staff so that they may still feel that he is their pastor. A pastor would love to have someone to whom he could pour out his heart and with whom he could share his weaknesses, but too much of this may forfeit his right to be pastor of a staff member. No one knows more than the pastor how lonely it feels not to have a pastor. Since the pastor cannot have a pastor, he knows the void that is in his life. Knowing this, let us be careful to provide a pastoral relationship even with our staff members. Let us not ask them to forfeit what we have had to forfeit in not having a pastor.

12. *The pastor should oversee the entire work of the church.* No staff member should pursue a program without the pastor's approval. The pastor should be pastor of the music, the youth, the Sunday school, the W. M. S., and every other phase of the church program. As the church gets bigger this is a very vital part of a pastor's responsibilities. He should oversee and approve everything that goes on. One of the titles given to the pastor in the Bible is the title of bishop. The word "bishop" means "overseer." It is an unhealthy condition when a music director feels that he can proceed without the pastor's approval. This same is true with any member of the staff or any phase of the church program.

In conclusion, the pastor may enlarge his ministry tremendously with the choosing and administrating of a good staff. When the proper love, respect, admiration, and loyalty is manifested by the staff to the pastor and by the pastor to the staff, the work of the Lord is increased, more souls can be saved, and the pastor has found a comradeship that he had not known before he had enlarged himself by choosing a staff.

27. The Invitation Time

After observing for nearly twenty-two years the preaching of hundreds of preachers across America, I have come to the conclusion that many of us need intensive help in the conduction of a public invitation. Many wonderful gospel messages can be rendered ineffective by a weak invitation.

On the other hand, many average preachers can be rewarded greatly with the use of an effective, pungent, public invitation. Though in many places a public invitation is seldom used and even considered out of date, it is still true that the greatest soul-winning churches utilize an effective, spiritual, Spirit-filled, powerful invitation as their greatest means of evangelism. May we look at a few practical pointers concerning the invitation.

Starting the Invitation

Do not reveal the closing of the sermon. When the sermon reaches a high point or a climax, then would be a good time to close abruptly. Even if the sermon is not completed, sometimes God may lead one to close prematurely in order to start the invitation from a high spiritual plane. This also prevents the unsaved from "digging in," so to speak, before the invitation is given.

Upon the completion of the sermon, ask the people to bow their heads and close their eyes. Such statements as these are sometimes effective: "Every head bowed, every eye closed, no one is leaving. No one is moving while God speaks to our hearts."

Now ask the congregation, "With heads bowed, how many can say under God, 'I know that if I died momentarily I would go to Heaven'?" Such an approach may be used, "Now while every head is bowed, every eye is closed, no one is leaving, no one is moving, with God being our witness, those of you who can say, 'If I died today, I know beyond any shadow of doubt that I would go to Heaven,' would you raise your hand?"

Ask lost people to raise their hands. A good way would be as follows, "Now while our heads are bowed, some of you could not raise your hands that you knew that if you died today, you would go to Heaven. You were too honest to raise your hand; you were sincere in not raising your hand, but would you say, 'Preacher, I want to know that I am saved. I wish I could say that if I died now, I would go to Heaven. I want to know that I'm a Christian. Please pray for me.' If you can say that while everyone is still and no one is looking, if you want me to pray that you may know that if you died today you would go to Heaven, would you lift your hand?" While the hands are being lifted, you may simply acknowledge each hand raised with a "God bless you," "I see you," "I'll pray for you," or some other acknowledgment.

While heads are still bowed, pray for them. Such a prayer as this would be fine: "Dear Lord, help the people who raised their hands to receive Christ today. May this be the biggest day in their lives and today may they have the joy of knowing that if they died they would go to Heaven. Bless the lady on the aisle near the front. Bless the man in the rear of the balcony. I pray that you would save those two on my left and the one in the back at the right of the auditorium. Speak to their hearts and may today be the biggest day of their lives as they receive Jesus as their Saviour."

At the conclusion of this prayer, do not give away the closing of the prayer and do not say "Amen," but continue speaking.

Lead them to pray silently where they are sitting, thusly: "Now while our heads are bowed; you raised your hand, you said that you wanted to know that if you died today, you would go to Heaven. You can know. The Bible tells of a man who prayed the sinner's prayer and put his faith in the Saviour. Would you right now simply pray this prayer silently, 'Dear Lord, be merciful to me a sinner and save me now. I do now receive Jesus as my Saviour from sin and trust Him to take me to Heaven when I die.'" Insist that they pray this prayer silently. You may even quote the prayer again to them.

The Public Profession

Lead them to a public profession in the service. Tell them exactly what they are to do. For example, "Now while every head is bowed and every eye is closed, you have raised your hand to admit your lost condition. You have said that you wanted to know that if you died you would go to Heaven. If you would make this the day of your acceptance of Christ and make this the red-letter day of your life by receiving Jesus as your Saviour, I'm going to ask you to do this: We're going to stand and sing in a minute; as we stand and sing, I'm going to ask you to leave your seat, come to the nearest aisle, walk down that aisle to the altar, give me your hand, and let me tell the people that you are receiving Christ as your Saviour today. I beg you in Jesus' name do not let Satan win the battle. Leave your seat when we sing, come to the aisle, down to the front, and let me tell the people that you are receiving Christ today."

Start the invitation hymn. Have the people stand. Have the choir lead the song militantly. This song should have been previously practiced by the choir. It should be rendered as a special number. It should not be dragged and it should not be whiny. It should be a very good musical presentation. At our services we always use the same song to open every invitation. "Just As I Am" is the song we use.

Continue singing the same song as long as folks are coming. As long as people are walking the aisle, it is not good to change the song. If God is blessing a certain invitation song, we often sing it four or five times all the way through. As soon as people quit coming on one song, it is good to change songs.

Let the people observe the invitation as long as folks are coming. If the invitation begins successfully and people are walking the aisle, it is good usually to let the congregation observe it. This will be a blessing to others and perhaps other lost ones can be won as they see people walking the aisle. As soon as people quit walking the aisle or if the invitation starts slowly, I would suggest an early time of asking the people to bow their heads in prayer. Once again, I would make an appeal of urgency and continue singing with heads bowed.

The pastor should control the invitation. We have found it advantageous for the pastor to decide when the songs should be sung. For example, the pastor may stop the choir by the lifting of his hand, ask the people to bow their heads, and say words such as this: "Now while our heads are bowed would you come? God loves you. Jesus wants to save you. This could be the greatest day in your life. As the choir sings, 'Softly and Tenderly Jesus Is Calling,' would you leave your seat, come down the aisle and receive Christ as your Saviour? Do not linger. Today is your opportunity." By that time the choir will have found the next song and can begin singing. Have the choir trained so that the rustling of pages will not interfere. Any moving on the part of the people or the choir can be a hindrance to an invitation. It is never good for the song leader to turn to the choir a few minutes before the end of the sermon and have them find the song as the pastor closes his message. The nearer the message gets to the end and the farther toward the invitation and into the invitation the pastor gets, the quieter the service should be. The pastor should also control the loudness or softness of the song. Our choir director is trained to have the choir sing the song loudly and at an average tempo unless otherwise directed by the pastor. The pastor may say, "While our heads are bowed, the choir will sing softly the next stanza," or he may say, "As our heads are bowed and God is working, the choir will sing softly and slowly the next stanza." In other words, the changes of songs, tempo, volume, etc., during the invitation should be controlled by the pastor.

Have soul winners at the altar to kneel with those who come forward. In many churches people often come down the aisles under con-

viction who never get converted. They need to be shown the Scriptures, prayed with at the altar, and led to Christ in the service. We
have some people trained to do this. The pastor may simply motion
for a soul winner as he sees the person coming forward. The soul
winner may kneel at the altar or have a seat on the front row and deal
with them. It is our opinion that it is much better to deal with people
in the service than to take them out of the service. The inspiration is
there, the singing is there, and we find it better to leave them in the
service until its completion. After the soul winner is satisfied, he
may lead the convert to a seat in the front and introduce the convert to
the church clerk or secretary who in turn will take his name and give
it to the pastor.

Make Much of Those Saved

The pastor then may read to the people the names of those coming.
This is a very important time. It should not be done quickly. Each
person should be presented to the people, asked to stand at the front,
and the pastor should say some sweet word of encouragement and
blessing to the people concerning the convert. Remember, a new
name has just been written down in Heaven. Hell has been robbed!
Heaven has been populated! Christ has seen the travail of His soul and
been satisfied! Heaven is rejoicing, and the angels are shouting! We
should also make much over people saved in our services.

Baptize the Converts Immediately

(See Chapter on Baptism)

This is not the only way, of course, to conduct an invitation. It may
not even be the best way. To be sure, there are many other good
ways. But this pastor has found through twenty-two years' experience
that this is the most profitable way for his ministry. Perhaps, some
of the aforementioned suggestions will help others in inviting the unsaved to come to the Saviour. One thing is certain: We need to put
more emphasis upon the public invitation in our churches.

May God help us to realize that this is a life-or-death proposition.
Eternity is at stake. Eternal values rest on our efficiency and the
anointing of God upon our methods and upon our message. May we
spend more time than the surgeon would and be more diligent than the
doctor would be as we wrestle, operate and work with the immortal
souls of men, women, boys and girls.

Publisher's note: For additional instructions concerning the personal work during the invitation and dealing with converts at the altar,
see the author's book, *Let's Build an Evangelistic Church*, chapters 8
and 9.

28. An Invitation

(Sunday, May 21, 1967)

An invitation is conducted in every Sunday service of the First Baptist Church. The following invitation is a very typical one given at a Sunday morning service after the message. Forty-eight people responded to this invitation, receiving Jesus Christ as Saviour. These were first-time decisions. The message of the morning was entitled, "He Will Abundantly Pardon."

The Message

May I ask you a question? What have you done with your sins? Are your sins charged to you this morning or to Him? If you have been saved, they are charged to Him. If you have not been saved, they are charged to you. Before you leave this building today, God could take your sins from you and put them against Christ's record, and you would be pardoned, forgiven, justified, blessed by God, and regenerated if you would put your faith in Christ this morning.

Let us pray together. Our Heavenly Father, speak to the hearts of the people, and grant that they will see so clearly and so plainly that all we do is provide the faith and God provides the salvation. I pray this morning that you would give faith to these dear ones all over this building. May people whose sins are charged to their own record be pardoned, forgiven, justified, and regenerated by putting faith in Christ this morning.

With heads bowed and eyes closed: Where are your sins today? WHERE ARE YOUR SINS TODAY? Either they are charged to your record and you are lost and on your way to Hell, or they are charged to Jesus and you will never see the fires of Hell. Where are your sins today?

With heads bowed, I wonder how many can say, "Brother Hyles, I know what you are saying. I have been pardoned, forgiven, justified, and regenerated. The penalty from sin has been lifted. God has forgiven me. He has taken my sins off my record and made me a new creature. My sins are blotted out, I know."

Gone, gone, gone, gone,
Yes, my sins are gone;
Now my soul is free
And in my heart's a song;
Buried in the deepest sea,
Yes, that's good enough for me;
I shall live eternally,
Praise God! My sins are gone.

"Brother Hyles, my sins are not charged to me today. I am saved, and I *know* I am saved. I could tell you when I was saved if you asked me. I could tell you what happened and how it happened if you asked me."

Would you raise your hands, please, all over the house. Your sins are blotted out, and you know it. You are saved and you know it.

Thank God. Lower your hands. If you would recommend to others what you have, would you say "Amen."

Ah, that is our testimony to you. If you have never been saved, God wants to pardon you today. God wants to forgive you today. God wants to justify you today. God wants to regenerate you and make you a new creature.

I wonder how many will say this morning, "Pastor, I could not raise my hand, for I do not know that I am saved. Preacher, I wish I knew. God knows that I wish I were saved. I want my sins pardoned. I want my sins forgiven. I want to be regenerated. Brother Hyles, my sins are charged to me. I don't know that I am saved. I want to be saved. Pastor, would you pray for me?"

Yes, yes, yes, I will. I wonder how many on the lower floor will say this morning, "Brother Hyles, I want to be a Christian. I want my sins forgiven. I want to know that I am saved. Pray for me."

Lift your hands, please, all over the building. Now on the lower floor. God bless you, fellow. God bless you, fellow. God bless this little lady over here. God bless these two here.

Who else on the lower floor would say, "Brother Hyles, pray for me." God bless you, fellow. God bless you, sir. My, how wise you are today. How wise you are to realize that something has got to be done with your sins. Jesus died for you. God bless you, lady.

Who else on the lower floor? You would say.... God bless that dear lady. God bless you, son. Oh, thank God! Who else would say, "Preacher, I want to know that I am saved. I have got to have...." God bless you, lad. Who else on the lower floor? Quickly raise your hand and say, "Include me in the prayer. I want to be saved and know it. I want my sins forgiven." God bless you, sir. I see your hand. Who else on the lower floor? God bless you, fellow. I see that hand. Who else on the lower floor? Quickly, would you raise your hand. God bless you. I see you back on my left. God bless you. On the lower floor, who else? "Preacher, I want to be saved and know it. If God can pardon, forgive, justify, and regenerate, it sounds like a good deal to me. If I will put my faith in Christ and God will do all the rest, it sounds like I can't lose on that bargain."

Who else on the lower floor will say, "Pray for me." God bless you, little lady. In the balcony on my left who would say, "Include me in the prayer." Raise your hand, please. In the balcony on my left, lift your hand way up high, and say, "Include me in the prayer." God bless you.

In the center balcony, raise your hand. God bless you and you and you. God bless you. God will forgive, pardon, justify, and regenerate this morning if you will put your faith in Christ.

In the balcony on my right? Yes, there are several. God bless you. I hope this morning that each of you will put your faith in Christ and trust Him as your Saviour.

Now with your heads bowed: Our Heavenly Father, I pray today that in the closing moments of this service you will bless each of these. Over here on my right there was a lady. She wants to know that her sins are forgiven and that she is pardoned. There is a man over here, two men in the center section and some over here on the right. There is a little boy down here on the front and a young fellow over here on the front and a young fellow over here on my right. Here on my left are several, a man back in the corner on my left and two or three in the balcony in the center. Over on the balcony on my right, yes, there are many. A man way back on the back seat, and others too. O God, today, I pray that you will help people to realize that something must be done with their sins and that through faith in Christ they can be pardoned, forgiven, justified, and regenerated. I pray today that they will say, "Yes, this is the day for me."

Now with heads bowed, right where you are, dear friends, would you say this prayer: "Dear God, I didn't understand it maybe, but I do now. Jesus died for me and I receive Him as my Saviour today."

In a moment we are going to sing. When we sing, if you want to receive Christ as your Saviour, come to the nearest aisle, down the aisle to the front, give me your hand, and give Christ your heart.

I hope you will do it. Don't let timidity or embarrassment keep you from it. Leave this building a new person, pardoned, forgiven, justified and regenerated. Do it this morning. Do it today.

If you have been saved, but not baptized, come for baptism. If you want to join this church by transfer and you are already saved, there is a way you can join. You come this morning.

Our Father, speak to our hearts. Flood these aisles with people getting their sins forgiven, their lives made new, and their records clear by faith in Christ. May scores of people find this thing which we have talked about today. In Jesus' name. Amen.

Shall we stand, please. I am not trying to high-pressure you into becoming a Baptist. I am not trying to talk you out of anything or into anything. I simply want you to be justified, pardoned, forgiven, regenerated. If you will put your faith in Christ, you can be. As the choir sings the first stanza, leave your seats now and come to the aisle. No one is leaving. Come while the choir sings, "Just As I Am, Without One Plea." (The choir sings all five verses about three times as the converts come forward and are dealt with at the altar.)

Now listen carefully. We are not talking to you about joining a church this morning. If you belong to a Presbyterian church back in Wisconsin, okay, but you have to do something with your sins, and that didn't necessarily happen when you joined the church. What are you going to do with your sins? You say, "I am going to turn over a new leaf." How about the old debts? Something has to be done. You have sinned against God as all of us have. You *have* to do something with those sins. They are charged to you or they are charged to God. They are not charged to Him unless you have come to a time and place in your life where you by faith committed your eternity to Jesus Christ. You didn't do that when you joined the church or got confirmed. Have you done it? Are you forgiven? Are you pardoned? Is your name written in Heaven? Let's bow our heads.

Our Heavenly Father, speak to the hearts of the people this morning. These others that raised their hands who have not yet responded to the Gospel, may they respond today. Oh, don't let anybody go out of this building not born again. Make it so. Save everyone whose hand was lifted. Help them to come and say "Yes" to God.

Now with heads bowed, you say, "Preacher, how will I feel?" You don't have to feel. It is faith. God provides the feeling. You just provide the faith. If God did not provide the feeling, you would still have His Word that you were saved. Place your faith in the finished work of Christ.

With our heads bowed and our eyes closed, the choir will sing "Softly and Tenderly Jesus Is Calling." We will not sing long. You will have to come quickly if you are going to come. Come and say this morning, "Preacher, I have been putting it off so long. I have wondered and wondered about it. Preacher, I have wanted to be saved and I have wanted to know it. I am not going to wait any longer to do it. I am just going to do it now."

Oh, for God's sake and your own soul's sake, do it today.

Come as the choir sings. Slip out from your seats. Come now. Come on, come on. The best step you will ever take will be that first step forward. Hurry. Heads are bowed and eyes are closed. Will you come? Come on, fellow.

(The choir sings all four verses of "Softly and Tenderly Jesus Is Calling.")

Hurry, hurry, come quickly. Just hum the chorus, choir. Hum the chorus one more time. Hurry. Come on. Come on.

(Choir hums the chorus.)

Thank you.

Thank you so much. Be seated, please, if you will. How we thank God for these who are coming. It is a little later than usual but many have had to think awhile and pray awhile. We thank God for every decision. As I call your name, would you please stand.

(The pastor then read the names of the forty-eight people who responded. Eighteen of these were then baptized.)

29. The Public Services

There are three types of services that a church needs. First, there should be an evangelistic service. Then there should be a service exhorting the Christians and instructing the saints. Third, there should be a service of Bible teaching. Since the average church has three public services, one service may be given to each of the above needs. In our generation there are more unconverted people who come to the Sunday morning service, so it is best to give the Sunday morning service to evangelism. This does not mean that the entire sermon and service should be geared to the unsaved. It does mean, however, that the service should be evangelistic in nature, warm, spiritual and powerful. A public invitation should be given urging upon the unsaved the importance of receiving Christ as Saviour. Below is a typical order of service for Sunday morning:

```
Sunday_____
Choir opening_____
Song no._____
Prayer
SPECIAL_____
Song no._____
Pastor's promotion
Announcements - Bro. Hand
SPECIAL_____
Song no._____
Intro. of man to pray-Bro. Fisk
Offering
Scripture - Bro. Colsten
SPECIAL_____
Message
Invitation
Song no._____
Baptisms
Prayer
Closing Chorus
```

Let us make these observations about the morning service.

1. *The choir opening.* Refer to the chapter on Church Music and read very carefully.

2. *The congregational song.* Again, please read with care the Church Music chapter.

3. *The opening prayer.* This is given by the pastor. This prayer is not read, but rather it is from the heart asking for God's blessings upon the service. It is direct, earnest, sincere and simple.

4. *The first special number.* (Again notice the chapter on Church Music.) This number should set the pace for the service. It should be a good solid selection, one that speaks to the heart rather than to the head, and one in which the words, melody and presentation will turn the hearers' thoughts to spiritual matters and unite them as one group ready for the service.

5. *The congregational song.* In the chapter on Church Music we emphasize that the congregational singing should be enthusiastic and spiritual. Care should be taken to avoid liturgical-type singing. Familiar hymns that exalt the Lord Jesus Christ and the Gospel should be used.

6. *Pastor's welcome.* At this point the pastor gives a word of greeting, makes a few necessary announcements, and welcomes the visitors. This is a very vital part of the service. This should relax the audience and warm the hearts of the people. Each visitor should feel that the pastor is speaking directly to him and that he is certainly a welcomed and honored guest in the services.

7. *Announcements.* We have found it wise to have mimeographed cards on which the people can write their announcements. They place these announcements on the pulpit before the service. A copy of such a card and an announcement is seen below:

DATE OF EVENT: *Saturday, December 2*   TIME: *7:00 pm*
LOCATION OF EVENT: *Fellowship Hall*
GROUP OR GROUPS INVOLVED: *High School and Junior High boys and girls.*
ANNOUNCEMENT: *Come to hear the Gospel singing Family, Mr. and Mrs. Harry Johnson and their four children. Bring your friends for a delightful evening of music and fellowship.*
ANNOUNCEMENT WRITTEN BY: *C. W. Fisk*

The announcements should be read briefly and with dignity.

8. *Special number.* This is the middle special since we have three in each of our Sunday services. If any of the specials are novelty numbers, spirituals, etc., this is the best place to use them. The special before the sermon should certainly be a sobering, devotional type that would blend the audience into a warm, spiritual group right before the message. This middle special is a good place for a peppy quartet number, a special singing group, etc. It, like all specials, should be well presented and well prepared.

9. *Congregational number.* It is usually wise to have the congregation to stand on this number as the ushers will come forward on the last stanza.

10. *Introduction of a deacon to pray.* At each public service we honor a deacon or leader of our church. Presently, we are asking a different deacon to pray at each public service. Sometimes we will go through the entire church membership and use every man who is willing to lead in public prayer. This acquaints the people with the church members. The man's name is given, his place of employment, his wife's name, the number of children they have, and his wife is asked to stand so the people may see her.

11. *The offertory.* This is a vital part of the service. (Please note the chapter on Church Music.)

12. *Responsive reading of the Scripture.* This is one of the most impressive parts of our service. The people are asked to stand and a portion of Scripture is read responsively. The pastor, or an assistant pastor, reads verse 1. The congregation reads, in unison, verse 2, etc., until the Scripture passage is completed. The people stand for the reading of the Word of God. This shows respect for the Bible and also gives the people another opportunity to stretch before settling down for the sermon. Following the reading of the Scripture, the pastor or assistant then offers a brief prayer asking God's blessings upon the service.

13. *Special musical number.* This should be a very spiritual number. If possible, it should blend in with the sermon. It should lift the hearers closer to God in preparation for the message.

14. *The message itself.* I have found that the Sunday morning sermon should be directed basically to the saints and yet have a strong appeal to the unsaved. It should be interesting, scriptural, pungent, and even folksy. The end of the message should direct itself to the unsaved and a definite, strong appeal should be made for the unconverted to receive Christ as Saviour. Following is a typical Sunday morning message.

30. A Sunday Morning Sermon

(Sunday, January 16, 1966—10:50 a.m.)

This sermon, "So You've Sinned," was preached by Pastor Hyles in a Sunday morning service. At the close of the service there were thirty-one conversions and additions and sixteen were baptized.

SO YOU'VE SINNED

I am preaching today on the subject, "So You've Sinned." The story that I am going to tell is one that would be descriptive of almost every person in this building today. You got saved. You were so happy. For the first time in your life you knew you were going to Heaven. You put your trust in the Word of God. The old life was not appealing as it once was, and suddenly new desires came. The things that you had wanted to do, you found fading. The things that you had never enjoyed before, you found yourself enjoying. Those were wonderful days. You quit the old way. You started a new way. The sun was brighter, the birds sang prettier, and the world looked more cheerful. Everything was viewed through rose-colored glasses. Everything looked beautiful. You were so enraptured with your newfound life! The preacher that once you did not like, all of a sudden, you liked. The church, you used to think, was made up of a bunch of fanatics. All of a sudden, you found yourself wanting to be one of those fanatics. This strange desire is one of the most joyous things that had ever come into your life.

You said, "I'll never go back to the old life. I am going to live for God."

So you came to church and you lived right. Your home was happier. Everything was going fine.

Suddenly you did something wrong. You found yourself, temporarily at least, sitting in the same hogpen from which you came.

You were shocked and said, "Could this be me? Could I still be a Christian? Could a Christian do what I have just done? I have sinned. I have done something wrong. Oh, I never thought I would do this again."

Maybe you said a bad word. Maybe you lost your temper or did something even worse.

You stopped in horror and said, "I've done wrong! I've sinned! I never thought it would happen to me again. Is this me? Am I lost?"

Maybe you thought you had overcome your temper. After you got converted you didn't throw a temper tantrum for weeks, but you stumbled.

Suddenly you said, "Oh, I thought that was behind me. Would a Christian do that? Why, am I lost again?"

So you've sinned. So you've sinned. So you've sinned. What about it? Are you lost again? Can you be reclaimed? Is all hope gone? So you've sinned.

You said when you awakened the next morning, "What happened? I thought I had changed, and here I am in the same old hogpen. Am I lost again? What happened to me?"

So you've sinned. So you've sinned.

The first thing I want to answer is this:

What Happened?

What really did happen? Now if you will listen carefully, I will tell you what happened. There is a logical explanation for your returning to your old life. When you got saved, a battle started. When you were born the first time, you were born of the flesh. All you had was the flesh and the physical appetites thereof. But when you got saved, a new person was born, and you were so enraptured with the new person that you forgot the old person existed. Before you knew it, you thought the new person was the only one there, but the old fellow had been sharpening his knife and getting ready for you. When you forgot he was there, he stabbed you in the back! You realized for the first time since you were saved that the old fellow was still around.

So a battle was started. In Romans, chapter 7, the Apostle Paul said, "For the good that I would I do not: but the evil which I would not, that I do." He also said that he found a constant warfare raging all the time in his life between the new man and the old man.

The Indian explained it so much better than I can.

Somebody asked, "Indian, what happened since you got saved?"

He said, "Ugh. Black dog in here. Black dog wants to do bad. Black dog don't do good. Black dog in here." But he said, "Ugh, white dog in here too. White dog want to do good. White dog don't want to do bad." Then he said, "Ugh, white dog fight black dog and black dog fight white dog. They fight all time."

Somebody asked, "Which one wins?"

He said, "The one I feed the most."

What you did not realize is that the Devil tried to make you forget that the old person was still there. Now listen, that fellow who liked to drink is still hanging around all the time. He will be there until you die. When you got saved, that fellow that loses his temper was still there; he didn't leave. Now you didn't pay him much mind because you were so happy with the new fellow.

Let me illustrate. Here is a fellow who gets married and he forgets all about himself. He forgets about everybody else in the world. All he is concerned about is that new bride. Her request is a command. Everything she wants to do is what he wants to do. She may have a new orchid every week. Gladly he offers to do anything for her.

But after a few months or a few years, it dawns upon him that he is still there too. After awhile that stuff gets old. After awhile he gets back to the realization that he is still there and needs to be cared for, and she ought to think about him. He comes back to the realization that he still has his desires.

Now listen to me. When you got saved, the sinful part of you did not die. You simply had another part born, and there is a warfare going on all the time.

Let me illustrate again with the marriage vows. When my wife and I were married, I had a habit of putting my clothes on the bedpost. (To me, it is the perfectly logical place to put the clothes.) When I got married, a new person came. This new person is clean. This new person is lovely. This new person is beautiful. This new person wants things done properly. The old fellow doesn't care. The new person cares. For the old fellow, the bedpost is fine; the new person—"Closet, please." The old person wonders why you have to straighten the towel if you are going to unstraighten it again. Why can't you, when you leave, throw it on a spot nearest the door so when you come back in, you can get it again? But this new person does not feel that way. A new person has come in.

Now then, here is the point. As long as I can keep this new person well and doing her job, our house runs fine. But when I feed myself more than I feed her, and the new person becomes weak and goes to bed, you have never seen such bedlam.

The other morning, I cooked breakfast on Christmas day. I went down and got some ham. I had three pieces of ham, so to me it was logical to get three skillets—one for each piece of ham. So I did. I had three skillets going at the same time.

I am like a fellow who had three holes in his floor and another fellow said, "What are those three holes for?"

He said, "I have three cats. When I say 'scat,' I want the cats to leave."

The fellow said, "Why don't you have one hole? They could go out one at a time."

He said, "When I say 'scat,' I mean scat!"

Well, brother, when I say "fry," I mean fry!

So I had three skillets going just fine. Now I did not realize that the room was as smoky as it was. I had the room closed and the doors shut. Then my wife came in and went for her gas mask, but I didn't realize it.

Now I find this: I find when this new person becomes weak, the old person takes over, and we have mass confusion. Before I know it, I find that old person even rejoicing that the new person is so fastidious.

The same thing happens in conversion. You become two people. Christ comes in you to live and you are a new person. The new person wants to live right; the old person doesn't. Now for a while you are infatuated with this new person, enraptured with only him, concerned about him alone. However, you have not made provisions for the old person, and suddenly the old person stabs you in the back and you find yourself cursing in a fit of temper or lying in a drunken stupor. You find yourself in lustful sin, and you wake up and say, "What happened? What happened? What happened?"

What has happened is simply what I have told you. You have not fed the new man enough. Now listen to me. You cannot, to save your life, live in the world where the cursing and the godlessness are, and where you hear people profane the name of God forty hours a week, and come to church only one hour a week and keep the new man strong enough to win the battle. You are going to have to feed him. That is one reason that I stress faithfulness. That is one reason that Sunday night is so important. That is one reason that Wednesday night, when we take the Word of God and have our Bibles open and our pencils and maps out, we will be feeding the new man.

If you do not take advantage of these opportunities, the new man is going to get sick and go to bed. The old man will take over, and you are going to have three skillets in a smoky kitchen!

Now that is what happens. That ought to be an encouragement to you. You are not lost at all. You are still saved. God hasn't kicked you out. You just lost round one; that's all. There are fourteen rounds. Get up and fight, but feed the new man!

The second question that I would like to answer is this:

What Can I Expect Now?

Here you are, lying in the gutter. What can you expect now? Now that you've found yourself in the hogpen, you've found yourself back in sin, and you've found yourself ashamed, what can you expect?

In the first place, as I said awhile ago, you are not lost because of it. First Corinthians 3 is a blessed chapter. Note verses 11 to 15:

"For other foundation can no man lay than that is laid, which is Jesus Christ. Now if any man build upon this foundation gold, silver, precious stones, wood, hay, stubble; Every man's work shall be made manifest: for the day shall declare it, because it shall be revealed by fire; and the fire shall try every man's work of what sort it is. If any man's work abide which he hath built thereupon; he shall receive a reward. If any man's work shall be burned, he shall suffer loss: but he himself shall be saved; yet so as by fire."

That means when a saved person doesn't live right, he loses his rewards but not his salvation.

The second thing you can expect is that Jesus is there to pick you up.

First John 2:1 says, *"My little children, these things write I unto you, that ye sin not. And if any man sin; we have an advocate with the Father, Jesus Christ the righteous."*

That word "advocate" means that you have a runner to your side. Jesus Christ runs along beside you everywhere you go. When you stumble, He picks you up.

He says, "My child, I understand. I know you are just flesh. I know you are weak. I know you didn't want to do it. I know the Devil tempted you. Let Me pick you up."

This morning He stands beside you. All you have to do is look up to Him and say, "Dear Jesus, I'm sorry."

Jesus will say, "Well, that's all right. Just come on back and I'll pick you up."

He'll give you strength, and the next time you will feed the new man. When you realize that the old man is there, you will start looking out for him.

If someone is out in front of your house with a knife in one hand and a gun in the other, and if he is looking meanly at your house, you know to call the police. But if you don't know he is there lurking in the darkness, you don't know to call the police.

Yes, Jesus comes to pick you up, but you may expect chastening if you don't *let* Him pick you up. In Hebrews, chapter 12, verses 4 through 8, we find a wonderful story, a wonderful truth:

"Ye have not yet resisted unto blood, striving against sin. And ye have forgotten the exhortation which speaketh unto you as unto children, My son, despise not thou the chastening of the Lord, nor faint when thou art rebuked of him: For whom the Lord loveth he chasteneth, and scourgeth every son whom he receiveth. If ye endure chas-

tening, God dealeth with you as with sons; for what son is he whom the father chasteneth not? But if ye be without chastisement, whereof all are partakers, then are ye bastards, and not sons."

Here we learn that if you are really a child of God and have really been born into God's family, when you do wrong and stay in that wrong, Jesus says, "Let me pick you up." If you say, "No, I will go ahead again, I'll curse again; I'll drink again; and I'll lust again," then Jesus Christ will do what any parent would do. He'll say, "Okay. Bend over."

You are going to get a tanning. You can expect it. You know, spankings are wonderful because they remind you that somebody owns you. I don't spank your children. Just in case I pick you up this morning and spank you, then you can say, "Well, he is still my daddy." I spank mine.

Oh, sometimes, if I ever do wrong and don't get a spanking for it, it worries me. Let me illustrate. When I decide I want to eat crackers, my wife says, "Where did the crackers go?"

I say, "I don't know."

(I love crackers. I am a cracker-holic. To me, cheese and crackers are the delicacy of life.)

Even though I love crackers, there is one thing about our place, and your place too: There are places we eat crackers and places we don't eat crackers. If I get some cheese and crackers, and start eating the crackers, I will hear a still small voice (not too still, not too small) saying, "We have a kitchen where we eat!" Even though I am a little peeved and want to say, "I'm providing for this house. I will eat where I want to" (That is what the old man always wants to say. He always wants to fuss.), there is one thing I can say: I am still married. I have no doubts about it. I mean I have sweet assurance that my wife is still here.

When you stumble in sin, the Lord says tenderly and lovingly, "I've come to pick you up." If you won't let Him pick you up, then He says, "Bend over!"

You mark my word, dear brother, you are going to have a car wreck; you are going to lose your job; you are going to go to the hospital. If you're a Christian and refuse to get back up, you are ruined for being happy in this world any more. God made you a new creature, and just as the old man fights against the new man when you are doing right, when you do wrong, the new man puts up a stiff battle. You will not be happy in the world because that new man is going to fight you and prick your conscience over and over again. So let me say, when you fall and stumble, let Jesus pick you up, lest He put His chastening rod upon you.

First, Jesus reminds you that He wants to pick you up. If you refuse, He will spank you. If you still refuse, God will take you on to Heaven.

You have said to your children, "Now listen, if you can't behave yourself, you have to come into the house. You are not going to play outside and be bad."

Finally you will say, "Come on in. If you can't behave yourself outside, come in and sit right here beside Mama."

If God asks you to get right and you don't, He spanks you. If He spanks you and you still don't do right, God will say, "Okay, come on up to Heaven where I can keep my eyes on you."

Christ is not going to let you continue to smear His testimony and His name. When it comes to the place that your life will do more harm to the Gospel of Jesus Christ than your death, He will take you Home. In John 15:2 we read, "Every branch in me that beareth not fruit he taketh away...."

You thought you would never go back. You said, "I'll never do that as long as I live," and you meant it. That was the new man talking. But the old man was working inside and you yielded to him. Now you find yourself full of sorrow. That sorrow is of God.

You say, "How can I face society? How can I face my wife? How can I face the church? How can I face the preacher? Oh, I'm so ashamed of myself. What will I do?"

First, you had better praise God that you feel that way. That's the way you ought to feel. You ought to feel sorrow for sin.

What Should I Do?

We have answered the questions, "What happened to me?" and "What can I expect?" Now we answer, "What should I do?"

You are back in sin. You are not happy. You are miserable. What can you do? First of all, realize the harm that your stumbling has done to your testimony. Somebody has been watching you. Somebody has had his eyes on you. Somebody has been saying that if he sticks, I am going to come to God. All of a sudden you hurt your testimony. Realize the awfulness of it!

Secondly, claim I John 1:9, "If we confess our sins, he is faithful and just to forgive us our sins, and to cleanse us from all unrighteousness."

If you have been in sin, confess it. Admit it.

When Becky, my oldest daughter, was a little child, she got into the jelly jar. She ate, and she ate, and she ate. It was grape jelly, and it was all over her face. She decided to scratch her head and you know how it is—she scratched it all over her head. It was all over her dress. It was all over her feet. It was all over her hands, and it was all over her face.

Mrs. Hyles came in and said, "Becky, have you been in the jelly jar?"

"No."

She wouldn't confess it. Now the first thing you need to do is get right with God. Confess it. Admit it.

A lady came one time to Mr. Moody, I think, and said, "Mr. Moody, pray for me. I exaggerate."

He said, "Let's pray for God to forgive you for lying."

"Oh, no," she said, "not lying, just exaggerating."

He said, "You will never get right until you admit it is lying."

Admit it. It is wrong. Confess it, ask God to forgive, and then believe what God says when He says He will forgive you. Believe Him. Claim forgiveness.

Thirdly, take up where you left off. If you get knocked down, just get up. If it seems like the old man has won round one, just look at him and say, "Buster, you will not win round two. I am going to feed this new fellow some more. I'll strengthen his muscles. We will go down to the spiritual Y.M.C.A. and do some push-ups and I'll strengthen him. You will not win round two." Listen, the battle is not over because you lost one round, so just feed the new man.

Fourthly, realize every day of your life that it could reoccur. It could happen again. If David could commit the sin of adultery, if Peter could curse and swear and deny the Lord, if Moses could lose his temper, if Solomon could go into lust, and Paul could get proud, it could happen to you. So let us be careful.

Now I come to the fourth question:

How Could It Have Been Avoided?

How could you have kept from crawling into the hogpen again? How could it have been avoided?

In the first place, many of you could have avoided it by getting baptized. Now listen to me carefully. Many people fall into sin between the altar and the baptistry. You will find a greater percentage, by far, of Christians who stick who have been baptized than those who have not been baptized. So if you refuse baptism after you are saved, you are disobeying God. You are feeding the old man, and he will win the victory.

Secondly, you could have avoided it some by joining a good church. Another great cause for backsliding is not belonging to a good church.

The third way you could have avoided it is by staying away from your weakness. Stay away from temptations. If your weakness is temper, don't get around things that make you mad. Don't discuss things that make you mad.

Let's suppose that lust is your problem. Don't get within forty yards of a girly magazine. Don't look at a calendar that is wicked and lewd.

If your temptation is liquor, don't even get around the drinking crowd. If it is cursing, don't hang around the cursing crowd. Whatever it is, now that you have gotten back up, you could avoid it if you will not get around it. Just don't stay around your weakness.

Fourthly, stay in the warfare and keep feeding the new man. How in the world can you lick the old fellow if you are feeding him all the time? The old man fights against the new man, and the new man fights against the old. A constant warfare is going on and you say, "I want to live right and I am going to live right," but all the time, you are feeding T-bone steaks to the old fellow. The new fellow is on a diet. You give him water and bread and put him in a cell, while you put the old fellow in the Waldorf-Astoria and feed him T-bones. When you stumble into sin, you say, "I wonder what happened." You starved the new fellow to death. The poor guy hasn't eaten. Feed him! Feed him! Feed him the Word of God, faithful attendance, and association with the right crowd. Be sure he is strong. The new man can't win if you don't feed him. Feed him! Feed him! Feed him!

Now, let me ask you a question: Are you two natures this morning? Can you say that you have been born again? Do you know in your heart you are God's child?

Last night about twelve o'clock our Mr. Boling went Home to be with Christ. I told his family (I was over at the house past midnight), "I loved Mr. Boling dearly." But I said, "More than that, I liked the guy." You know, there are folks you love, but some folks you love and like too. I liked him. I liked to be around him. I will never forget the night he got up and testified. He is in Heaven. He hears me. He will chuckle when I say this. I would not bring reproach against him, but it is so like him. Mr. Boling got up and said, "I've been saved now so long. Before I was saved, I used to smoke and curse." Then he said, "Thank God, I haven't smoked since I was saved and I am doing a lot better on my cursing."

Now really, do you know what he was saying? What he was saying was this: The old man is dead as far as cigarettes are concerned, but I have him on a rope as far as the cursing is concerned.

I don't know if you remember or not, but when Mr. Boling used to come in the old building, most every Sunday night I would preach on little sins, and he was so sensitive. I can see him now, nearly 78 years of age, leaving his seat Sunday night after Sunday night coming to kneel at the altar. He would come as if he were looking for the right spot. He would find the right spot, and slowly (because of illness and old age) he would kneel at the altar and confess his sins.

Four days ago they said he turned his face toward the wall. He wouldn't talk to anybody all day.

They asked, "Dad, what's wrong?"

And he said, "I've got to get some things settled with God. I have got some things that I have to take care of now."

He turned his face toward the wall, and he spent a day feeding the new man and asking God to forgive him for the old man. Now he is in Heaven. One reason I know the old fellow is in Heaven is that it was so obvious he was fighting a war all the time—the old nature against the new nature. He was saved when he was in his seventies, but now he is in Heaven.

Are you a child of God? Do you know, if you died today, that you would go to Heaven? If you will receive Christ by faith, He will come into your heart to live, and then you can say, "I am born again." You will have in you Christ, the hope of Glory.

Last night, before I left Mrs. Boling, I patted her precious cheeks and prayed with her and the family. When I left them, it was almost one o'clock. I drove down the street and I was singing:

> Oh for a thousand tongues to sing,
> Blessed be the name of the Lord,
> The glories of my God and King,
> Blessed be the name of the Lord!

I said, 'Blessed be the God and Father of our Lord Jesus Christ, who hath called us to sit together in heavenly places.' Thank God it is real! Thank God, He is in Heaven! Thank God, you can be too! Let us pray.

Our Heavenly Father, probably the message this morning comes nearer hitting everybody than anything we could have talked about. All of us have this battle—the old and the new. Every one of us has looked at himself after he became a Christian and said, "Is this me? Is this me?" I pray that You will help the message to strengthen some of us, many of us, yea, all of us. Then for those, dear Lord, who have not been saved, who do not know this new nature, I pray You will help them this morning to come to Christ and become new creatures.

31. A Sunday Evening Sermon

The Sunday evening service is conducted exactly as the Sunday morning service. Since there is usually a little more time, the sermon can be a little longer and there can be a bit more music, announcements, etc., in the service.

The only addition that we make to the Sunday evening service is made right after the recognition of the visitors. At this point we spend a few moments honoring people in our church who do their jobs well. One Sunday night we read a list of the ushers. We ask them to stand and we express to them our appreciation and gratitude. Another Sunday night we may honor the nursery workers; another Sunday night, the public address men. Another Sunday night may find the choir being honored. This is done until every group in the church has been adequately honored.

The Sunday evening sermon is somewhat different from the Sunday morning sermon. It is usually longer, and it is usually not directed as much toward sinners. It is the exhorting kind of sermon. At the Sunday evening service we would preach on prayer, Bible study, separation, etc. Following is a typical Sunday evening sermon:

The Message

(Sunday, April 24, 1966—7:00 p.m.)

This sermon, "Praise the Lord!" was preached by Pastor Hyles in a Sunday evening service. At the close of the service there were six conversions and additions and six were baptized.

Take your Bibles and notice the last five of the Psalms—Psalms 146, 147, 148, 149 and 150. There is something unusual about these Psalms. There is something that each of these Psalms has in common. Notice the first four words of Psalm 146, *"Praise ye the Lord."* Notice the last four words of Psalm 146, *"Praise ye the Lord."* Notice the first four words of Psalm 147, *"Praise ye the Lord."* Notice the last four words of Psalm 147, *"Praise ye the Lord."* Notice the first four words of Psalm 148, *"Praise ye the Lord."* Notice the last four words of Psalm 148, *"Praise ye the Lord."* Notice the first four words of Psalm 149, *"Praise ye the Lord."* Notice the last four words of Psalm 149, *"Praise ye the Lord."* Notice the first four words of Psalm 150, *"Praise ye the Lord."* Notice the last four words of Psalm 150, *"Praise ye the Lord."* To me it is very interesting that all of these Psalms begin and end with praise to the Lord.

If the translators had translated this a little more carefully, they would have said, "Praise ye Jah," which is the word "hallelujah." Then, Psalms 146, 147, 148, 149 and 150 would have been started and ended with "Hallelujah" or "Praise ye Jah."

By the way, hallelujah is one of the very few words in all the Bible that is the same in any language. The German, when praising the Lord, says, "Hallelujah." The Frenchman, when praising the Lord, says, "Hallelujah." When Spanish people praise the Lord, they say, "Hallelujah."

The psalmist says, "Hallelujah." Then he lists the things for which he praises God and closes by saying, "Hallelujah." Then he starts the next Psalm with "Hallelujah." After telling how we ought to praise God, he closes again with "Hallelujah." So out of his heart of love and praise, the psalmist says over and over again, "Hallelujah."

I said last Sunday, and I've said it several times lately, that for some unknown reason I find myself increasingly praising the Lord in my heart. I find myself more and more overflowing. Now I have never shouted (perhaps I should have), but I find more and more my own heart wanting to praise the Lord. I find myself walking down the street sometimes and thinking how good God is to me. I guess the Lord must be better to me than to anybody. When I think how good God is to me, I want to clap my hands. I do not quite understand it, for it seems that praise swells up more and more in my own heart. Sometimes I just want to weep and praise the Lord at the same time.

There was a man in our service this morning who is blind and deaf. Sign language means nothing to him. He came over to the office to "see" me after the baptismal service, and Miss Jeffries, our interpreter, introduced him to me. He had a man with him who was deaf. I would talk to Miss Jeffries. She, in turn, would talk in the sign language to the deaf man who could see. He would then take the palm of the hand of the blind, deaf man and by some kind of signs by touching, he would make the man understand. Think of it—blind and deaf! As I walked out of the office, I just wanted to shout and say, "Praise the Lord! Glory to God!"

Is that dear man here tonight? God bless him. Please "tell" him to stand. God bless him. I want you to meet him. Maxine, tell him somehow that we are glad he is here, and that we love him in the Lord. Ask him if he is saved. Isn't that wonderful! Ask him if he would just say a word of testimony for Christ tonight.... That's wonderful! Please thank him for us.

Brother, you ought to shout, clap your hands, and say, "Bless the Lord!" This man cannot hear what I am saying. He cannot see what the interpreter is doing. He is totally dependent upon someone to see the sign language for him and to tell him by the touch of the hand what is going on. God has been good to you. You ought never complain again. We act like spoiled children. We ought to look at that brother and say, "Glory to God!" We have so much!

Queen Victoria went to hear the great Handel's *Messiah*, one of the greatest pieces of music ever written in the world. At the conclusion the choir sang the great "Hallelujah Chorus." As they swelled on the "Hallelujah, Hallelujah, Hallelujah, the Lord omnipotent reigneth," the Christian Queen stood to her feet, as was the custom, with a heart full of praise to her God. From this thing that she had done, people around the world still stand to pay respect to Him, the Lord omnipotent, when the "Hallelujah Chorus" is sung.

Let us discuss for a few minutes the matter of praise. You ought to read the Psalms. If you do, you will find yourself rejoicing and praising God. You cannot fellowship long with the Psalmist David without shouting.

We had a fellow in our church in Texas whose name was J. B. Combest. J. B. said, "AMEN," over and over again as I preached. I would preach along, and J. B. would say, "Amen. That's what it says. That's right. Yes sir; I see it. It's in the Bible. There it is. AMEN!" When I would preach against dancing, he would say, "Amen, pull over and park there awhile, Preacher." One day a pulpit committee from the First Baptist Church of Mt. Pleasant, Texas, came to look me over. After the morning service they came to my house to talk to me awhile. They said, "Brother Hyles, would you be interested in coming to the First Baptist Church in Mt. Pleasant, Texas?"

I said, as I always say, "I'm not interested in going anywhere." One of the committee said, "Brother Hyles, I want to talk to you about one thing." He said, "Did you notice a strange fellow sitting in front of me this morning?"

I said, "No, I didn't."

He said, "There was a fellow sitting in front of me that talked more than you did, and he bothered me!"

That night the committee member sat about the same spot, and J. B. was really happy. "AMEN!" J. B. would say as he shook his head. He said, "Amen, Preacher. That's what it says, Preacher. Go ahead, Preacher. Let'em have it, Preacher!"

Before long I looked over at the pulpit committee member, and he was shaking his head and saying "Amen, Amen, Amen!" (He caught it.)

Now look, you just can't hang around some folks without getting happy. You run around with David for awhile and you will find yourself praising the Lord. Listen, read the Psalms every day. It is my habit to read from the Psalms every day.

When I read Proverbs, I want to go pay all my bills. I jump over to the book of Acts, and I want to go out and build something. Then I read the Psalms again, and I want to give praise to God. David said:

"Praise ye the Lord. Praise God in his sanctuary: praise him in the firmament of his power. Praise him for his mighty acts: praise him according to his excellent greatness. Praise him with the sound of the trumpet: praise him with the psaltery and harp. Praise him with the timbrel and dance: praise him with stringed instruments and organs. Praise him upon the loud cymbals: praise him upon the high sounding cymbals. Let every thing that hath breath praise the Lord. Praise ye the Lord."

Then praise the Lord there is a Heaven to which you can go.

You say, "Brother Hyles, I have troubles."

Then praise the Lord for the Holy Spirit He has given to comfort you.

If you have health, food, a home, and a loving family, and if you are born of God, praise the Lord for it!

Oh, let everything that has breath praise the Lord! That is what the pulpits in America need. The other day somebody sent me a book entitled *Sermons for the Year*. It even listed sermons for the children— one for the big folks and one for the little folks. Preachers all across the nation are using these books for their sermons. Their folks go home with no lilt, no joy, no praise, no tears, no heartbreak, no sorrow while America languishes. Where are those prophets of old? Where are the men whose hearts overflow? Where are the Paul Raders, the Dwight Moodys, and the Billy Sundays? Where are the Charles G. Finneys, the Jonathan Edwardses, and the John Wesleys? Where are they?

O God, give us again a pulpit on fire with praise and love to God Almighty for what He has done. Give us churches that praise! I am not talking about rolling down the aisle and doing two flips and four handsprings and making a fool out of yourself. I am talking about a heart that beats with praise to God.

I am talking about Mr. Cunningham over here. He just cannot help it. If anybody in the world works on being quiet, it is he! One day God saved him, but he could not read so he opened the blessed Word of God and God gave him the ability to read! Now he can read the Bible. You would praise the Lord too. As I preach, Cunningham begins to swell and swell until after awhile he has to say, "Hallelujah! Hallelujah!" Let him praise the Lord!

When I first came to Hammond, one Sunday morning a fellow came down the aisle and threw himself face down on the altar. Somebody said that it was ruining the worship. I said it ought to be ruined. That is the kind of worship God loves. God loves a heart that is overflowing. Billy Bray used to say, "Don't blame me because I am overflowing. Blame the fellow that is pouring into the vessel! Don't blame the vessel! If God keeps pouring, I can't help it. It is not my fault. I'm just the vessel. If God overflows me, I've got to say something about it."

Now I am not talking about sensationalism, but I am talking about sincere praise. Listen, are you saved? If you are, you are going to Heaven. Oh, this dead, dry religion is sweeping America!

The Philistines had stolen the ark of the covenant from Israel. The glory of God had departed, and old men were weeping because the blessings of God were gone. That sweet ark of the covenant, over which rested the holy breath of God and the Shekinah glory of God, had been gone all this time. How the people hungered and thirsted for the power of God! How they hoped that some day maybe the ark of the covenant and the glory of God could come back. One day David looked down into the street and saw the ark of the covenant coming back. He ran down the steps into the street, ran around the ark of the covenant, praised the Lord, rejoiced and said, "The glory of God is back! The ark has come home!"

His wife looked out the window and said, "You idiot! You are the King of Israel. Look what a fool you are making out of yourself." David could not help it. The ark was back. David had to praise the Lord!

There were others in the Bible who praised the Lord. In Genesis 29:35 Leah said, "Now will I praise the Lord." In Isaiah 25, verse 1, the prophet said, "I will praise thy name." In Jeremiah 33:11 Jeremiah said, "Praise the Lord of hosts." In the dungeon at midnight in the Philippian jail, Paul and Silas, who were suffering from being beaten, began to sing praises to God.

I say to you, my precious friend, I do not know your burdens. I know you have them, and my heart goes out to you. Let me say this: The very fact that you could come to church tonight should cause you to praise the Lord.

I was in the home last week of a man who lost his wife of many years. The man said, "What am I going to do? What am I going to do?" That is the cry of the world tonight, "What am I going to do? What am I going to do?"

Mothers and fathers of boys in Vietnam are sitting in this building right now. God bless you as you cry, "What are we going to do?"

One of our young men said this morning that he would be in to see

me after awhile. He is in the Navy. I said, "Where are you going
when you go back in a few days?"

He said, "I go back to a certain camp and on to Vietnam." He cries,
"What am I going to do?"

Two of our own children from our Sunday school were walking down
the street and a car hit them. Both of them are lying in the hospital in
Chicago tonight. The parents cry, while looking at the little children,
"What are we going to do? What are we going to do?"

He said, "All you beasts of the field, fowl of the air, and fish of the
sea—everything that breathes, praise ye the Lord." You can't be
around a fellow like that without praising God after awhile. I spend
time daily with David.

Who Should Praise the Lord?

We now answer the question, "Who should praise the Lord?" In the
Bible so many praised the Lord. Of course, David praised the Lord,
and we have to start with him. In Psalm 71:14 David said, "...and will
yet praise thee more and more." In Psalm 63:3 he said, "...my lips
shall praise thee." In Psalm 67:3 he said, "Let the people praise thee,
O God; let all the people praise thee." In Psalm 148:2, "Praise him,
all his angels...." In Psalm 148 he said the sun and the stars should
praise Him, the dragon should praise Him, the fish should praise Him,
and the animals should praise Him. He even said the hail and snow
should praise the Lord. David must have looked up, saw the snow
coming down and said, "Don't just drop down, snowflakes, praise the
Lord!" He saw the hail and said, "Hail, praise the Lord." He said in
Psalm 107:8, "Oh that men would praise the Lord...." In Psalm 107:
15 he also said, "Oh that men would praise the Lord...." Then in
Psalm 107:21 he said, "Oh that men would praise the Lord...." Then
in Psalm 107:31 he said, "Oh that men would praise the Lord...." In
Psalm 74:21 he said, "...let the poor and needy praise thy name." In
Psalm 119:164 he said, "Seven times a day do I praise thee...." At six
o'clock in the morning David praised the Lord. At nine o'clock in the
evening he praised the Lord. At midnight he praised the Lord. He
praised the Lord seven times a day.

Listen, young preachers, if you lose your praise, you will not be
worth much for God. Many of you have heard me tell how I got my
praise. I haven't always been like this. I used to be normal! When I
surrendered to preach, I surrendered to be a normal preacher. I went
out to the country one time to an old Negro church. There they got
happy. While I was preaching, Deacon Busey would get happy and start
to shout. After awhile the folks would form a line around the building
—the ladies on one side and the men on the other. They put their
hands on the waist of the person in front of them. The ladies would go

around this way and the men around the other way and they would sing, "What Could I Do Without the Lord?" I saw something! Those folks were sincere. Those Negro people had something in that St. Mary's Baptist Church, ten miles from Marshall, Texas, way out in the country. The more I thought about this, the deader the churches got that I had been to and the more I wanted to praise the Lord. Many a night at eleven o'clock I would walk into the building through the back door and couldn't see a thing. Everything was pitch dark and they were pitch dark. Soon they would turn around and look at me, and I would just count the eyes and divide by two! We just praised the Lord together. Deacon Busey would lift his hands toward Heaven. His eyes would start rolling, and he would praise the Lord.

I'm not saying that you and I ought to get our hands on each other's waist and go around hollering, "Praise the Lord!" I don't want any hypocrisy, but I will tell you one thing: There are many services going on now that could use a Deacon Busey! I had rather have a Deacon Busey than high church ritual. God says that He hates it, despises it, and can't stand the smell of it. We need a generation of preachers and churches that will praise God again and rejoice in the good things of life.

God must look down from Heaven and want us to praise Him with hearts overflowing with praise. David said in Psalm 147:12, "Praise the Lord, O Jerusalem...." In Psalm 148, verses 11-13, he said, "Kings of the earth, and all people; princes, and all judges of the earth: Both young men, and maidens; old men and children: Let them praise the name of the Lord...."

How long has it been, young folks, since you praised the Lord? I don't mean how long since you sang, "Praise Him, praise Him, all ye little children, God is love." How long has it been since you sat down and realized what you have?

If you could go with me to Egypt tonight and see what boys and girls your age have, you would praise God for that which you have. If you could go with me to Jamaica, or if you could go with me to Jordan, where young people like you beg food on the streets and little boys and girls like you on the front row beg for cigarettes, you would look to God and say, "Praise the Lord for what He has done for me."

David said the young should praise the Lord.

How long has it been, dear saints up in years, with your hair turning silver and your age creeping up on you, since you looked up and said, "Praise the Lord! Praise the Lord!"?

Oh, you say, "Brother Hyles, I am getting old."

Our precious Deacon Penley and his wife have a little boy with leukemia. I am sure that they have said, "What are we going to do?"

Tonight in homes all over this area people lie on beds of affliction. Their bodies are racked by pain. They would give anything in the world to be in this service tonight. They would give anything in the world just to be able to lift their feet out of bed and walk across the room or be able to sit down again at the table. Their world is just four walls. Their activity is just looking at the ceiling. What are they going to do? Those of us who were privileged to come tonight ought to clap our hands and say, "Praise the Lord! Praise the Lord!"

Second Chronicles 29:30 tells us that the Levites sang praises to God. In Acts 2:47 we find the great church at Pentecost was "praising God, and having favour with all the people."

The king of England came with his wife to our country to the White House many years ago. A born-again Indian, Chief White Feather, came to the White House and sang for the king and queen of England, "I'd rather have Jesus than silver or gold, I'd rather be His than have riches untold...." When he started to leave, the King of England stood and walked in front of all the people and said, "I'd rather have Jesus, too!"

Notice again, if you would please, David said that the old, the young, the poor, the needy, the men, the women, the preachers, the teachers, the kings, and the judges ought to praise the Lord.

Oh, I cannot help but say that when the Pastors' School came, I was so sick I thought that I would not be able to go to the School. The day the Pastors' School started I walked over to the building across the street on the first night, and I could hardly hold myself up. Perspiration was flowing off my face even though it was cool outside. I said, "Dear Lord, just let me get through tonight."

That Monday night we had that great service in which Dr. Rice preached and I baptized. I thought I would not get down the steps. I said, "Lord, let me have one more service. Just give me strength for the next one...and the next one...and the next one...." After about five times I forgot I was sick.

The last day of the School an old preacher (I do not think I will ever forget him. I guess he was seventy years of age) came, took my hand and said, "Young man, this was a wonderful week!" He said, "I wish I had had it twenty years ago."

His ministry is almost over now. It is too late now. He didn't know how to win souls. He didn't know how to get the job done, and so he said, "I wish I had had it twenty years ago."

I was walking down the alley thinking about him when suddenly it dawned on me that I was sick! I had forgotten about it for three days. I began to clap my hands. I said, "PRAISE THE LORD! PRAISE THE LORD!" I just overflowed a little bit.

Oh, listen, the longer I preach, the longer I see the blessings of God, the longer I see folks kneel at this altar, the more I must praise the Lord!

In little churches and big churches, country churches and city churches, folks have come down the aisles trusting Christ. All through these years it has been like a great army of people. Why shouldn't I praise the Lord?

Why shouldn't we here at First Baptist praise the Lord? What we saw this morning, millions of people would give their right arm to see. I suspect we had more folks saved this morning than many will have saved all the year. Oh, we yawn, go home before baptism, and do not care one bit! We ought to be ashamed. God is so good!

Why Should We Praise the Lord?

We have said who should praise the Lord. Now we answer the question, "Why should we praise the Lord?"

In Psalm 103:3 the psalmist said we ought to praise the Lord, "Who forgiveth all thine iniquities; who healeth all thy diseases." We ought to praise the Lord for a useful life. Psalm 103:4 says, "Who redeemeth thy life from destruction...." I am glad that God redeemed my life as well as my soul. The psalmist said to praise the Lord for a useful life.

David said in verse 4 of Psalm 103 to praise the Lord for the love and mercy of God. In verse 5 he reminds us to praise the Lord for food and strength. In Psalm 147:8 he says to praise the Lord for the rains, the clouds and the grass. In Psalm 147:3 he says to praise the Lord because He heals broken hearts. In Psalm 147:2 he says to praise the Lord because He loves outcasts. Aren't you glad He loves outcasts? Aren't you glad that God loves the poor?

David said to praise the Lord because He made the stars and calls them by their names—Psalm 147:4. Sometime go out and look at the stars. Try to count them. The Lord knows them every one by name. I don't know what He names them, but each star has a name. If God can keep account of those stars, I know God can keep account of us.

I'll tell you what to do. Everybody in the building close your eyes for a minute. Don't bow your head, just close your eyes. I want to talk to you with your eyes closed. Now we are all like our dear blind Mr. Foreman is. He is here tonight, and he praises the Lord more than most of us do. Now with your eyes closed take your fingers and put them in your ears. Everybody do it. Push them real hard. Now take them out. For awhile we lived in the world of our blind and deaf friend back in the corner. How would you like to live in that world all the time? Now open your eyes. We all ought to shout! How long has it been since you touched your eyes and said, "Praise the Lord!"

I'll tell you what to do. Look down at your legs. Look! Move them, and then praise the Lord that you can walk.

Is your mother or father here tonight? If so, look at them, wherever they are in the building. Just look at them. I see my mother here tonight. Now we ought to bless God that we still have them.

Look around at the crowd tonight. You ought to thank God for this church. I mean that. I know people by the tens of thousands who would give almost everything they own just to be able to come to this church every once in awhile.

I will tell you something else you ought to do. I know America has her faults, but you ought to get the flag out and look at it and thank God for America. You leave here, as we did, and travel to France, Italy, Greece, Egypt, Jordan, Israel, Turkey, Austria, Germany, England, and Canada. Brother, when you return and set your foot on American soil, you will want somebody to play the "National Anthem," and you will want to look at the flag waving and say, "Bless God, I am in America! Bless God, I was born in this country!" Why don't we bless God and praise Him for his goodness?

Then we ought to praise God, of course, for our salvation and the salvation of our families. How many ladies are with your husbands in the service tonight? Every one of you ought to shout. Many would give anything they own tonight to have the joy of having their husbands sit by them in church Sunday after Sunday.

Then we ought to bless God that we have help when troubles do come. Whenever we have burdens and heartaches, He says, "My yoke is easy, and my burden is light." The Word says, "Casting all your care upon him; for he careth for you." Whenever we are lonely He says, "I will never leave thee, nor forsake thee." When death comes and He sends His angels to take us over Jordan, we read, "Precious in the sight of the Lord is the death of his saints." When times of weakness come He says, "My grace is sufficient for thee." How we ought to praise the Lord.

When I first started preaching, what I preached was in the Book, so I preached it, but I didn't know from experience that it was true. The Bible says that He will comfort us, so I believed the Lord would comfort but I didn't *know* it. Now I have preached long enough to *know* it is true.

We also ought to praise the Lord for our salvation. The apostles had received power so they were casting out devils. They came back with joy and said, "Lord, even the devils are subject unto us through thy name."

Jesus said, "...in this rejoice not, that the spirits are subject unto you; but rather rejoice, because your names are written in heaven."

Is your name written in Heaven? How many of you know it is? Raise your hand. As your hand goes back down, you ought to shout! Your name is in Heaven! In that verse "rejoice" is the same word that is used where it says, "God loveth a cheerful giver." It includes jumping up and down and clicking your heels. Clap your hands and say, "I am going to Heaven! My name is written there!"

I would not want to live one minute without my name written in Heaven. I would not want to go to bed tonight. Oh, I know what some of you men do every time a pain hits you. You say, "It is indigestion, isn't it? Isn't it? Isn't it?" You wonder what would happen if you would not wake up in the morning. You wonder where you would be. You wonder if you are right with God. Nobody in this building has to go to bed tonight not knowing if his heart is right with God. Salvation is to all men. Jesus will save all men who will come by faith. You, too, can have your name written in Heaven.

How Should We Praise the Lord?

Now I hasten to answer the last question, "How should we praise the Lord?"

First, we should praise Him by being saved. If you are not saved, you cannot praise the Lord because you are stealing yourself from Him. He bought you with a price. You are not your own. You are His! You are supposed to glorify God in your body. If you are not saved, you cannot glorify God. You take God's air, breathe God's air, eat God's food, enjoy God's sunshine, drink God's water, and enjoy God's rain, but you turn your back on God! That is not praise, that is ingratitude!

The second way you can praise God is by obedience.

Another way to praise the Lord is by singing. Psalm 146:2 says, "While I live will I praise the Lord: I will sing praises unto my God while I have any being." That is one reason that we try to sing songs here that praise the Lord. We sing songs about Jesus and songs that magnify Him.

Psalm 149:3 says, "Let them praise his name in the dance."

People used to tell Billy Bray, "Billy, don't shout! Just shut your mouth."

Billy would say, "If I did shut my mouth, my feet would shout." He said, "When my left foot hits the ground it says, 'Amen.' When my right foot hits the ground, it says 'Glory!' My feet would shout if my mouth were shut up." I am not talking about somebody here getting up tonight and making a fool out of himself. I am talking about getting in your prayer closet at home, bowing your head, and saying, "O God, look at my hands—they are strong. Look at my eyes—I can see. Look at my ears—I can hear. Look at my tongue—I can speak. Look at my legs—they can walk and move. As far as I know, dear Lord, I am in good health. I have food in my cupboard, and my family is well and strong. I am going to Heaven. I am Your child. I live in America. I have this blessed Book and freedom to read it. I go to a Bible-preaching church. I have friends who love me. Oh, dear Lord, you have been so good!"

How long has it been since you overflowed with the praise of God? How long has it been since you spent some time alone and said, "Well, praise the Lord!"

In Psalm 150, it says that we should praise the Lord with a musical instrument.

Then it says in Psalm 149:5 that the saints ought to "...sing aloud upon their beds."

I love to look at the stars at night. I love to go outside and look up at the stars. I have done it for many years. Almost every night when I am away from home and many nights when I am at home I just look out the window or go outside and look at the stars. The psalmist said that we ought to lie on our beds and just look up and meditate. On our beds we ought to stop and think what we have, how good God is, and how much He has done for us. Sing on your bed. When you go to bed tonight, look up and say, "Praise the Lord!"

I was over in the old auditorium one day reading Isaiah 9:6. I was sitting in the chair studying it in the empty building. I was reading a commentary on it. The commentary said the words "Prince of Peace" mean "tranquilizer." I said, "Praise the Lord!"

Somebody came in and said, "Preacher, what's wrong?"

I said, "Nothing. I just learned that I have a tranquilizer that I can take any time I want."

'...his name shall be called Wonderful, Counsellor...TRANQUIL-IZER.'

You folks who have to take tranquilizers—I have *the* Tranquilizer! He is always here. He lives in me—"Christ, in me, the hope of glory!"

Have you praised the Lord today?

32. A Wednesday Evening Bible Study

Following is a typical order of service for Wednesday evening with a few observations:

1. The letters from the missionaries, college students, and servicemen are a very vital part of this service. One of the assistant pastors reads excerpts from a letter from a missionary. Each member of the missionary family is called by name and special prayer is offered for them. Then another assistant pastor reads excerpts from a letter from a serviceman, and the church spends a season of prayer for him and other servicemen. Another assistant pastor then reads a letter from a college student, and the church offers prayer for this and all college students. This is a very important part of our service.

2. The Wednesday evening message is a Bible-study type. Following is a typical Wednesday evening Bible study:

(Wednesday, March 23, 1966—7:30 p.m.)

Each Wednesday at 7:30 p.m. Pastor Hyles teaches a portion of the Bible to the entire congregation in the auditorium. The audience participation used here is the typical method of teaching. The Sunday school lesson is taught to the Pastor's Class in the same manner.

Turn in your Bibles, please, to the book of Proverbs, chapter 1. We are going to look at a good portion of the first chapter of Proverbs tonight. Normally on Wednesday night we spend about fifty minutes to an hour just teaching the Bible. That is all. We just teach the English Bible verse by verse. We usually start about this time and then we go until nine or a few minutes past nine.

The book of Proverbs will be our textbook for many Wednesday nights. I have never actually taught this entire book before. If you are one of our own people and if you need the page number, it is on page 672. We will start reading with verse 1.

Chapter 1, verses 1-10:

"The proverbs of Solomon the son of David, king of Israel; To know wisdom and instruction; to perceive the words of understanding; To receive the instruction of wisdom, justice, and judgment, and equity; To give subtilty to the simple, to the young man knowledge and discretion. A wise man will hear, and will increase learning; and a man of understanding shall attain unto wise counsels: To understand a proverb, and the interpretation; the words of the wise, and their dark sayings. The fear of the Lord is the beginning of knowledge: but fools despise wisdom and instruction. My son, hear the instruction of thy father, and forsake not the law of thy mother: For they shall be an ornament of grace unto thy head, and chains about thy neck. My son, if sinners entice thee, consent thou not."

Let us pray. Father, open our eyes to the teachings of Thy Word and make it easy for us to understand, especially this tremendous book of Proverbs. In Jesus' name. Amen.

There are three books in the Bible that I read perennially. The three books are Proverbs, Acts and the Psalms. The Psalms will keep my heart warm and my spirit sweet. The book of Proverbs will do more to build character and integrity than any other book in the Bible. God knows we could use much of that today. The third book I read is the book of Acts because it keeps me knowing how to keep the church going and what kind of program we ought to have. It keeps me living in New Testament Christianity.

Now I want you to notice the tremendous teaching of the book of Proverbs. By the way, Proverbs is taught basically to young people. You young people listen very carefully. I want everybody to get your pencils and mark your Bibles as we teach the book of Proverbs.

Let us begin with verse 1. *"The proverbs"*—Circle the word "proverbs" please. The word "proverbs" comes from two words—"pro" and "verbam." "Pro" means "far." "Verbam" means a "word," or actually it means more than a word, a little more than a word, or beyond a word. If you circled the word "proverbs," write beside it "more than meets the eye." These are sayings that have an underlying meaning.

"The proverbs of Solomon...." I want you to circle the word "Solomon" in your Bible, please, and write "peaceable," for that is what the word Solomon means. All of these proverbs were not written by Solomon. Many were collected by Solomon. They were a collection of proverbs that had been given down through many years. Especially along the middle part of the book we have Solomon's proverbs, but all of them are not his.

"...the son of David...." Now I want you to circle those words, please. Circle the words "son of David" and write "and Bathsheba." Solomon was the youngest son of David and Bathsheba. You recall that

Bathsheba was the lady whom David saw bathing. He lusted after her, had her husband Uriah killed, took her unto himself, and she became his wife. This was the awful sin of David's life. It is the sin that caused the writing of the Fifty-first Psalm.

PASTOR: Solomon was the son of whom?

AUDIENCE: The son of David.

PASTOR: Who was his mother?

AUDIENCE: Bathsheba.

PASTOR: Was he the oldest boy, the youngest boy, middle boy, or what?

AUDIENCE: Youngest boy.

PASTOR: "Proverbs" means what?

AUDIENCE: More than meets the eye.

PASTOR: Solomon means what?

AUDIENCE: Peaceable.

PASTOR: Who was his father?

AUDIENCE: David.

PASTOR: Who was his mother?

AUDIENCE: Bathsheba.

PASTOR: Okay. David named Solomon "Peaceable" for this reason: David had known war. David had had many, many battles. His kingdom had been one of ups and downs. David's reign was one of warfares and many battles, so David hoped that Solomon would not have such problems.

You know it is a funny thing. I have one son, David. He is twelve years old. He is a preacher. God has already called him. He has a file of sermon outlines. He is outlining my sermon right now. I am sure he has his pencil out and is outlining it and marking in his Bible. It is a funny thing about David. I want David to be a hard-hitting, knock-down, drag-out, Hell-fire and damnation, soul-winning, sin-fighting, Hell-hating, Devil-fighting, God-honoring preacher; but I don't want him to have any trouble. I don't want anybody to get mad at him. Do you see what I mean?

I want David to hate the movies, hate tobacco, hate dancing, hate cursing, hate lying, hate stealing, etc., but I don't want him to get into trouble. I don't want anybody to get mad at him. I guess all of us are that way about our boys.

My mother has said many times, "Son, I want you to preach hard, but couldn't you preach where everybody would like you?" She used to worry so much about it.

Let us go back to verse 1 again. The word "proverbs" means what?

AUDIENCE: More than meets the eye.

PASTOR: "Solomon" means what?

AUDIENCE: Peaceable.

PASTOR: The son of whom?

AUDIENCE: David.

PASTOR: And...?

AUDIENCE: Bathsheba.

PASTOR: Which son?

AUDIENCE: Youngest son.

PASTOR: Okay. "...*king of Israel.*" Circle the words "king of Israel" and write "at age twenty." Solomon was about twenty years of age when he became the king of Israel.

Now circle the first verse and write, "the introduction." Then place brackets around verses 2 through 4 and write, "the purpose of the book."

In verses 2-4 we find the ten purposes for the writing of Proverbs. Look at it and follow me carefully. *"To know wisdom and instruction; to perceive the words of understanding; To receive the instruction of wisdom, justice, and judgment, and equity; To give subtilty to the simple, to the young man knowledge and discretion."*

Now take your pencils and circle ten words. Remember and memorize these ten words, for in these ten words we have the purpose for the writing of the book of Proverbs.

You tell me the first word we ought to circle.

AUDIENCE: Wisdom.

PASTOR: Okay, write it down and also circle the word "wisdom" in your Bibles. What is the next word we ought to circle?

AUDIENCE: Instruction.

PASTOR: Circle the word "instruction." All right, keep reading. What is the next word you think we ought to circle?

AUDIENCE: Perceive.

PASTOR: I think so. I have written "perception." Circle the word "perceive" and write the word "perception." All right that is three— wisdom, instruction, and perception. What is the next word we want to circle? What is it? Say it.

AUDIENCE: Understanding.

PASTOR: Circle the word "understanding." That is the fourth word. In verse 3, what is the next one? We already have instruction circled, haven't we? That was in verse 2. Justice is the next word. Circle the word "justice." That is number five. What is the next word?

AUDIENCE: Judgment.

PASTOR: Circle the word "judgment." That is number six. What is the next word?

AUDIENCE: Equity.

PASTOR: Circle the word "equity." That is number seven. Now read verse four. What is the first word in this verse we ought to circle?

AUDIENCE: Subtilty.

PASTOR: Okay. Circle the word "subtilty," which is number eight. The next word?

AUDIENCE: Knowledge.

PASTOR: That is number nine. Circle the word "knowledge." The next word is...?

AUDIENCE: Discretion.

PASTOR: That is number ten. Number one is...?

AUDIENCE: Wisdom.

PASTOR: Number two is...?

AUDIENCE: Instruction.

PASTOR: Number three is...?

AUDIENCE: Perception.

PASTOR: Number 4 is...?

AUDIENCE: Understanding.

PASTOR: Number five is...?

AUDIENCE: Justice.

PASTOR: Number six is...?

AUDIENCE: Judgment.

PASTOR: Number seven is...?

AUDIENCE: Equity.

PASTOR: Number eight is...?

AUDIENCE: Subtilty.

PASTOR: Number nine is...?

AUDIENCE: Knowledge.

PASTOR: Number ten is...?

AUDIENCE: Discretion.

PASTOR: Yes, those are the ten purposes for the book of Proverbs. Now look at verse 2. *"To know wisdom..."* I want you to circle the word "wisdom" and somewhere along there write what this particular word "wisdom" means—"to know one's self, one's God and one's neighbor." That is what the word wisdom means, "to know one's self, one's God, and one's neighbor."

God said, "I want you to have wisdom. I want you to know yourself, I want you to know God, and I want you to know your neighbor. I want you to know how to handle yourself. I want you to know how to judge yourself, how to handle yourself. I want you to know how to relate yourself properly with God. Then I want you to know how to relate yourself properly with your neighbor."

Let's go on. "...and instruction; to perceive the words of understanding; to receive the instruction of wisdom, justice, and judgment, and equity...." Circle the word "equity" and write "to weigh properly." Equity means to weigh properly. It means to weigh carefully the decisions of life.

Let us go further. "...to give subtilty...." That means "prudence." "...to give subtilty to the simple...." Circle the word "simple." This is the key statement in all the book of Proverbs—"to give subtilty to the simple." What does that mean? Does that mean to give subtilty to Brother Terry? No, we are supposed to comfort Brother Terry, for the Bible says plainly that we are supposed to comfort the feeble-minded (Laughter.) The word "simple" here is an interesting word. Circle it and write "no folds—N-O F-O-L-D-S." It comes from a root word which means "no pleats, no folds, just plain."

Let me see if I can illustrate. Who in the choir has a pleated skirt on tonight? Stand up. Come up here. Who has one that is just plain? Come on up here. Now you stand right there. Now look. This one is just plain. It has no folds. This one has pleats in it. Life at an early age has no folds in it. Life is very simple. It is not very complex. You may think it is complex, but you just wait. It is very simple. While you have no folds, God wants to talk to you. Before you get your life pleated, God wants to talk to you. Before life becomes folded, interwoven, and complex, and before things begin to fold on top of each other, problems begin to stack up, and life becomes folded and pleated, God says that He wants to talk to you. Okay, thank you, girls.

Now what does that mean? It means that God says the book of Proverbs is a book of instruction to young people. Young people, you read this book. YOU READ THIS BOOK!

Look! If there is anything we need today in the world—in Congress, in the Supreme Court, in the pulpit, and in business—it is integrity, honesty, decency and character! The only time to get it is at the age of these boys and girls—before life gets its pleats, before life gets its folds, before life gets complicated.

So the book of Proverbs is written to the simple or the unfolded to give them subtilty and prudence. In these days, we are going to be talking to the boys and girls, the juniors, junior highers, the primaries, the high schoolers, and the young people before life gets folded and before life gets complicated.

Let us go further. *"...to the young man...."* Circle the words "young man." Those are very interesting words. The words "young man" here mean "the big boy." It means a fellow who has a body of a man but the mind of a boy. Let me illustrate. Come up here, Wainscott. Now I am proud of Rick Wainscott. I mean this when I say this: I know of no young man right now in the country for whom I have more hopes than I have for Rick Wainscott. To those of you who don't know him, Rick was the starting half-back on the Northern Indiana Conference football team. He is clean. God has called him to preach. One brother is already at the Tennessee Temple Schools and Rick is on the way. Another brother will be going on before long. Now look at Rick. Is Rick as tall as I am? Rick, how much do you weigh?

"One-hundred-seventy-five."

I weigh a little more than you do, but we are about the same size. How old are you?

"Eighteen."

I am thirty-nine. That means that you and I both have bodies that are man-sized. We both look like men, but I know some things that you do not know. This book of Proverbs was written to you, while you are young, you see? That is what it means when it says to give subtilty to the simple. There are not as many folds in your life as there are in mine. My life is folded. I have had a lot of pleats. Thank you, Rick.

Consequently, when it says to the young man, it means "to the big body, but young mind." It is written to the young people.

Let us go further. *"...To give subtilty to the simple, to the young man knowledge and discretion."* This is interesting. Verses 5 and 6 are parenthetical verses. Look what it says. *"A wise man will hear...."* The Lord is saying, "You young people, read this. Young people, get these ten things. Young people, sit up and listen." Then it says that wise folks don't have to be begged to listen. A wise man will listen.

All of us are supposed to get Proverbs, but to the young people we are supposed to say, "Sit still and listen to this!" To the wise people we are supposed to say, "We know you will listen."

Let us see what a wise man will do! *"A wise man will hear, and will increase learning; and a man of understanding shall attain unto wise counsels: To understand a proverb, and the interpretation; the words of the wise, and their dark sayings."* Circle the words "dark sayings" and write "riddles."

Turn to Proverbs 9:9. I want you to see a verse that teaches us about the same thing. Proverbs 9:9: "Give instruction to a wise man, and he will be yet wiser: teach a just man, and he will increase in learning." So the Bible is saying back in Proverbs that we have ten things for the young people to learn. Now if a person is wise, he will also listen to it. That means, mammas and daddies, if you are wise you will listen to what it says too. However, it says, "Young people, now you listen. It is written to you!"

Let us review the ten purposes. Let's see how many of these ten things you can remember. The book of Proverbs is written for ten reasons which are wrapped up in ten words. Call out the ones you remember.

AUDIENCE: Wisdom.

PASTOR: What is another?

AUDIENCE: Instruction.

PASTOR: What is another?

AUDIENCE: Knowledge.

PASTOR: Let's let the young folks do it.

TEEN-AGERS: Perception.

PASTOR: What else?

TEEN-AGERS: Understanding. Equity.

PASTOR: What does equity mean?

TEEN-AGERS: To weigh properly.

PASTOR: What else?

TEEN-AGERS: Judgment. Subtilty. Discretion. Justice.

PASTOR: Yes, those are the ten purposes God has for us in this book.

Now let's try to get them all. *"To know wisdom and instruction; to perceive the words of understanding; To receive the instruction of wisdom, justice, and judgment, and equity; To give subtilty to the simple, to the young man knowledge and discretion."*

Now starting with verse 7 and going through chapter 9 and verse 18, we have a division of the book known as the father-and-son relationship. Mark verse 7 and make a little note there: "through chapter 9, verse 18—the father-and-son relationship." Again and again in these verses and chapters Solomon says, "My son."

Look at verse 8 for the first one. *"My son, hear the instruction of thy father, and forsake not the law of thy mother."*

Verse 10: *"My son, if sinners entice thee, consent thou not."* When I was a boy, I had a Sunday school teacher named Dr. Rutherford. Dr. Rutherford was a veterinarian. He gave me a little New Testament one time and wrote inside of it, "Jack, read Proverbs 1:10." I was a teen-age boy, and I decided to take Proverbs 1:10 for my motto. I wrote Proverbs 1:10 on a card. I had an old car that I used to drive and on the windshield I had "My son, if sinners entice thee, consent thou not.—Proverbs 1:10."

When I was in the army, I kept on my shelf above my bunk Proverbs 1:10. "My son, if sinners entice thee, consent thou not."

So we have the relationship between the father and the son. The instructions are given from the father.

I am going to give you very quickly the first four of these instructions that the father gave the son.

You already know who wrote the book of Proverbs, who his parents were, and what the book means. He was the king of Israel. We have had the ten reasons for the writing. Now we are going to have the first four pieces of advice given to these simple ones—to these "grown-up young people"—these with physical bodies of men but with minds of boys.

Look at verse 7. *"The fear of the Lord is the beginning of knowledge...."* You cannot have wisdom if you do not have the fear of God. You cannot have equity if you do not have the fear of God. You cannot have justice if you do not have the fear of God. You cannot have judgment if you do not have the fear of God. You cannot have understanding if you do not have the fear of God. You mark it down. You say what you want to say, but if you don't have the fear of God, you are not wise. The very beginning of knowledge, the very beginning of judgment, and the very beginning of justice is the fear of God!

Young people, hear me. Hear Solomon who said, "You people, big of body, young in mind, you people, simple ones, with not many folds in life, not many pleats in your life, hear me. Start off by fearing God."

Verse 8 is the second instruction that he gives. *"My son, hear the instruction of thy father, and forsake not the law of thy mother."* Now put a "2" beside that verse. That is the second thing that God tells young people. Hear the "what" of thy father?

AUDIENCE: Instruction.

PASTOR: And the "what" of thy mother?

AUDIENCE: Law.

PASTOR: That is interesting—instruction of thy father.
I never will forget when our youngest daughter Cindy was about three years old. I had been to Wyoming and I was going to Florida. I got in on Wednesday night at 5 o'clock. I rushed in and met Mrs. Hyles in the Teachers' and Officers' Meeting. She had a bag of clean clothes packed to go with me and she got the dirty clothes from me. I had been gone Monday through Wednesday, got in, met my wife over here, kissed her good-bye in front of all of the people and took off the next direction.
However, little Cindy said, "Where have you been, Daddy?"
I said, "Wyoming."
She said, "Where are you going now?"
I said, "Florida."
She put her little hands on her hips and said, "Well it was mighty nice of you to drop by a few minutes."
Yes, Dad works all day and comes home at night, but Dad ought to instruct the children. Dad ought to be an example.
Mother is there all the time. It says to listen to the instructions of your dad, but hear the law of your mother. The mother is the queen of the house. The mother determines the spirit of the home. The second thing God said was that if you want judgment, if you want equity, if you want knowledge, mind your mommy and daddy!
Listen, young people, you will not have any of these things if you don't obey them. You check your Bible and you will find right beside the sins of drunkenness, adultery and fornication will be listed, "disobedience to parents."
You say, "My daddy is not perfect."
Neither was Solomon's. What kind of daddy did Solomon have? Well, he stole a wife and killed a husband, but yet Solomon said to listen to the instructions of your daddy.
Well, you say, "My daddy is out of date."
You had better get out of date then and hear his instruction.
You say, "Well, my mother is not what she ought to be."
You are still supposed to listen to the law of your mother. Solomon's mother was Bathsheba.
Look at verse 9, a beautiful verse: *"For they shall be an ornament of grace unto thy head, and chains about thy neck."* What does it mean? The victors in battle wore ornaments and chains of victory around their necks. Solomon said that if you would listen to your mamma and daddy and have the fear of the Lord, they will be like the victor's wreath, like the chains of royalty, and like the chains of victory around your neck.
The third advice is found in verse 10. *"My son, if sinners entice*

thee, consent thou not. " The third advice Solomon wants to give these whose lives are not pleated, whose lives are not folded, is to walk with the right crowd.

First, you are supposed to fear God. Secondly, obey your parents. Now number three, walk in the right crowd.

"If they say, Come with us, let us lay wait for blood, let us lurk privily for the innocent without cause: Let us swallow them up alive as the grave; and whole, as those that go down into the pit: We shall find all precious substance, we shall fill our houses with spoil." Now the modern version: "If they say, Let's get a duck-tail haircut; if they say, Let's hang around the malt shop and whistle at the girls as they go by; if they say, Let's go down to the store and get us a cigarette; if they say, Let's go out and pet and neck; if they say, Let's cheat; if they say, Let's smoke a cigarette, if they say, Let's do wrong: Don't even walk with them! Don't do it!" That is the next piece of advice.

Now, notice verse 14. This is interesting. *"Cast in thy lot among us."* That is what they say. If you will check that very carefully, you will find it is the same word from which we get our words, "to fraternize." The world says, "Fraternize with us." Solomon said, "Don't fraternize with the world." What it really means is, "Don't swear in with them." You check it in the original language. You will find it says, "Don't swear in with a worldly fraternal organization." Don't line up with the world. Don't fraternize with the world! Do not cast in your lot with them.

Then look at the next line. *"...let us all have one purse."* Brother, that is what the world says tonight. The world says, "All the churches should go together. All the nations should go together." Now look, it sounds good, but, brother, it is not good!

"My son, walk not thou in the way with them; refrain thy foot from their path." Remember, the third advice is walk in the right crowd.

Now look to verse 20 for the fourth advice. *"Wisdom crieth without ...."* Get wisdom! *"Wisdom crieth without; she uttereth her voice in the streets: She crieth in the chief place...."* Then we have wisdom's message through the rest of the chapter. You ought to read what wisdom says.

Remember these four things:

1. Fear the Lord.

2. Obey your mother and father and hear what they say.

3. Walk in the right crowd.

4. Get wisdom. James 1:5 says, "If any of you lack wisdom, let him ask of God, that giveth to all men liberally, and upbraideth not; and it shall be given him."

Listen carefully. Let us see how well you know what we have learned so far.

The book of Proverbs means...?

AUDIENCE: More than meets the eye.

PASTOR: They were collected by...?

AUDIENCE: Solomon.

PASTOR: The word "Solomon" means...."

AUDIENCE: Peaceable.

PASTOR: How many proverbs did Solomon write?

AUDIENCE: Three thousand.

PASTOR: Who was Solomon's father?

AUDIENCE: David.

PASTOR: Who was his mother?

AUDIENCE: Bathsheba.

PASTOR: He was which child?

AUDIENCE: The youngest son.

PASTOR: He was the king of what nation?

AUDIENCE: Israel.

PASTOR: He became king when he was what?

AUDIENCE: Twenty years old.

PASTOR: How many reasons for writing the book?

AUDIENCE: Ten.

PASTOR: Give me some of them.

AUDIENCE: Wisdom, instruction, knowledge, equity, judgment,
justice, subtilty, perception.

PASTOR: Okay, that's enough. To whom was the book of Proverbs written basically?

AUDIENCE: Young.

PASTOR: It was written to those who do not have what in their lives?

AUDIENCE: Pleats, folds.

PASTOR: Who else will listen and do what it says?

AUDIENCE: Wise.

PASTOR: Give me the first four things he says to the young.

AUDIENCE: Fear the Lord. Obey your parents. Walk with the right crowd. Seek wisdom.

PASTOR: Father, help us to know the Bible. Amen.